THE CARTOON HISTORY
OF THE
UNIVERSE
II

THE CARTOON HISTORY OF THE

Volumes 8-13
From the Springtime of China to the Fall of Rome
Larry Gonick

INDIA TOO!

Broadway Books
NEW YORK

BROADWAY

VISIT OUR WEBSITE AT WWW.BROADWAYBOOKS.COM

FIRST BROADWAY BOOKS TRADE PAPERBACK EDITION
PUBLISHED 2001.

LIBRARY OF CONGRESS CATALOGING-IN-PUBLICATION DATA
(REVISED FOR VOLUME 2)
GONICK, LARRY
THE CARTOON HISTORY OF THE UNIVERSE.

CONTENTS: [1] VOLS. 1-7: FROM THE BIG BANG
TO ALEXANDER — 2. VOLS. 8-13: FROM THE SPRINGTIME OF CHINA
TO THE FALL OF ROME.
1. WORLD HISTORY—CARICATURES AND CARTOONS.
I. TITLE.
D21.1.G66   1990   902'.07   89-27397
ISBN 0-385-26520-4 (V. 1)

ISBN 0-385-42093-5

17 16 15 14 13

ACKNOWLEDGMENTS

THE MIDWIFE OF THIS WORK WAS GILBERT SHELTON, CREATOR OF *THE FABULOUS FURRY FREAK BROTHERS*. HE WAS THE FIRST TO SEE THE POTENTIAL OF A CARTOON HISTORY OF THE UNIVERSE. HE ALSO HELPED NAME IT, WAY BACK WHEN...

VIKRAM JAYANTI SHOWED THE ORIGINAL COMIC BOOKS TO EVERYONE... KARL KATZ PASSED THEM TO HIS FRIEND JACKIE... NANCY EVANS AGREED TO COMPILE THEM UNDER THE DOUBLEDAY IMPRINT... AND MY AGENT, VICKY BIJUR, HAS OFFERED CONSTANT ENCOURAGEMENT, PATIENCE, GOOD SENSE, AND FRIENDSHIP. IN THE ABSENCE OF ANY ONE OF THESE PEOPLE, THIS BOOK PROBABLY WOULDN'T EXIST.

GABRIELA KOTARSKI, JESSE BUNN, JODY OKUMURA, AND RHODE MONTIJO PROVIDED PRODUCTION ASSISTANCE. SHARON SMITH WAS ALWAYS READY TO OFFER GRAPHIC CONSULTATION. SCOTT MOYERS KEPT HIS COOL AS DEADLINES CAME AND WENT. JOANN COSTELLO, ANN HOOD, AND JERRY SONTAG HELPED ME KEEP BODY AND SOUL ALIGNED DURING THE FINAL STAGES OF PRODUCTION. THE SAN FRANCISCO PUBLIC LIBRARY WAS THE SOURCE OF MOST OF MY RESEARCH MATERIALS.

AND FINALLY, FINALLY... MY EDITOR, JACQUELINE ONASSIS, CHAMPIONED THIS STRANGE PROJECT FROM THE MOMENT SHE SAW IT, THROWING ALL HER ENTHUSIASM, HUMOR, ENERGY, DETERMINATION, AND CONSIDERABLE PERSUASIVE POWER BEHIND THE BOOK. IN PUBLISHING AS ELSEWHERE, FRICTIONLESS WORKING RELATIONSHIPS ARE RARE ENOUGH; EVEN RARER ARE THOSE IN WHICH ONE IS THE BENEFICIARY OF SUCH UNWAVERING SUPPORT AND UNSTINTING ADVOCACY. I WILL MISS HER VERY MUCH.

THE CARTOON HISTORY
OF THE
UNIVERSE
II

INTRODUCTION

HELLO AGAIN! TODAY WE'RE GOING TO TRY SOMETHING *STRANGE*: VISIT A COUNTRY *WITHOUT A HISTORY* – ANCIENT INDIA. TO HELP US, WE HAVE MY *GURU*, SWAMI GOANANDANANDANDA!

OUCH!

SNAP

OF COURSE, INDIA REALLY *DOES* HAVE A HISTORY, BUT THE ANCIENT HINDUS LEFT US *VERY LITTLE* OF IT. INSTEAD OF DESCRIBING HISTORICAL PROGRESS, THEY SAW THE WORLD AS GOING IN *CYCLES*, ROUND AND ROUND...

IN HINDI, THE WORD FOR *TOMORROW* IS THE SAME AS FOR *YESTERDAY*!"

AGH!

SQUISH

THE GREAT THINKERS OF ANCIENT INDIA CONCENTRATED ON *SPIRITUAL THINGS* AND CONCLUDED THAT THE *DIVINE IS EVERYWHERE,* INCLUDING *WITHIN OURSELVES!*

STEADY!

THERE ARE *MANY PATHS* TO THIS SPIRITUAL AWARENESS. ONE WAY IS TO TWIST OURSELVES INTO *REALLY UNCOMFORTABLE POSITIONS,* ISN'T IT, SWAMI-JI?

WUF!

ISN'T IT, SWAMI-JI?

HEY! COME BACK WITH MY WRIST WATCH!

"DESIRE IS SUFFERING; ATTACHMENT IS PAIN..."

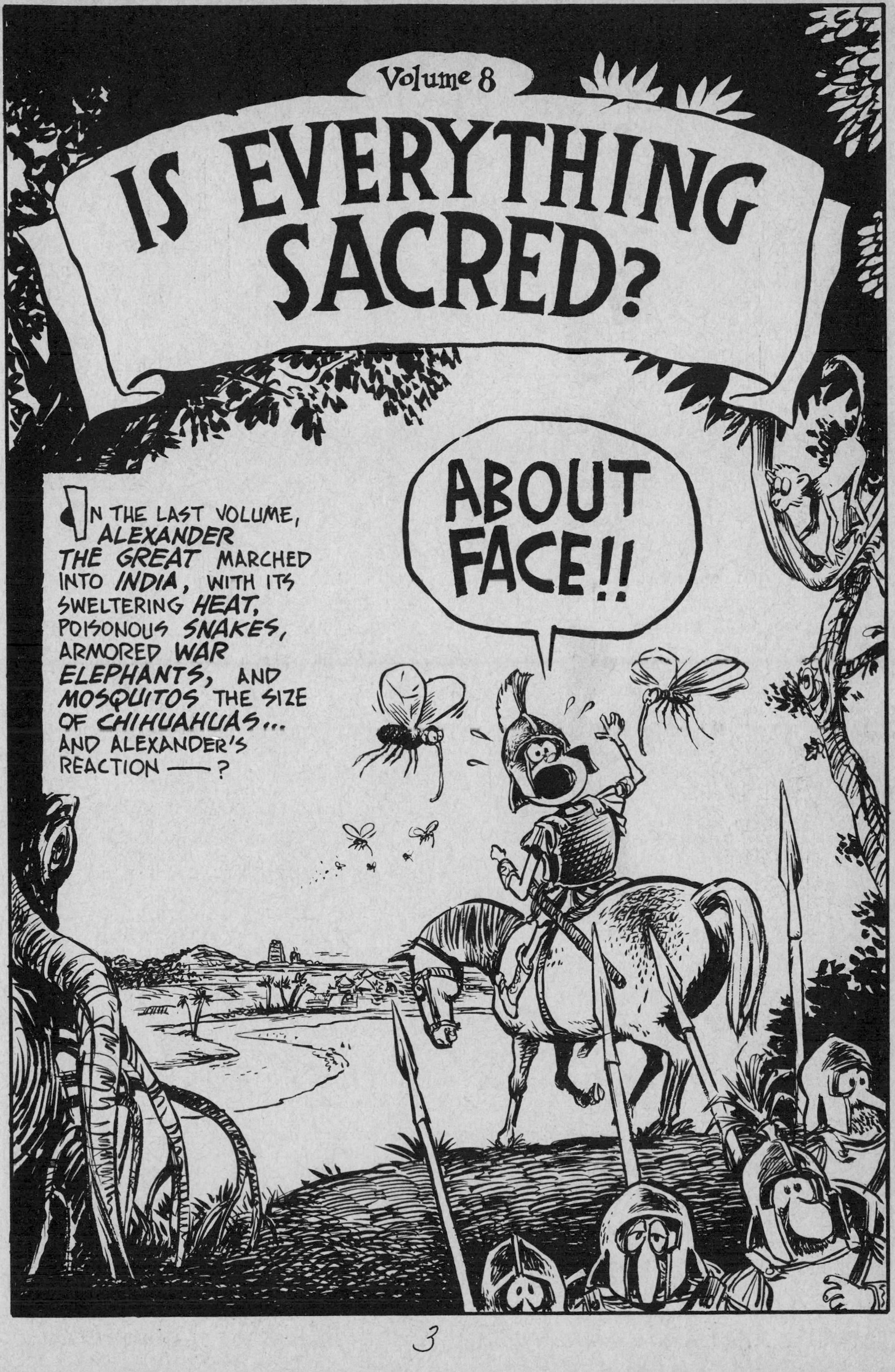
Volume 8
IS EVERYTHING SACRED?
IN THE LAST VOLUME, ALEXANDER THE GREAT MARCHED INTO INDIA, WITH ITS SWELTERING HEAT, POISONOUS SNAKES, ARMORED WAR ELEPHANTS, AND MOSQUITOS THE SIZE OF CHIHUAHUAS... AND ALEXANDER'S REACTION —— ?
ABOUT FACE!!

AND THE *INDIAN* REACTION? IN ALL THE VAST
LITERATURE OF THIS VAST SUBCONTINENT,
ALEXANDER THE GREAT IS *NEVER* MENTIONED.
ZERO TIMES HE APPEARS! IN FACT, INDIAN
MATHEMATICIANS MAY HAVE INVENTED THE NUMBER
ZERO JUST TO DESCRIBE SITUATIONS LIKE THESE...

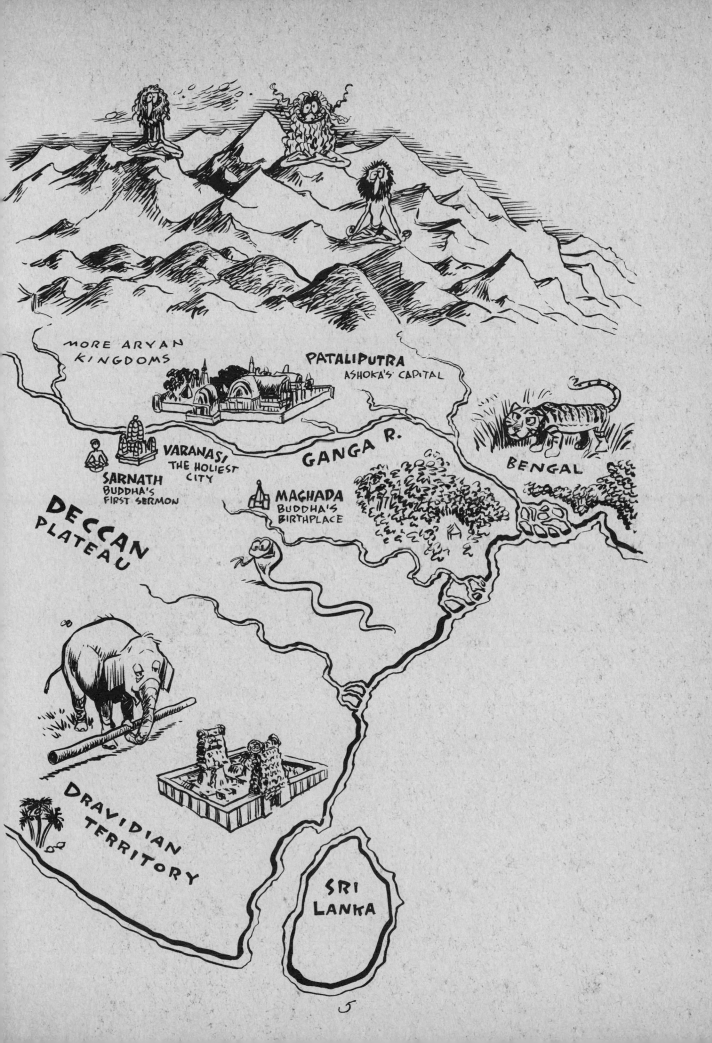

MORE ARYAN KINGDOMS

PATALIPUTRA
ASHOKA'S CAPITAL

VARANASI
THE HOLIEST CITY

GANGA R.

BENGAL

SARNATH
BUDDHA'S FIRST SERMON

MAGHADA
BUDDHA'S BIRTHPLACE

DECCAN PLATEAU

DRAVIDIAN TERRITORY

SRI LANKA

5

INDIA WASN'T ALWAYS WHERE IT IS NOW: DURING THE AGE OF DINOSAURS, IT WAS FIRMLY ATTACHED TO THE *AFRICAN* CONTINENT.

BUT SOME 100 MILLION YEARS AGO, A GIANT TRIANGULAR SLAB DECIDED TO *SPLIT.*

HISS CRACK SHUDDER

DRIFTING VAGUELY NORTHEAST, THE SLAB CLOSED IN ON THE ASIAN BEACH SOME 60 MILLION YEARS AGO.

CONTINENTS MOVE SLOWLY — BUT THEY CAN STILL DO A LOT OF DAMAGE!

RUMBLE

!

AFTER ALL, INDIA WEIGHS AT LEAST 45,000,000,000,000,000,000 POUNDS!

BLUNFF

SO THERE WAS MELTING, SHAKING, CRACKING, BUCKLING, TWISTING, SINKING, AND ESPECIALLY *RISING!!*

WOW! GEOLOGY IS UPLIFTING!

THE RESULT WAS THE *HIMALAYAS*, THE WORLD'S HIGHEST MOUNTAIN RANGE, HOME OF THE GOD *SHIVA*.

HM. WHERE DID ALL THESE *FISH* COME FROM?

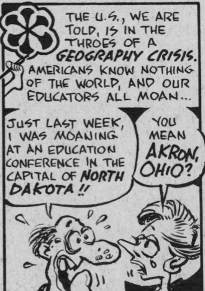

THE U.S., WE ARE TOLD, IS IN THE THROES OF A *GEOGRAPHY CRISIS*. AMERICANS KNOW NOTHING OF THE WORLD, AND OUR EDUCATORS ALL MOAN...

JUST LAST WEEK, I WAS MOANING AT AN EDUCATION CONFERENCE IN THE CAPITAL OF *NORTH DAKOTA*!!

YOU MEAN *AKRON, OHIO*?

THEY RIGHTLY REMIND US THAT GEOGRAPHY AFFECTS PEOPLE'S *FOOD, CLOTHES, HOUSES, HABITS*, AND EVEN THEIR *IDEAS*.

GOD IS *WATER*.

SO? WHAT *ISN'T*?

MAYBE WE HAVE LOST INTEREST IN GEOGRAPHY BECAUSE IT MEANS LESS AND LESS TO OUR HOMOGENIZED, ELECTRONIC CIVILIZATION...

HEY, NO, MOUNTAINS CAN *RADICALLY* AFFECT T.V. RECEPTION!

NOT WITH *CABLE*, DUDE...

AND YOUR FINAL "JEOPARDY" CLUE: *EDUCATOR*.

WHAT IS A SOUTH AMERICAN COUNTRY?

1

THE HIMALAYAN MASS BLOCKS NORTHERN ASIA'S WEATHER FROM GOING SOUTH. INSTEAD, INDIA HAS THE THREE SEASONS OF THE *TROPICS:*

HOLD IT!

A *HOT* SEASON (MAY-JULY)...

A *WET* SEASON, OR *MONSOON* (AUGUST-SEPTEMBER)...

AND AN *IN-BETWEEN* SEASON (THE REST OF THE YEAR).

SPROING!

A FINE CLIMATE FOR NOURISHING *GROWING THINGS,* WHETHER THEY BE *LARGE MAMMALS, MOSQUITOS, MICROBES,* OR *MOLD...*

WHAT? YOU'VE NEVER SEEN A RHINOCEROS WITH A SKIN CONDITION?

...AND, AROUND THE YEAR *2500 B.C.,* A *CIVILIZATION* SPROUTED ALONG THE *INDUS,* ONE OF THE MIGHTY RIVERS FLOWING DOWN FROM THE HIMALAYAN BROW.

SECOND CITIES

THE DRAVIDIAN PEOPLE, WHO BUILT THE FIRST INDIAN CIVILIZATION, SEEM TO HAVE VISITED THE CITIES OF SUMER FIRST, TO SEE HOW IT WAS DONE.

GOOD LORD! :CHOKE!:

THERE THEY FOUND CROOKED STREETS, EMPTY LOTS USED AS GARBAGE DUMPS, AND SEWERS SERVING AS A WATER SUPPLY...

SPLOOK

IT'S PRETTY OBVIOUS WHAT THE VISITORS THOUGHT OF SUMERIAN CIVILIZATION...

HEY...GIVE US SOME CREDIT FOR TRYING...

...BECAUSE OF WHAT THEY DID WHEN THEY GOT HOME!

I HAVE ONLY THREE THINGS TO SAY: WORLD'S BIGGEST BATHTUB!

PHEW! YUP!

COMIN' RIGHT UP!

WE KNOW LITTLE OF ANCIENT DRAVIDIAN GOVERNMENT, BUT THEY MUST HAVE HAD ONE POTENT PLANNING DEPARTMENT...

O.K...FIRST, WE NEED SEVEN MILLION IDENTICAL BRICKS...

THEY LAID OUT A GRID OF STRAIGHT STREETS, EACH WITH A BRICK-LINED DRAINAGE DITCH.

THEY BUILT SUBSTANTIAL PRIVATE BATHS WITH SUNKEN DRAINS FLOWING INTO THE SEWER.

REMEMBER, SON, A BRICKLAYER WILL NEVER LACK WORK!

AND THEN — THE **WORLD'S BIGGEST BATHTUB** — A 13-METER LONG PUBLIC POOL IN A LUXURIOUS BATHHOUSE (LIKE THE TEMPLE TANKS OF MODERN INDIA).

AH... BATHS, PUBLIC AND PRIVATE... GOOD WATER SUPPLY... NICE, STRAIGHT SEWERS... ANYTHING WE'VE **FORGOTTEN**?

UM... HOUSES?

OH, STOP IT! THIS IS SUPPOSED TO BE A CLEAN CIVILIZATION!

OH RIGHT, THE HOUSES! BUILT ALL ALIKE ON FEATURELESS STREETS, OPENING ONTO COURTYARDS, THE DOOR TO THE REAR...

IT'S CLEAN, BUT WHERE AM I?

...AND THE **GREAT GRANARY,** WHERE JARS OF GRAIN WERE BANKED ABOVE A SYSTEM OF BRICK DUCTS WHICH ALLOWED AIR TO CIRCULATE.

EXCUSE ME— WHERE'S MY HOUSE?

WHEN IT WAS ALL DONE, THEY PRONOUNCED IT GOOD.

IT'S SIMPLE — JUST TAKE A LEFT AND A RIGHT AND A LEFT AND A RIGHT AND A LEFT AND A RIGHT AND A RIGHT AND A LEFT...

SO THEY BUILT SEVERAL MORE CITIES ON THE SAME PLAN! THE TWO BIGGEST ONES ARE NOW CALLED **HARAPPA** AND **MOHENJO-DARO,** BUT THESE ARE MODERN NAMES. THE ORIGINAL NAMES ARE LOST FOREVER.✳

...AND A RIGHT AND A LEFT...

THE HARAPPAN RUINS CONTAIN HARDLY ANYTHING **WRITTEN.** THE FEW SHORT INSCRIPTIONS ARE BARELY ENOUGH TO IDENTIFY THE LANGUAGE AS DRAVIDIAN, RELATED TO PRESENT-DAY SOUTH INDIAN LANGUAGES.

CAN SUCH A COMPLEX CULTURE HAVE EXISTED WITHOUT TEMPLE RECORDS, BOOKKEEPING, INVOICES, PLANS, STORIES, LETTERS, SPREADSHEETS ....?

HOW CAN WE REMEMBER OUR PAST?

PAST, PRESENT, FUTURE — ALL ILLUSIONS!

OR DID THEY WRITE ON PERISHABLE MATERIALS THAT HAVE DISINTEGRATED IN THE INDIAN CLIMATE?

OR WERE THEY THE FIRST CIVILIZATION TO INVENT THE SHREDDER?

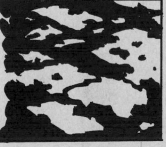

MAN! CLAY TABLETS ARE TOUGH ON SHREDDERS!

CRUNK CRACKITY

FOR ABOUT A THOUSAND YEARS, THESE "HARAPPANS" BATTLED GEOGRAPHY. THERE WERE **FLOODS**...

AH! WOTTA BATH!

AND RIVERS SHIFTING IN THEIR BEDS...

WHOA!

...BUT THESE ARE STANDARD PROBLEMS OF LIFE ON THE RIVER... THERE WERE ALSO SOME **UNIQUE** SURPRISES, CAUSED BY THE SAME **TECTONIC** FORCES THAT MOVED INDIA AND LIFTED THE HIMALAYAS...

RMM

SURPRISES LIKE **MUD VOLCANOES**...

VORP

GOOD LORD!

...AND THE CONSTANT **UPLIFT**, WHICH MOVED THE ENTIRE **SEACOAST** AWAY!

AND, THEN, AROUND 1500 B.C., WHEN EVERYONE HAD BEEN SOFTENED UP BY ENVIRONMENTAL STRESS, CAME THE FINAL BLOW — **NORTHERN BARBARIANS**. IN INDIAN HISTORY, INVASIONS USUALLY ROLL IN FROM THE NORTHWEST — ANOTHER HIMALAYAN EFFECT WE FORGOT TO MENTION!!

COWBOYS AND INDIANS

YOU MAY RECOGNIZE THESE PARTICULAR BARBARIANS BY THEIR HORSES, CHARIOTS, AND GENERAL ATTITUDE. THEY'VE GALLOPED THROUGH THIS HISTORY BEFORE, AS THE **HITTITES, GREEKS,** AND **PERSIANS** (AND THERE ARE OTHERS YET TO COME). THE *INDIAN* BRANCH OF THIS *INDO-EUROPEAN* FAMILY CALLED THEMSELVES **ARYAN,** MEANING *"PURE."*

AT LEAST THEIR **AGGRESSION** WAS PURE! THEY PICKED THEMSELVES UP AND CONQUERED THE DARKER-SKINNED DRAVIDIAN-SPEAKERS OF THE INDUS VALLEY..

THIS IS WORSE THAN A MUD VOLCANO!!

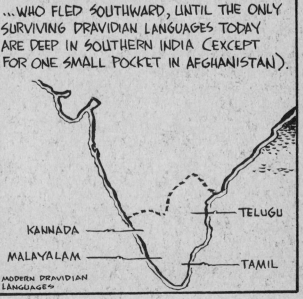

...WHO FLED SOUTHWARD, UNTIL THE ONLY SURVIVING DRAVIDIAN LANGUAGES TODAY ARE DEEP IN SOUTHERN INDIA (EXCEPT FOR ONE SMALL POCKET IN AFGHANISTAN).

KANNADA

MALAYALAM

TELUGU

TAMIL

MODERN DRAVIDIAN LANGUAGES

THEY CALLED THEMSELVES "ARYAN"— HOW DO WE **KNOW** THAT? BECAUSE THE ARYANS' SACRED SONGS AND PRAYERS HAVE SURVIVED, MEMORIZED AND TRANSMITTED **ORALLY** FROM PRIEST TO PRIEST, RIGHT DOWN TO THE PRESENT DAY!

WHY NOT WRITE 'EM DOWN?

THAT WOULD BE **AUTOMATIC TRANSMISSION!** THEN ANYONE COULD LEARN THEM...

THE COLLECTIONS OF THIS ANCIENT **SANSKRIT** * LORE ARE CALLED THE **VEDAS**, AND THIS ERA OF ARYAN CONQUEST IS KNOWN AS THE **VEDIC AGE** (1500-1000 B.C.).

OR POSSIBLY THE **IN·VEDIC** AGE !!

THE VEDAS GIVE A VIVID IMPRESSION OF THE ARYANS, AS FUN-LOVING, MEAT-EATING, ACTIVE, OPTIMISTIC FOLKS WITH HIGH SELF-ESTEEM, FOND OF HORSE RACES AND PILLAGING.

HUP!

AS MUCH AS THEY LOVED THEMSELVES, THEY HATED OTHERS, ESPECIALLY **DARK-SKINNED** OTHERS. **ARYAN** ALSO MEANT **WHITE**...

AND DARK MEANS DIRTY! BAD! LOW!

SO IT'S O.K. TO HAVE SLAVES! IT'S FUN! WE DON'T GIVE IT A SECOND THOUGHT!

I MISS MY BATHTUB...

IN THE 18TH AND 19TH CENTURY, SCHOLARS NOTICED THE CLOSE RESEMBLANCE BETWEEN **SANSKRIT** AND MOST EUROPEAN LANGUAGES.

ZEY MUST ALL COME FROM ZE SAME RRROOT!

SANSKRIT	SOME EUROPEAN LANGUAGE OR OTHER	SANSKRIT	S.E.L.O.O.
PITR	FATHER	DO, TIN	TWO, THREE
AGNI (FIRE)	IGNITE	CHAR	QUATRE
ASURA	SPIRIT	MIDHA	MEAD
VARUNA	URANUS	DYAUS	ZEUS
BAS (ENOUGH)	BASTA	DYAUS·PITR	JUPITER

HISTORIANS IMAGINED A CONQUERING ARYAN RACE, WHICH HAD SPREAD ITS LANGUAGE FROM IRELAND TO INDIA — AN IDEA SEIZED UPON BY **HITLER**, WHO INSISTED THE ARYANS WERE **NORDIC**.

THE MASTER RACE, THAT MUST BE US!

THE RACIAL INTERPRETATION OF LINGUISTIC EVIDENCE IS EVEN SHAKIER THAN HITLER'S GEOGRAPHY...

wie?

ER, UM... IS ONE OF US AN ARYAN?

THE VEDIC ARYANS WORSHIPPED MANY GODS, THEIR FAVORITE BEING **INDRA**, A WAR GOD, NATURALLY.

HE'S ONE OF US!

STILL, THESE PEOPLE ALSO HAD A SENSE OF WONDER AND SPECULATION. ONE FAMOUS VEDIC HYMN ASKS, "**WHO** IS THE GOD WE SACRIFICE TO?"

"WHO OWNS THESE SNOWY MOUNTAINS AND THE OCEAN...? WHO HAS THE QUARTERS OF THE SKY AS HIS TWO ARMS?"

?

AND THE SURPRISING ANSWER —?

UM—IT'S A HYMN TO THE GREAT GOD **WHO**!

WHAT? WHAT'S HIS NAME?

NO— WHO'S HIS NAME!

WHERE IS WHO?

ON FIRST...

THIS SHOWS HOW THE VEDIC ARYANS TEND TO SEE **EVERYTHING** AS SACRED— EVERY SYLLABLE OF THE VEDAS, FOR EXAMPLE, ESPECIALLY THE COSMIC "**OM.**"

OMMMMMM

WOA!

GET DOWN!

THEIR SPIRITUAL QUEST EVENTUALLY LED THE INDIANS TOWARD MANY REFINED SYSTEMS OF MEDITATION... BUT IN VEDIC DAYS, ARYAN WARRIORS ALTERED THEIR PERCEPTIONS THE **OLD-FASHIONED** WAY...

GLUG GLUG

WITH **DRUGS**...

BLAST

NOBODY KNOWS EXACTLY WHAT "*SOMA*" WAS — ONLY THAT SIPPING ITS SACRED JUICES PUT ARYAN WARRIORS IN THE MOOD TO *BESTRIDE THE UNIVERSE!*

BY INDRA, I COULD SACRIFICE A *HORSE!* *

THEN, AFTER COMMITTING SOME HEINOUS ACT OF PLUNDER, A WARRIOR *MEASURED* HIS *TREASURE.*

ONE, TWO... OOO, MY HEAD...

HE WASN'T COUNTING SLAVES OR GOLD, BUT *COWS.*

SEVENTY-TWO... HOLD STILL...

EVERY SO OFTEN, AN ARYAN PRINCE WOULD TURN HIS FAVORITE HORSE LOOSE TO ROAM THE COUNTRYSIDE-

FOR A YEAR, THE PRINCE AND HIS ARMY FOLLOWED, PILLAGING AND DEMANDING SUBMISSION FROM WHOEVER CROSSED THEIR PATH.

BRING OATS!

AT THE END OF THE YEAR, THE HORSE WAS SACRIFICED TO THE GODS.

THANKS FOR ALL YOUR HELP, REALLY!

YOU OBVIOUSLY ONLY PERFORMED THE GREAT HORSE SACRIFICE IF YOU THOUGHT YOU COULD WHIP ANY PRINCE WITHIN A RADIUS OF ONE HORSE-YEAR.

GALLOP -
GALLOP -
GALLOP -

YOW! HERE COMES ANOTHER ONE!

TO THE ARYANS, **COWS** EQUALLED **WEALTH** — AND NO WONDER! COWS GAVE MILK AND BUTTER TO EAT, DUNG TO BURN, URINE FOR MEDICINE (STILL USED!), AND LEATHER TO WEAR.

AND BESIDES, THEY'RE JUST PLAIN PURTY TO LOOK AT!!

IN SANSKRIT, TO "MAKE WAR" LITERALLY MEANT TO "SEEK COWS." TO "PROTECT" WAS TO "GUARD COWS." EVEN THE ENGLISH WORD "DAUGHTER" COMES FROM A ROOT MEANING "MILKMAID!" (DUDH = MILK.)

SECOND FIDDLE TO A COW — SHEESH!

IF YOUR LIFE REVOLVES AROUND COWS, AND YOU'RE A VEDIC ARYAN, THERE'S ONLY **ONE** THING TO DO: **WORSHIP THE COW** — AND SO IT'S BEEN IN INDIA FOR THE LAST **3500 YEARS!!**

HARM A SINGLE, DIVINE HAIR ON MY COW, AND I'LL KILL YOU!

HOLY MACKEREL!

SO ONWARD THE ARYANS PUSHED, BEYOND THE INDUS VALLEY AND INTO THE VAST, MAGICAL MOTHERLAND, THE INDIA OF JUNGLE, MOUNTAINS, SACRED RIVERS, VILLAGES, AND WHO KNOWS WHAT VANISHED CITIES?

WE'RE NOT IN KANSAS ANY MORE, MEN! MEN?

THE CONQUERORS BEGAN TO **HEAR** THINGS...

?

BZZOINNNG

AND **SEE** THINGS...

BZZONNG   POOT   TWEEDLE

NATIVE DIETIES BEGAN TO MINGLE WITH THE ARYAN GODS, SOMETIMES ECLIPSING THEM.

NAGA   GANESH   HANUMAN

THE ARYANS BEGAN TO HEAR ABOUT THE LOW-BORN, BLACK-SKINNED **KRISHNA**, A POPULAR HERO SAID TO BE A SORT OF GOD ON EARTH...

UM...PLEASED TO MEET YOU?

YOU SHOULD BE.

(MORE ON KRISNA LATER, I PROMISE!)

18

THE ARYANS FINALLY SETTLED DOWN AND EMBRACED INDIA IN ALL ITS GLORIOUS VARIETY — BUT THEY STILL WORRIED ABOUT **RACIAL PURITY** — SO THEY DIVIDED SOCIETY INTO FOUR SEPARATE "COLORS" (SANSKRIT VARNA) OR CLASSES: **SUDRA** WORKERS, **VAISYA** MERCHANTS, **KSHATRIYA** WARRIOR-ARISTOCRATS, AND **BRAHMIN** PRIESTS.

AH, INDIA IN ALL ITS GLORIOUS VARIETY — AND ON TOP, THE **BRAHMINS!**

KSHATRIYAS, YOU MEAN...

BRAHMINS...

BRAHMINS...

KSHATRIYAS...

KSHATRIYAS...

ETC...

SOAP?

AND SO THE STAGE IS SET FOR THE **CLIMAX** OF THE VEDIC AGE: A GREAT **WAR**, RECORDED AND MYTHOLOGIZED IN THE IMMENSE SANSKRIT EPIC, THE **MAHA-BHARATA** ("GREAT BHARAT"). LONGER THAN THE BIBLE, NOW A PBS MINI-SERIES, THIS POEM IS THE NATIONAL EPIC OF INDIA!

YEEOW!

COMMITTED AS WE ARE TO BRINGING ENLIGHTENMENT IN THE SMALLEST POSSIBLE SPACE, HERE — WITH A FANFARE OF RAMPAGING ELEPHANTS — IS THE **MAHABHARATA** IN TWO PAGES:

MAHABHARATA

THE STORY CONCERNS TWO SETS OF BROTHERS CONTENDING FOR THE THRONE. ONE SET, THE HUNDRED **KAURAVAS**, WERE THE SONS OF **DHRITARASHTRA**, WHO WOULD HAVE BEEN KING, EXCEPT THAT HE WAS **BLIND**, AND BLIND GUYS COULDN'T BE KING.

I DON'T SEE WHY NOT!

THE OTHER BROTHERS WERE THE **PANDAVAS**, OR FIVE SONS OF **PANDU**, DHRITARASHTRA'S YOUNGER BROTHER. PANDU, WHO ACTUALLY WAS KING, GAVE UP THE THRONE BECAUSE HE WAS LIVING UNDER A CURSE. THE OLDEST PANDAVA BOY, NAMED **YUDHISTHIRA**, WAS SUPPOSED TO BE KING WHEN HE CAME OF AGE...

...BUT THE KAURAVAS' CONSTANT ATTEMPTS TO **KILL** YUDHISTHIRA PERSUADED THE PANDAVAS TO RUN AWAY, TAKING UP A CAREER AS WANDERING **SOLDIERS OF FORTUNE**. THEY ENTERED A CONTEST, AND MIDDLE BROTHER **ARJUNA** WON THE PRIZE, PRINCESS **DRAUPADI**.

JUST CALLING THEM TO BREAKFAST IS LIKE READING RUSSIAN NOVEL!

FOLLOWING THEIR MOM'S ORDERS, **ALL FIVE** BROTHERS MARRIED DRAUPADI AT ONCE. BUT BEFORE THE WEDDING, THEY MADE FRIENDS WITH **KRISHNA**, WHO HIRED ON AS ARJUNA'S CHARIOTEER AND SPIRITUAL ADVISER.

UNCLE DHRITARASHTRA INVITED THE PANDUS HOME AND SPLIT THE KINGDOM BETWEEN THEM AND HIS OWN SONS. BUT YUDHISTHIRA LOST IT ALL AT **DICE** TO HIS UNPLEASANT COUSIN **DURYODHANA**.

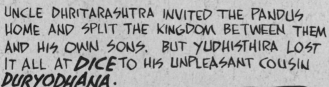

DRAUPADI AND HER FIVE HUSBANDS WENT TO LIVE IN THE WOODS. AFTER **13 YEARS**, THEY RETURNED FOR THE KINGDOM (THAT BEING THE DEAL). DURYODHANA SAID NO DICE, SO THE COUSINS PREPARED FOR **WAR**.

ENOUGH IS **ENOUGH!**

BUCKLE SNAP FASTEN

AT THE LAST MINUTE, **ARJUNA** WAS FROZEN WITH **DOUBT**: CAN IT BE **RIGHT** TO KILL **COUSINS, UNCLES, TEACHERS?** THE GOD KRISHNA, HIS DRIVER, ANSWERED, **DEFINITELY.**

THE BATTLE RAGED FOR 18 DAYS... THE PANDAVAS PREVAILED, AND THEIR STRANGE LITTLE FAMILY LIVED HAPPILY EVER AFTER — AND **THEN** CLIMBED THE HIMALAYAS TO JOIN THE GODS.

YO!

KRISHNA IS THE CUTEST, SEXIEST, AND TOUGHEST HERO IN HINDU MYTHOLOGY. MOTHERS PICTURE HIM AS AN ADORABLE INFANT STEALING BUTTER.

EVEN AS A CHILD, HE MOVED MOUNTAINS (LITERALLY).

GIGGLE

BUT HIS MOST FAMOUS TRICK WAS MAKING 99 EXTRA KRISHNAS, SO HE COULD SHARE HIMSELF WITH 100 COWGIRLS!

FOR HIS SPIRITUAL SIDE, SEE P. 45

21

THAT OLD-TIME NEW-AGE RELIGION

IN THE BEGINNING, THE ARYANS SAW NEW WORLDS TO CONQUER EVERY DAY... BUT AS INDIA'S ENDLESS CYCLES BECAME THEIR OWN, THEY CAME TO AN *OVERWHELMING REALIZATION:*

THIS IS **IT!**

...WHICH LED TO THE OBVIOUS QUESTION:

BUT—WHAT **IS** "THIS"?

AFTER A FEW MINUTES' DEEP THOUGHT, THE BRAHMIN SAGES GAVE THEIR OPINION: THE UNIVERSE HAD A *SOUL,* CALLED *BRAHMAN.*

HM..."BRAHMIN"... "BRAHMAN"... THE SIMILARITY BETWEEN YOU AND THE DIVINE ESSENCE IS A COINCIDENCE, NO DOUBT?

GOD ALONE KNOWS...

IT WAS EASIER TO SAY WHAT BRAHMAN *WASN'T* THAN WHAT IT *WAS.* IT WASN'T ANYTHING YOU COULD SEE, HEAR, OR TOUCH. WHATEVER IT WAS, IT WASN'T FOUND IN THE HOME!

WHERE'S DADDY GOING?

SIGH... SEEKING BRAHMAN AGAIN...

WHERE *IS* THIS BRAHMAN STUFF, ANYWAY? HOW CAN WE MERE MORTALS FEEL THE TOUCH OF THE UNIVERSAL SOUL? THE ANSWER WAS BRILLIANT!

IT LIES *WITHIN!*

LET'S SEE! SOMEONE HAND ME MY FISH KNIFE!

THERE IS ALSO AN *INDIVIDUAL* SOUL, OR *ATMAN* (LIT. "BREATH," AS IN "ATMOSPHERE"). EVERY LIVING BEING HAS ONE. AND THE EQUATION IS —

BRAHMAN = ATMAN!

THIS WAS COOL! TO PROBE THE SECRETS OF THE COSMOS, ALL YOU HAD TO DO WAS CONCENTRATE ON YOUR BREATHING!!

THE BRAHMINS ALSO NOTED THAT MORTIFYING THE FLESH WITH **STARVATION** AND **COLD** PRODUCED HEIGHTENED STATES OF CONSCIOUSNESS.

INHALE... EXHALE...

IN FACT, IF YOU DID IT RIGHT, SELF-DENIAL WAS SUPPOSED TO GIVE YOU **MYSTIC POWER!**

I WILL NOW SMITE THIS **RAKSHASI** WITH A DEATH-BOLT FROM MY THIRD EYE!

ZORT

IN THIS WAY, **GURUS** (TEACHERS) ACQUIRED FOLLOWERS.

DID YOU SEE HOW SHE DROPPED IN HER TRACKS? YOU DIDN'T? YOUR ASTRAL EYES NEED TRAINING ... ETC ETC ..

JUST ONE QUESTION, MASTER: IF YOU GET ENLIGHTENMENT AND POWER, WHY IS IT SELF-DENIAL?

BRAHMAN IS **IMMORTAL,** SO WHAT HAPPENED TO AN INDIVIDUAL SOUL AFTER DEATH? CLEARLY, IT LEFT THE BODY, BUT THEN—?

ANSWER: IT WENT TO **ANOTHER** BODY?! IN THIS SYSTEM, SOULS LEAP STRAIGHT FROM CORPSES TO NEWBORN BABIES! VERY ECONOMICAL!

ZIP

WAH!

I'M ALIVE!

THE SOUL'S ENDLESS CYCLE OF REBIRTH WAS THE KEY TO ANOTHER PROBLEM: THE ORIGIN OF **SUFFERING.**

NEVER IN SHORT SUPPLY... SIGH...

"TWITCH" TWITCH..

OVER THE COURSE OF A LIFETIME, ONE'S **GOOD** AND **BAD DEEDS,** OR **KARMA,** ACCUMULATED LIKE CREDITS AND DEBITS TO A SPIRITUAL BANK ACCOUNT.

LET'S SEE... **WOW!** THIS GUY WAS A **SAINT!** O BOY O BOY..

KARMA NAT'L BANK

AT DEATH, A **GOOD KARMIC BALANCE** WAS REWARDED WITH A **HIGHER REBIRTH,** A BETTER LIFE, ETC...

SO YOU WERE A SAINT, PREVIOUSLY?

BAD KARMA LED TO A WRETCHED FUTURE EXISTENCE.

WHAT WERE YOU?

SOMETHING MEDIUM-EVIL, I GUESS... A USED-HORSE DEALER OR A CARTOONIST...

SKRITCH ITCH

IN OTHER WORDS, **SUFFERING WAS YOUR OWN FAULT —** IN A PREVIOUS LIFE!! YOU DESERVED IT!

MAN, **YOU** SURE MUST HAVE SCREWED UP THE LAST TIME AROUND...

THE WHOLE, TIDY SYSTEM WAS EXPLORED IN MINUTE DETAIL IN THE HINDU CLASSICS KNOWN AS THE **BRAHMANAS, PURANAS,** AND **UPANISHADS,** COMPILED BETWEEN 800 AND 300 B.C.

O.K., I'LL BE GENEROUS, AND **GIVE** YOU A LESSON FROM THE UPANISHADS...

IF EVERYTHING SPIRITUAL IS MADE OF THE SAME STUFF, **GOD** MUST BE **ONE**. ALL THE POPULAR GODS — WHO NUMBERED **330 MILLION** BY OFFICIAL COUNT — WERE ALL REALLY DIFFERENT FORMS OF THE SAME UNIVERSAL ESSENCE. THE VEDIC **NATURE GODS** NOW BEGAN TO SEEM LESS IMPORTANT, WHILE THE **BIG THREE** OF HINDUISM CAME TO THE FORE:

← **BRAHMA** HE CREATED THE UNIVERSE, BUT WHAT HAS HE DONE LATELY? (HIS FIVE HEADS ARE TO KEEP AN EYE ON HIS WIFE.)

HONEY? HELLO? HONEY?

MARVEL COMICS? HAVE YOU CONSIDERED REPLACING "THE MIGHTY THOR?"

SHIVA HIS DANCE DESTROYS → EVERYTHING (AND SQUASHES A DWARF), GIVING BRAHMA A CHANCE TO TO START OVER.

VISHNU PRESERVES THE UNIVERSE BY COMING TO EARTH IN HUMAN OR SEMI-HUMAN FORM, AS NEEDED.

THE GOD **SHIVA**, DESPITE HIS DESTRUCTIVE SIDE, IS ALSO A **SEX GOD** WHO MAKES CROPS GROW. HIS PHALLIC EMBLEM, THE **LINGAM**, APPEARS IN EVERY SHIVA TEMPLE.

EVEN SHIVA'S LONG HAIR PILED HIGH IS SUPPOSED TO MAKE HIS **HEAD** LOOK LIKE A LINGAM...

OF COURSE, THERE IS **NO** EQUIVALENT TO THIS IN **ANY** EUROPEAN RELIGION.

SEX?! WHERE? HELP?!

 NOTE HOW THE OLD ARYAN OPTIMISM HAD SUNK INTO *PESSIMISM* AND *RESIGNATION!* IN THE OLD DAYS, YOU WANTED SOMETHING, YOU SACRIFICED A HORSE! NOW... YOU JUST GIVE UP *WANTING*...

 WHY TAKE PITY ON THE *LEPER*, THE *HUNGRY*, THE *UNTOUCHABLE*? IT'S THEIR *KARMA!*

 THIS ENDLESS CYCLE OF REBIRTHS IS A *DOWNER* TOO... WHO WANTS TO *DIE* AGAIN AND AGAIN AND AGAIN...?

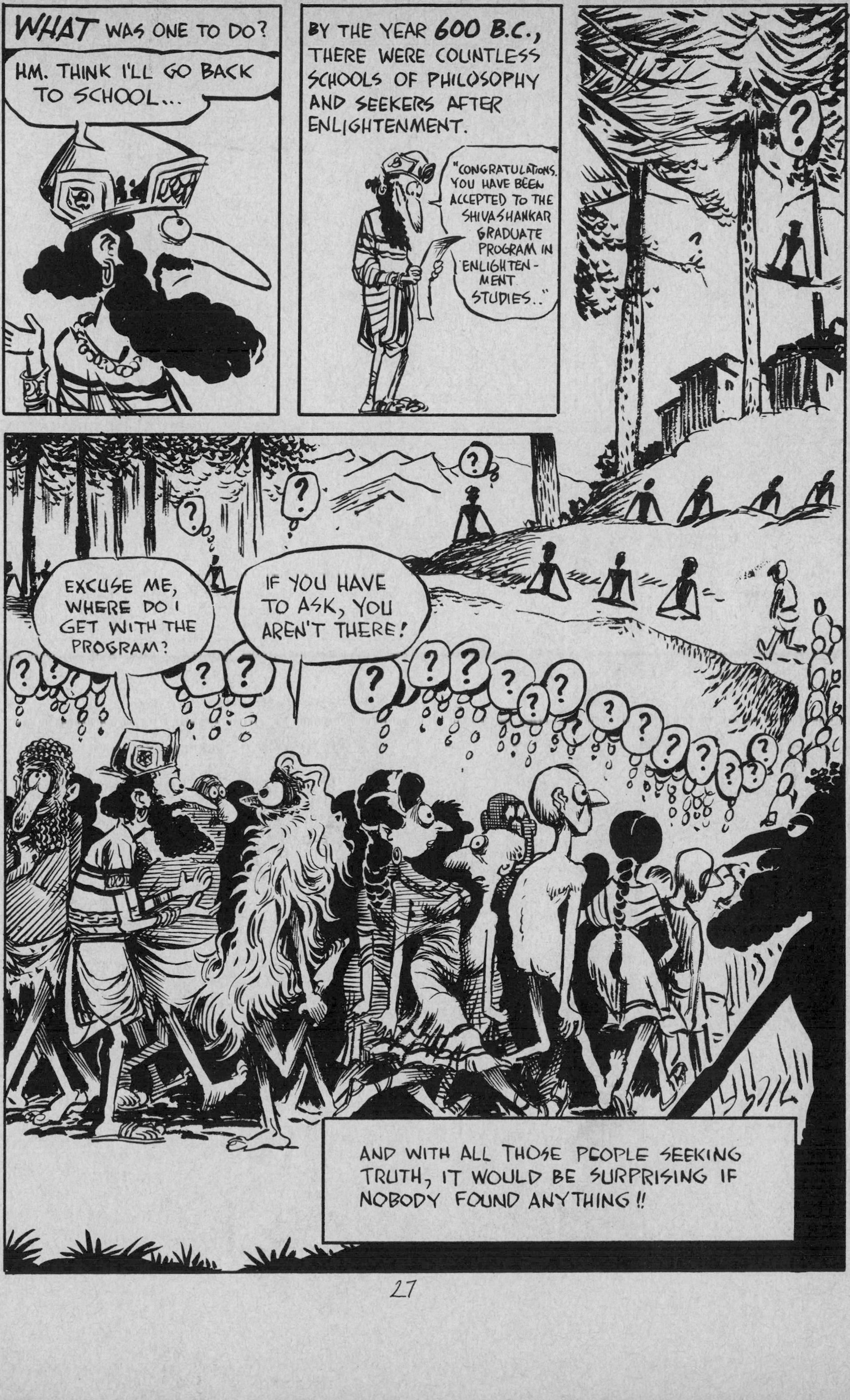
WHAT WAS ONE TO DO?
HM. THINK I'LL GO BACK TO SCHOOL...
BY THE YEAR 600 B.C., THERE WERE COUNTLESS SCHOOLS OF PHILOSOPHY AND SEEKERS AFTER ENLIGHTENMENT.
"CONGRATULATIONS. YOU HAVE BEEN ACCEPTED TO THE SHIVASHANKAR GRADUATE PROGRAM IN ENLIGHTEN-MENT STUDIES.."
EXCUSE ME, WHERE DO I GET WITH THE PROGRAM?
IF YOU HAVE TO ASK, YOU AREN'T THERE!
AND WITH ALL THOSE PEOPLE SEEKING TRUTH, IT WOULD BE SURPRISING IF NOBODY FOUND ANYTHING!!

Two Who Found It

THE PRINCE **GAUTAMA**, THE FUTURE BUDDHA, WAS BORN AROUND **567 B.C.** IN EASTERN INDIA TO OVERPROTECTIVE PARENTS. THEY VOWED HE WOULD NEVER SEE ANYTHING ICKY OR UNPLEASANT!

THAT WAY, HE'LL ALWAYS BE HAPPY!

MY SWEET QUEEN!

THE YOUNG PRINCE SLIPPED OUT OF THE PALACE ONE DAY — AND GOT THE **SHOCK** OF HIS LIFE. HE SAW —

WHAT'S THAT?

A **SICK** PERSON...

ECH!

AN **OLD, SICK** PERSON...

GHASP!

A **DEAD** PERSON...

WHOA!

...AND A WANDERING HOLY MAN!!

EH?

PRINCE GAUTAMA CONCEIVED AN **INSTANT** DESIRE TO BECOME A WANDERING HOLY MAN!

HARDLY SURPRISING, CONSIDERING THE ALTERNATIVES!

KOF!

HE BECAME OBSESSED WITH THE PROBLEM OF **HUMAN SUFFERING.** WHERE DOES IT COME FROM? WHY DOES IT CONTINUE?

AND MOST IMPORTANT, HOW CAN I **AVOID** IT??

STILL, HE WAS A GOOD BOY: HE DUTIFULLY MARRIED AND HAD A CHILD — AND **THEN** FLED TO SEEK TRUTH!

SON!

HUSBAND!

YUP. THIS IS WHAT WE'RE TRYING TO AVOID...

WAA

(BEING A PRINCE, HE TOOK A FRIEND WHO WAS ALSO A SERVANT!)

TOGETHER WE'LL DO THE MOST **ATROCIOUS** AUSTERITIES!!

UM...

HE TRIED OUT VARIOUS HINDU SCHOOLS... GOT **A's** IN STARVING, BEGGING, AND PENANCE... AND SOON HAD FIVE DISCIPLES OF HIS OWN...

BODY'S GETTING LIGHTER, ANYWAY!

...UNTIL, THAT IS, HE ADMITTED —

UM...THIS ISN'T REALLY "IT"... I DON'T HAVE A CLUE WHAT **IS**... THOUGHT I DID... SORRY!

GOOD. BYE!

HIS DISCIPLES LEFT, AND GAUTAMA SAT DOWN IN THE SHADE TO THINK THINGS OVER.

GET ME SOMETHING TO EAT, PREFERABLY **PORK**...

AND A RAZOR...

HE VOWED TO SIT THERE UNTIL ENLIGHTENMENT CAME, HOWEVER LONG IT TOOK!

B-BUT, MASTER... WOULDN'T YOU PREFER THE INFINITELY LESS COMFORTABLE **SUN**?

I'M SEEKING ENLIGHTENMENT, NOT **DISCOMFORT**! NOW GO!

RETURN AT DINNER TIME.

29

THE SEEKER HAD TRIED EVERYTHING ELSE, SO NOW HE DID THE ONLY THING LEFT: *NOTHING.* FOR 49 DAYS GAUTAMA MEDITATED, TORMENTED BY DEMONS...

AND, IN THE END, HE HAD IT!!

AFTER HE GOT IT, GAUTAMA PONDERED HIS IDEAS FOR SEVERAL MORE WEEKS...

BRING ME A *SMALL* PLATE OF PORK...

...BEFORE GETTING UP TO LOOK FOR HIS FORMER FOLLOWERS.

OW! ONE MORE SOURCE OF SUFFERING!!

HE FOUND THEM IN THE EXQUISITE VILLAGE OF *SARNATH*, NEAR VARANASI.

HEY, GUYS! GUESS WHAT?

HEY!

LOOK WHO'S LOOKING *PLUMP!*

WELL? ISN'T *ANYONE* GOING TO FALL AT MY FEET IN A WORSHIPFUL ATTITUDE?

WELL?

GIVE US A MOMENT... WE HAVE A BIG PSYCHIC INVESTMENT IN DISCOMFORT...

HERE HE GAVE HIS FIRST SERMON, "SETTING IN MOTION THE WHEEL OF THE LAW," AND FOREVER AFTER GAUTAMA HAS BEEN KNOWN AS THE *BUDDHA*, THE ENLIGHTENED ONE!

WOW! HE REALLY *DID* GET IT!!

BEFORE LOOKING AT BUDDHA'S IDEAS, LET'S MEET ANOTHER YOUNG NOBLEMAN, **VARDHAMANA**, FOUNDER OF THE **JAIN** SECT. BORN AROUND 540 B.C., A QUARTER CENTURY AFTER GAUTAMA, VARDHAMANA ALSO LEFT A WIFE AND CHILD TO SEEK TRUTH.

HEY, DUDE! THIS **IS** TRUTH !!

VARDHAMANA JOINED A SECT CALLED "FREE FROM BONDS," WHICH PRACTICED **RADICAL SELF·DENIAL.**

WHAT IT MEANS — "FREE FROM BONDS?"

WE INVEST ONLY IN STOCKS. NOW GIVE ME ALL YOUR POSSESSIONS...

WHEN VARDHAMANA WAS DEEMED READY, HIS **GURU** SENT HIM INTO THE WORLD WITH ONLY A SINGLE ROBE.

ONLY ONE ROBE? PRETTY RADICAL...

IT GETS WORSE...

FOR TWELVE YEARS, THE SEEKER WANDERED, THE ROBE HIS ONLY POSSESSION.

IN THE THIRTEENTH YEAR, HIS ROBE WAS EITHER STOLEN, OR IT DISINTEGRATED— ANYWAY, IT WAS GONE···

?

...AND **ENLIGHTENMENT STRUCK!!**

THIS IS RADICAL!

USING THE NAME **MAHAVIRA** ("GREAT HERO") HE PREACHED A DOCTRINE OF **SELF-DENIAL**. HIS FOLLOWERS WENT NAKED AND PLUCKED THEIR BEARDS OUT HAIR BY HAIR.

B·BUT... ISN'T SELF-TORTURE A FORM OF SELF·PROMOTION?

LEAVE THE SECT.

MAHAVIRA'S **REVERENCE FOR LIFE** WAS EQUALLY EXTREME. JAINS TAKE NO ANIMAL LIFE, NOT EVEN AN INSECT.*

THAT MOSQUITO MIGHT HAVE BEEN YOUR GRANDMOTHER!

IN FACT, MAHAVIRA BELIEVED IN **MICROBES**. HE SHUNNED ONIONS, FOR FEAR OF EATING INVISIBLE, SOIL·DWELLING ANIMALS!

BESIDES, I DON'T REALLY **LIKE** ONIONS...

AND, SOMEWHAT SURPRISINGLY, ALTHOUGH THE MAHAVIRA BELIEVED IN SPIRIT AND KARMA, HE NEVER MENTIONED **GOD** AT ALL...

OOPS.

HEY, IF WE BELIEVE IN INVISIBLE BEINGS ON ONIONS, WHY NOT IN THE SKY?

ONCE UPON A TIME, SAYS INDIAN FOLKLORE, ALL THE ANIMALS MET TO DECIDE WHAT TO DO ABOUT **HUMAN BEINGS**. THE VOTE WAS ALL BUT **UNANIMOUS**.

KILL 'EM!

WIPE 'EM OUT

ANNIHILATE 'M

DESTROY

EXPUNGE

ONLY THE MOSQUITO SPOKE UP FOR US.

MMMM... THEY'RE **SO** DELICIOUS...

SO — THEY LET US LIVE, AND HINDUS HAVE BEEN **GRATEFUL** TO MOSQUITOS EVER SINCE!

JUST DRINK YOUR FILL, AND **LEAVE ME ALONE!!**

NOW BACK TO THE BUDDHA AND HIS SPEECH. UNLIKE MAHAVIRA'S EXTREME SELF-DENIAL, THE BUDDHA RECOMMENDED **MODERATION.** THIS WAS TRULY **REVOLUTIONARY!**

MODERATION? ARE YOU SURE THIS IS A **RELIGION?**

NO...

HIS SERMON LAYS OUT THE ORIGIN OF **SUFFERING** — AND A PLAN OF **ESCAPE** THROUGH MODERATION.

MODERATION! I CAN'T GET OVER IT!!

BIZARRE!

SUFFERING OR UNHAPPINESS, HE SAID, COMES WHEN WE ARE SEPARATED FROM PLEASURE.

THE REASON IS THAT WE ARE **ATTACHED** TO PLEASURE... WE **DESIRE** IT... AND THIS DESIRE IS WHAT CAUSES OUR MISERY.

EH?

HUH?

WHAT?

YOU'RE NOT UNHAPPY BECAUSE YOU LACK EXPENSIVE SHOES OR ELECTRONIC GEAR, BUT BECAUSE YOU **WANT** THEM.

AND HAVING THINGS DOESN'T HELP, BECAUSE THERE'S ALWAYS MORE TO WANT...

THE OBVIOUS THING TO DO IS TO **ABANDON ALL DESIRE.**

ABANDON DESIRE? OH, YEAH, **RIGHT!**

THIS WAS ALL PRETTY HINDU SO FAR... BUT THE BUDDHA'S RECIPE FOR ESCAPE WAS UNIQUE: HE CAUTIONED **AGAINST EXTREMES.** TOO MUCH PLEASURE IS VAIN...TOO MUCH SELF-DENIAL IS WORTHLESS.

WE HAVE TO GIVE UP GIVING UP?

HIS PROGRAM WAS THE **MIDDLE WAY** OR **8-FOLD PATH.**

1. RIGHT VIEWS
2. RIGHT INTENTION
3. RIGHT SPEECH
4. RIGHT CONDUCT
5. RIGHT LIVELIHOOD
6. RIGHT EFFORT
7. RIGHT RECOLLECTION
8. RIGHT MEDITATION

THERE IS A DEEPER REASON WHY DESIRE CAUSES PAIN, HE WENT ON. IT IS THAT "**REALITY**" IS AN **ILLUSION,** A SORT OF MOVIE CREATED BY OUR MIND AND SENSES. HOW CAN ANYTHING BUT **PAIN** COME FROM EMBRACING A **HALLUCINATION**?

THE BUDDHA BELIEVED THAT, IN REALITY, THE COSMOS IS CEASELESSLY **CHANGING,** BLINKING ON AND OFF... ALWAYS BEING CREATED — **NOTHING IS PERMANENT.**

ANYONE WHO THINKS OTHERWISE DOESN'T KNOW QUANTUM PHYSICS!

THE IMMORTAL SOUL? AN ILLUSION! REINCARNATION? **FORGET** IT!! KARMA? **OUT!?** AND...AND...

GOD?

A **REALLY** IMMODERATE IDEA!!

NOTHING BUT MODERATION —... WHAT A CONCEPT! NO BEDS OF NAILS... NO PAINFUL POSTURES... NO SELF-STARVATION...WASN'T THERE **SOMETHING** A BUDDHIST MONK COULD RENOUNCE?

OH, ALL RIGHT... **WOMEN.** YOU CAN'T HAVE ANY WOMEN.

WELL, THERE'S SOME CONSOLATION AT LEAST...

ALTHOUGH BUDDHA PREACHED RENUNCIATION OF DESIRE, HE DID NOT RENOUNCE THE WORLD. FOR THE NEXT 40 YEARS, HE TRAVELED, SPOKE, AND BUILT HIS ORGANIZATION.*

FORWARD, MONKS, TO THE FUNDRAISER!!

MAHAVIRA DID LIKEWISE.

ONWARD TO THE — HOLD IT! I HEARD SOMEBODY SWAT A MOSQUITO!

EVEN THEIR DEATHS WERE IN CONTRAST: MAHAVIRA FASTED TO DEATH AT AGE 72...

OOPS!

... WHEREAS THE BUDDHA OVERDOSED ON PORK AT THE AGE OF 80. (487, B.C.).

BURP! WELL... MAYBE I WAS A LITTLE ATTACHED TO PORK!

THE BUDDHIST ORDER REJECTED MANY OLD CUSTOMS. INSTEAD OF SACRIFICING ANIMALS, THE BUDDHISTS SIMPLY PRAYED, MEDITATED, OR WALKED CLOCKWISE AROUND SHRINES!

HEY! OTHER WAY!

SORRY. I'M A HERETIC.

THOUGH MONKS VOWED POVERTY AND CHASTITY, THEY SAID NOTHING ABOUT OBEDIENCE. MAJOR ISSUES WERE DISCUSSED AT MEETINGS WITH REGULAR RULES OF ORDER.

MOST OUTRAGEOUS TO TRADITION, PEOPLE FROM ALL SOCIAL CLASSES COULD JOIN THE ORDER AND EAT TOGETHER!

WHAT'S THAT SOUND?

ORTHODOX RETCHING...

BOTH TEACHERS' *BUREAUCRACIES* LIVED ON... THE *JAINS* KEPT ESSENTIALLY THE SAME PURE, TOUGH DOCTRINE LAID DOWN BY MAHAVIRA.

WHY NO CHANGES?

THE GREAT ONE, IN HIS PERFECTION, IS NOW EVERYWHERE, LOOKING OVER OUR SHOULDERS...

(THERE WAS ONE SPLIT, BETWEEN THE ORTHODOX *SKY-CLAD*, WHOSE PRIESTS WENT NAKED, AND THE MORE PRAGMATIC "WHITE-CLAD"... BUT THIS WAS A MERE QUIBBLE... THEY AGREED ON ALL ELSE.

SIGH... THIS WORLD IS CORRUPT...

TODAY THERE ARE SOME 2 MILLION JAINS IN INDIA, INCLUDING FOR SOME REASON A DISPROPORTIONATE NUMBER OF STOCKBROKERS.

ARE YOU STILL "FREE FROM BONDS?"

:AHEM: EVEN THE SKY-CLAD WEAR ROBES IN TODAY'S IMPERFECT WORLD...

THE BUDDHISTS, ON THE OTHER HAND, ADDED HEAPS OF SUPERNATURAL BEINGS TO THE BUDDHA'S FIRST DRAFT.

ONCE YOU GET STARTED, IT'S HARD TO STOP!

THEY ACTIVELY WENT AFTER THE *RICH* AND *POWERFUL* AS A WAY TO SPREAD THE WORD.

YOU ARE TOO *ATTACHED* TO WEALTH, HIGHNESS! WHY NOT GIVE IT TO *US*, WHOSE ATTITUDE IS BETTER...?

BUT FOR THE TIME BEING, THEY WERE JUST *ONE* INDIAN SECT AMONG *MANY*.

WE HAVE THE *ANSWER!*

WHAT A COINCIDENCE — SO DO *WE!*

IN THE YEARS AFTER 500 B.C., THE BUDDHISTS AND JAINS WERE NOT THE ONLY SECTS PROMOTING THEMSELVES AND INSULTING EACH OTHER AS THEY VIED FOR POPULAR SUPPORT AND ROYAL FAVOR...

NEXT!

THERE WERE ALSO THE **AJIVIKAS**, VERY JAIN-LIKE, FOUNDED BY ONE OF MAHAVIRA'S OLD BEGGING BUDDIES. EVIDENTLY, THEY PARTED ON BAD TERMS.

HALF YOUR IDEAS YOU **STOLE** FROM ME!

YEH... AND NOW THEY'RE **MINE!**

THE **MATERIALISTS** BELIEVED ONLY IN THE PHYSICAL WORLD. TO THEM, THE ONLY **ILLUSION** WAS THE SPIRIT WORLD PREACHED BY EVERYONE ELSE!

THEIR "SPIRIT WORLD" IS NOTHING BUT AN **INVENTION** DESIGNED TO **SCARE** PEOPLE INTO **SUBMISSION!**

THE MATERIALISTS ALWAYS HAD A HARD TIME GETTING GOVERNMENT GRANTS AND EVENTUALLY SANK OUT OF SIGHT.

HEY! WE **LIKE** SCARING PEOPLE INTO SUBMISSION. NOW GO...

YESSIR!

THEN THERE WAS A SMORGAS-BORD OF DIFFERENT **YOGAS** ("PRACTICES"). SOME OF THEM EMPHASIZED **BREATHING** AND **MEDITATION**.

YOGA FOR SAX PLAYERS!

OTHERS WERE BASED ON DOING **GOOD DEEDS.**

LIKE HELPING THE POOR?

NO... LIKE GIVING GIFTS TO BRAHMINS...

STILL OTHERS INVOLVED CONTORTED POSTURES...

HELP ME UP!!

AND **TANTRISM** CELEBRATED **SEX** WITH TYPICAL HINDU THOROUGH-NESS!

O.K... POSITION #133...

EVERY FOUR YEARS, ALL THE SECTS WOULD GATHER AT THE JUNCTION OF INDIA'S TWO MOST SACRED RIVERS, THE *GANGA* AND *JUMNA*. THIS IMMENSE FESTIVAL, CALLED THE *KUMBH MELA,* CONTINUES TODAY, DISPLAYING RELIGIOUS INDIA IN ALL ITS TOLERANT, TEEMING DIVERSITY. (JUST DON'T MESS WITH THE COWS!*)

I AM *HOLIER* THAN *THOU!!*

WHAT WAS THAT?

I *SAID*, "I AM HOLIER THAN THOU!"

OH, NEVER MIND. I THOUGHT YOU SAID, "I AM HOLIER THAN A COW."

AFTER THE BUDDHA, THE IDEA OF *AHIMSA* (NONVIOLENCE) SPREAD THROUGH INDIAN RELIGION. THIS MEANS DOING NO HARM TO ANY ANIMAL, EATING NO MEAT, WEARING NO LEATHER SHOES.

SHOES? WHO CAN AFFORD *SHOES?*

FOR HINDUS, THE PERFECT SYMBOL OF NONVIOLENCE IS THE *COW,* A GENTLE CREATURE.

ACTUALLY, WE'RE JUST VERY GOOD AT INTERNALIZING OUR ANGER...

YET TODAY'S MOST MILITANT HINDUS USE THE SLOGAN *"COW PROTECTION"* AS AN EXCUSE FOR VIOLENCE AGAINST MOSLEMS...

RUN! HERE COME THE NONVIOLENT!

39

HOLY TERROR

So... THIS WAS THE COMPLEX, TRADITION-LADEN IMMENSITY THAT **ALEXANDER OF MACEDON** THOUGHT HE COULD CONQUER IN **328 B.C.**

YO! WAIT! NOT SO FAST!!

I'M GREAT, BUT I'M GONE!

INDIA BRUSHED HIM OFF LIKE AN ELEPHANT WHISKING AWAY A MOSQUITO.

FWOP

BUT AT LEAST **ONE** INDIAN PRINCE ADMIRED ALEXANDER'S HUMONGOUS **CHUTZPAH.** HIS NAME WAS **CHANDRA-GUPTA MAURYA.**

HE **WAS** INSPIRING!!

RIGHT AFTER ALEX LEFT, CHANDRAGUPTA CONQUERED MOST OF INDIA, FOUNDING THE **MAURYAN EMPIRE AND DYNASTY,** CAPITAL **PATALIPUTRA** (MODERN PATNA).

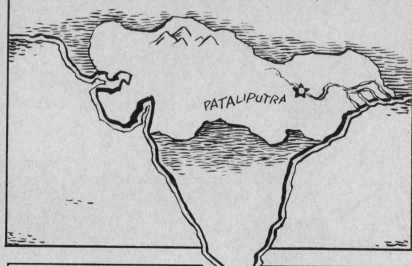

PATALIPUTRA

IN THE 6TH CENTURY B.C., NORTH INDIA, CONQUERED BY **DARIUS,** BECAME PART OF THE **PERSIAN EMPIRE** (SEE VOL.6). PERSIAN INFLUENCE INCLUDED SUCH ARCHITECTURAL ITEMS AS THE **1000-PILLAR HALL** (WITH PERSIAN PILLARS!):

WHEN **ALEXANDER** TOOK OVER PERSIA IN THE 300's, THE INDIANS GOT A LOOK AT **GREEK SCULPTURE.**

HEY! TWISTY!

FOR A TIME, THE NORTH INDIAN **GANDHARA** SCHOOL COPIED THE GREEKS, BUT EVENTUALLY QUIT.

I JUST COULDN'T DO ONE MORE OF THOSE **BLOCKY** WOMEN!

CHANDRAGUPTA'S GRANDSON **ASHOKA** INHERITED THE EMPIRE, AS WELL AS THE URGES THAT DROVE HIS GRANDPA TO CONQUER IT.

MORE...

I MUST HAVE MORE...

IN THE FIRST FEW YEARS OF HIS REIGN, HIS ARMIES CONQUERED MERCILESSLY.

PLEASE, I PREFER TO THINK OF IT AS "THOROUGHLY."

BUT THEN — AFTER AN ESPECIALLY *THOROUGH* EXTERMINATION, ASHOKA NOTICED SOMETHING *ODD* FOR A MAN IN HIS POSITION...

HEY! I FEEL REALLY BAD!

41

ASHOKA IMMEDIATELY BECAME A BUDDHIST AND A VEGETARIAN.

WHENEVER I LOOK AT **MEAT**, IT REMINDS ME ~ **WHFGH!**

HE DECREED THAT THE NATIONAL POLICY WAS TO BE ONE OF **NON VIOLENCE**.

ESPECIALLY FOR **YOU** GUYS!!

HE DREW UP LAWS AND HAD THEM INSCRIBED ON POLISHED STONE ALL ACROSS THE REALM. HIS PILLAR AT SARNATH CARRIES THE NATIONAL EMBLEM OF TODAY'S INDIA!

AN ALL-SEEING BEAST OF PREY? IS THAT NON VIOLENT?

WELL, HE WAS AS BUDDHIST AS A KING CAN BE... OF COURSE, ASHOKA STILL HAD **POLICE, JAILS,** AND **TAX COLLECTORS,** BUT HIS REIGN IS STILL REMEMBERED AS A **GOLDEN AGE** OF PEACE AND PROSPERITY. *

ARE VEGETARIANS REALLY LESS VIOLENT?

UNTIL YOU WAVE A **SALAMI** IN FRONT OF THEM!

DURING THE MAURYAN DYNASTY, THE COURT HIRED SCHOLARS TO PONDER PRACTICAL PROBLEMS NOT COVERED IN THE HINDU SCRIPTURES.

WRITE ME SOMETHING ON HOW TO RUN A GOLDEN AGE WITH POLICE, SPIES, AND TAX COLLECTORS...

THEY STANDARDIZED A SCRIPT AND WROTE SOME **CLASSICS:** THE **ARTHASHASTRA,** ON GOVERNMENT, A SANSKRIT **GRAMMAR,** AND THE FAMOUS SEX MANUAL **KAMA SUTRA.**

THERE GOES THE STAFF OF THE KAMA SUTRA, OFF TO WORK~

BUT RELIGIOUS CLASSICS LIKE THE **VEDAS** CONTINUED TO BE PASSED ALONG BY WORD OF MOUTH.

REPEAT AFTER ME, SON: "MEMORY — USE IT OR LOSE IT!"

*@# BOOKS!

WAIT. I ALSO LOST MY PENCIL...

FWAP

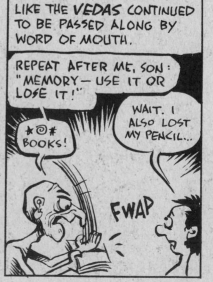

HE LAVISHED DONATIONS ON THE BUDDHISTS.

AH... WHAT DO WE **DO** WITH IT?

BUILD SOMETHING **STUPENDOUS!**

B-BUT THAT WOULDN'T BE **MODERATE**...

WHAT? YOU REFUSE MY MONEY?

SIGH... NO...

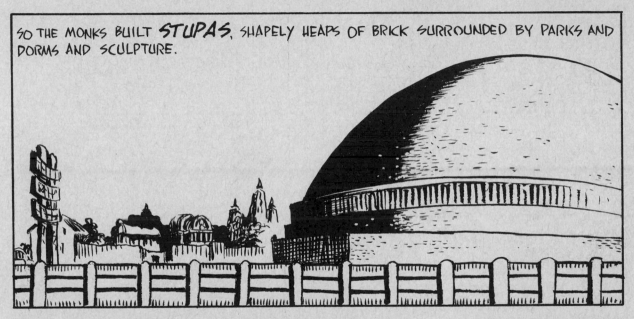

SO THE MONKS BUILT **STUPAS**, SHAPELY HEAPS OF BRICK SURROUNDED BY PARKS AND DORMS AND SCULPTURE.

THEY TOOK CUTTINGS FROM BUDDHA'S FAMOUS TREE AND TRANSPLANTED THEM ACROSS INDIA. THERE ARE STILL A COUPLE OF THEM GROWING HERE AND THERE.

MISSIONARY WORK STEPPED UP — AND **UP**, OVER THE HIMALAYAS, AND INTO NEPAL, TIBET, AND CHINA.

IF YOU DON'T BELIEVE IN AUSTERITIES, THEN WHAT ARE YOU DOING **HERE**?

DESPITE THE BUDDHISTS' NEW IDEAS, HINDU TRADITIONS HAD **DEEP ROOTS**: THE OLD GODS, BRAHMIN PRESTIGE, AND ESPECIALLY THE **CASTE SYSTEM**.

A CASTE IS NOT THE SAME AS THE ARYAN SOCIAL CLASSES MENTIONED ON P. 17... A CASTE IS SMALLER... LIKE A **CLAN**... AND MORE: **EVERYONE IN A CASTE DOES THE SAME WORK.** IN TRADITIONAL INDIA, YOUR **NAME** IS YOUR **BIRTH** IS YOUR **JOB!**

WITHIN THE CASTE, IT'S ALL FOR ONE AND ONE FOR ALL. BUT **BETWEEN** CASTES, RELATIONS WERE FORMAL, CAUTIOUS, EVEN SUSPICIOUS... EVERYONE WORRIED ABOUT WHAT CASTE HAD HANDLED THEIR **FOOD**.

IT'S OKAY — I'M YOUR MOTHER!

THE MERE SIGHT OF SOMEONE LOW-CASTE COULD SEND A **BRAHMIN** INTO A FRENZY OF **SELF-PURIFICATION**.

NEXT TIME SHOUT, SO I CAN GET OUT OF THE WAY!

COW PIES

IF A BRAHMIN **MURDERED** A LOW-CASTE VICTIM, THE PUNISHMENT WAS A SLAP ON THE WRIST.

WAIT — BEFORE YOU **TOUCH** ME — ARE **YOU** A BRAHMIN, TOO?

BUT KILLING A BRAHMIN — THIS WAS ALMOST AS BAD AS KILLING A **COW!**

SAYS SO RIGHT HERE IN THIS **LAW BOOK**, WRITTEN BY BRAHMINS...

AND WITHIN THE CASTE, WHAT WAS THE POSITION OF WOMEN?

I'LL GIVE YOU ONE GUESS...

AS MOTHERS, OF COURSE, THEY WERE VALUED. EVERYONE LOVES HER OWN MOTHER!)

HEY, MOM! LOVE YOU! GOIN' OUT!

BUT DAUGHTERS WERE A NET MINUS. A BRIDE'S FAMILY PAID FOR HER WEDDING, WHICH HAD TO BE LAVISH. DAUGHTERS WERE EXPENSIVE!

A WIFE WAS NOT SUPPOSED TO CALL HER HUSBAND BY NAME, LOOK HIM IN THE EYE, OR WALK BESIDE HIM!

YO! HEY! LISTEN!

AND WIDOWS WERE CONSIDERED BAD LUCK.

TSK TSK TSK

IN FACT, IT WAS GOOD FORM FOR A WIDOW TO JUMP INTO HER HUSBAND'S CREMATION.

OOH AH

CLAP CLAP

(THERE WERE SOME EXCEPTIONS... AT LEAST ONE WIDOW BECAME A PRIME MINISTER IN SOUTH INDIA... BUT THIS WAS RARE...)

WELL-DONE IS MORE USUAL...

IN THE CENTURIES AFTER ASHOKA (200 B.C.- 100 A.D.) BRAHMINISM REVIVED, MOST NOTABLY IN THE *DEVOTIONAL* YOGA CENTERED ON *KRISHNA*.

WE'LL FIX THOSE *BUDDHISTS!*

THE IDEA HERE WAS NOT AUSTERITY, ETHICS, OR EXERCISE. ALL YOU HAD TO DO TO WIN *COSMIC MERIT* WAS TO KEEP GOD *CONSTANTLY IN MIND!!* *

O.K.! THINK OF GOD NOW!

YES... *O.K.*... LET'S SEE... THINK ABOUT GOD *NOW*... MM... THIS IS HARDER THAN IT SOUNDS...

THE MORE FOCUSED ON GOD YOU WERE, THE BETTER YOUR CHANCES OF *ESCAPING* THE TEDIOUS CYCLE OF *REBIRTH.*

HA! YOU'RE PROBABLY COMING BACK AS A *DUNG BEETLE!*

IN PRACTICE, THIS TRANSLATED INTO A LOT OF *CHANTING* KRISHNA'S VARIOUS NAMES:

HARE KRISHNA HARE RAMA HARE HARE KRISHNA KRISHNA RAMA RAMA HARE KRISHNA KRISHNA HARE RAMA KRISHNA HARE RAMA KRISHNA HARE KRISHNA KRISHNA HARE RAMA KRISHNA RAMA HARE HARE KRISHNA KRISHNA RAMA KRISHNA HARE RAMA KRISHNA RAMA RAMA RAMA...

CAN'T ARGUE WITH THAT!

* A FAMOUS FABLE DESCRIBES AN *ATHEIST* WHO HATED GOD.

GOD? THERE IS NO GOD!

ALL HIS LIFE, WHATEVER HE DID, HE KEPT REMINDING HIMSELF——

THERE *IS* NO GOD THERE IS *NO* GOD THERE IS NO *GOD* THERE IS NO...

UNTIL HE DIED.

THERE IS NO GOD THERE IS NO GOD THERE——

SURPRISE!

OF COURSE, HIS SOUL WAS INSTANTLY UNITED WITH GOD!

BY CONSTANTLY DENYING GOD, HE HAD KEPT THE THOUGHT OF GOD CONSTANTLY IN MIND!

IS MY FACE RED!

HERE WE DON'T EXACTLY HAVE FACES...

SAY... HOW DID ANYONE KNOW WHAT HAPPENED AFTER THE GUY DIED?

46

IT WAS PROBABLY SOMEONE FROM THE DEVOTIONAL KRISHNA CULTS WHO COMPOSED THE **BHAGAVAD GITA,** OR "SONG OF GOD." THIS FAMOUS RELIGIOUS POEM, LIKE SO MUCH IN ANCIENT INDIA, IS HARD TO DATE PRECISELY!

THE POEM APPEARS IN THE **MAHABHARATA,** BUT MOST HISTORIANS THINK IT WAS WRITTEN LATER AND THEN INSERTED INTO THE HUGE EPIC LIKE A POETRY SANDWICH!

RECALL (P. 19) THAT JUST BEFORE THE FINAL BATTLE, THE WARRIOR **ARJUNA** STANDS FROZEN WITH DOUBT.

ARE YOU SURE IT'S OKAY TO KILL ALL MY COUSINS?

THE **GITA** IS KRISHNA'S LITTLE PEP-TALK.

OF COURSE IT IS...

KRISHNA EXPLAINS THAT EVERYONE HAS TO ACT ACCORDING TO HIS DUTY AND THE LAW. SECOND THOUGHTS ARE USELESS. ARJUNA FINDS THIS CONFUSING, SO KRISHNA, LIKE BUDDHA, ANNOUNCES THAT EVERYTHING IS **ILLUSION—** DEATH, FOR EXAMPLE...

♪ NOTHING TO GET HUNG ABOUT... ♪

THEN WHAT ASKS ARJUNA, IS **REAL?** THAT IS, **REALLY, REALLY REAL?** HERE KRISHNA'S ANSWER IS VERY DIFFERENT FROM BUDDHA'S:

YOU **REALLY** WANT TO KNOW?

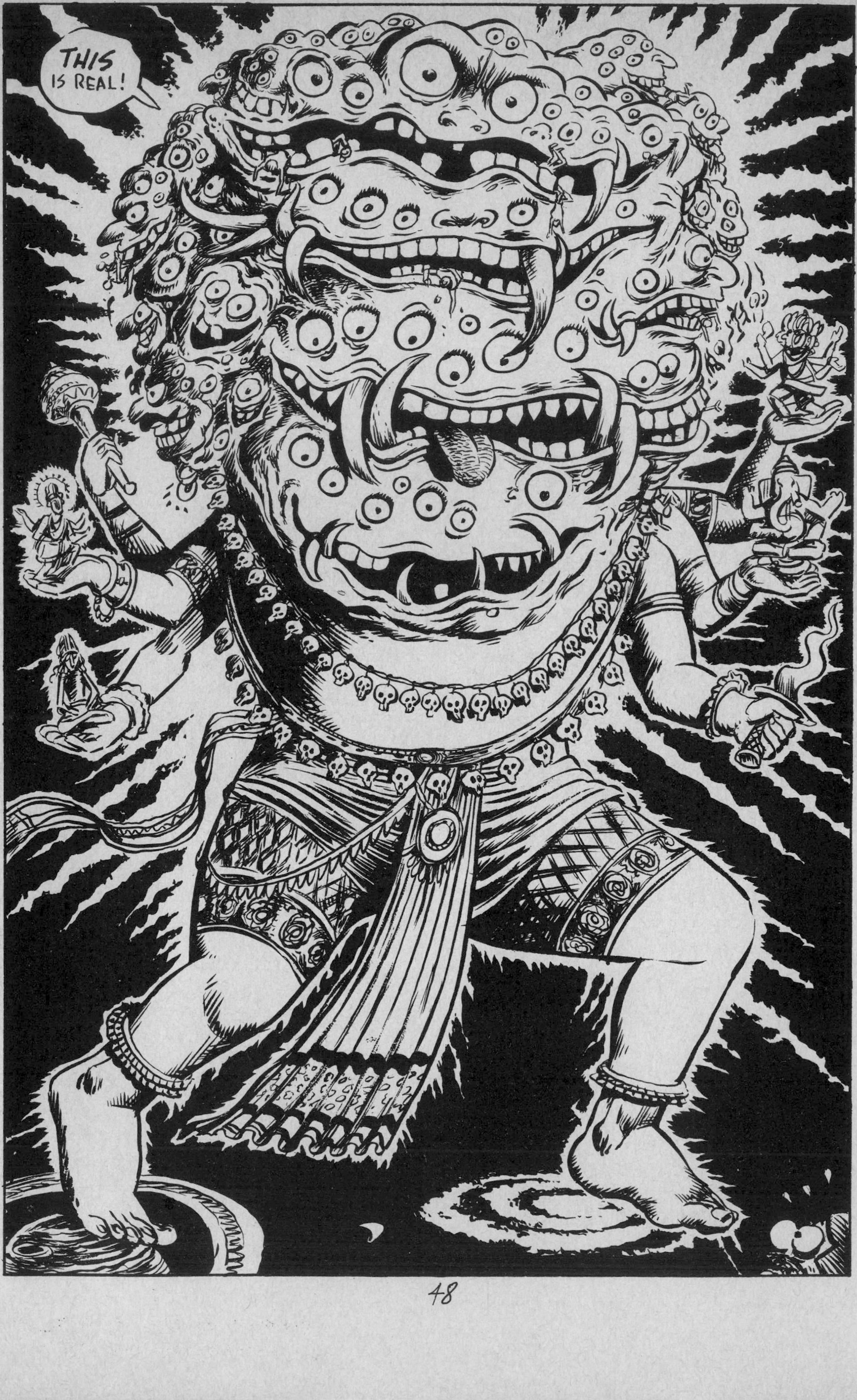
THIS IS REAL!

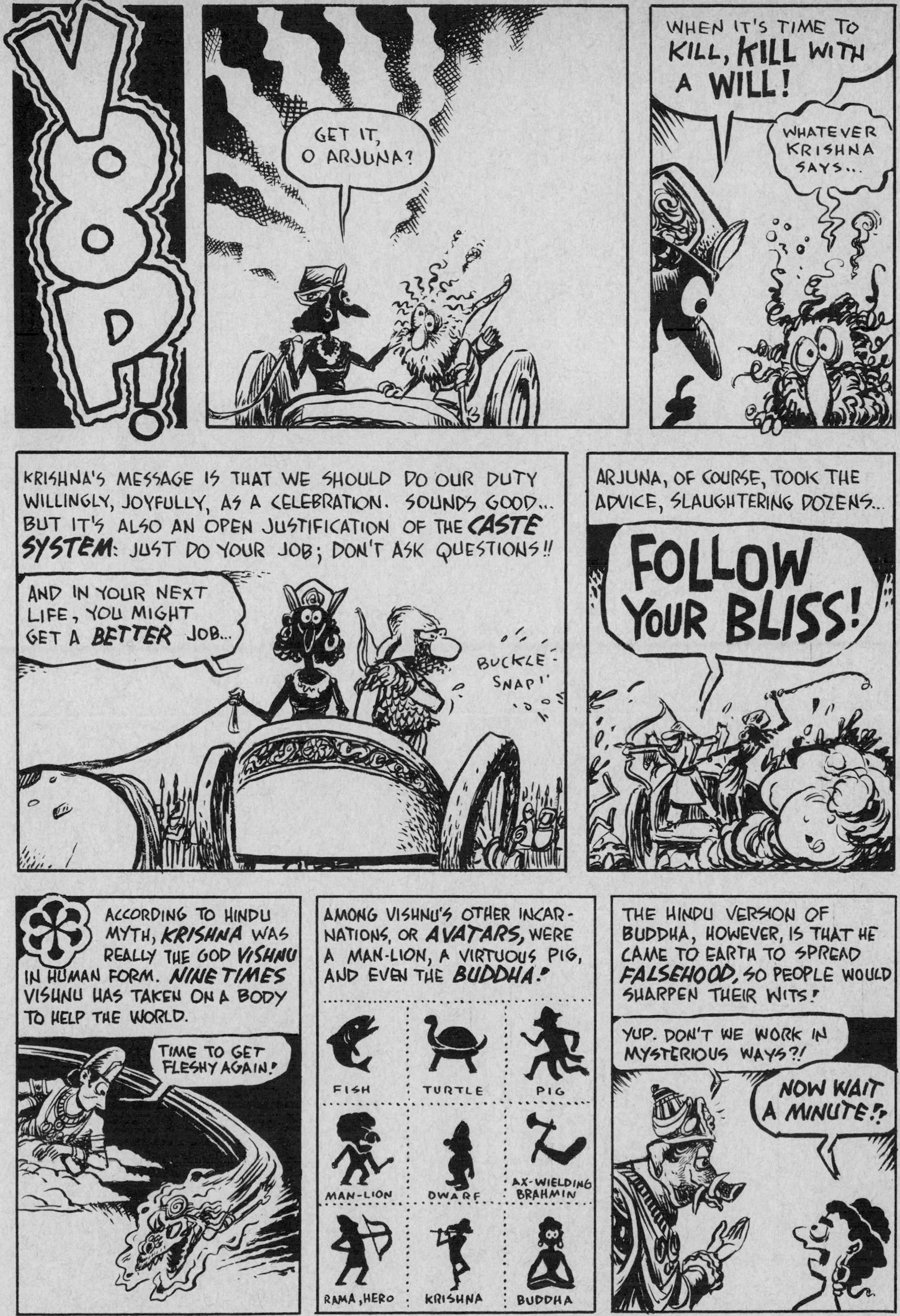
VOOP!
GET IT, O ARJUNA?
WHEN IT'S TIME TO KILL, KILL WITH A WILL!
WHATEVER KRISHNA SAYS...
KRISHNA'S MESSAGE IS THAT WE SHOULD DO OUR DUTY WILLINGLY, JOYFULLY, AS A CELEBRATION. SOUNDS GOOD... BUT IT'S ALSO AN OPEN JUSTIFICATION OF THE CASTE SYSTEM: JUST DO YOUR JOB; DON'T ASK QUESTIONS!!
AND IN YOUR NEXT LIFE, YOU MIGHT GET A BETTER JOB...
BUCKLE SNAP!
ARJUNA, OF COURSE, TOOK THE ADVICE, SLAUGHTERING DOZENS...
FOLLOW YOUR BLISS!
ACCORDING TO HINDU MYTH, KRISHNA WAS REALLY THE GOD VISHNU IN HUMAN FORM. NINE TIMES VISHNU HAS TAKEN ON A BODY TO HELP THE WORLD.
TIME TO GET FLESHY AGAIN!
AMONG VISHNU'S OTHER INCARNATIONS, OR AVATARS, WERE A MAN-LION, A VIRTUOUS PIG, AND EVEN THE BUDDHA!
FISH
TURTLE
PIG
MAN-LION
DWARF
AX-WIELDING BRAHMIN
RAMA, HERO
KRISHNA
BUDDHA
THE HINDU VERSION OF BUDDHA, HOWEVER, IS THAT HE CAME TO EARTH TO SPREAD FALSEHOOD, SO PEOPLE WOULD SHARPEN THEIR WITS!
YUP. DON'T WE WORK IN MYSTERIOUS WAYS?!
NOW WAIT A MINUTE!?

SO THE VIEW FROM THE HIMALAYAS 2000 YEARS AGO WAS OF AN INDIA DIVIDED INTO COUNTLESS BELIEFS, TRADITIONS, AND CUSTOMS.

MEANWHILE, IN THE YEAR *202 B.C.*, ON THE OTHER SIDE OF THE MOUNTAINS, ANOTHER GREAT EMPIRE HAD BEEN FOUNDED.

THE PEOPLE OF THE EAST COULD NOW TRAVEL WEST... THEY HEARD RUMORS OF BUDDHISM... AROUND THE YEAR **65** THE EMPEROR DREAMED OF A GOLDEN BUDDHA... HE SENT A TEAM TO INDIA TO COPY THE SACRED TEXTS AND BRING THEM HOME, ACROSS THE IMMENSE MOUNTAINS AND STEPPES, TO *CHINA*.

OH! WOWWW... WHERE *AM* I? WHERE *WAS* I? OH... RIGHT... *INDIA*... WHERE ANCIENT HISTORY IS ALL MIXED UP WITH TALES OF GODS, DEMONS, AND MYSTIC POWERS...

NOW WE *MOVE ON* TO A COUNTRY THAT IS *ALL HISTORY:* CHINA!

AFGH! MY KNEES!

CRAK

I WAS BORN IN *SAN FRANCISCO* AND RAISED WITH *CHOPSTICKS* IN MY LITTLE HANDS (DOWNSTAIRS IN *YEE JUN*, THE OLDEST RESTAURANT IN CHINATOWN).

IT CLOSED YEARS AGO SNURF!

BUT LIKE MOST WESTERNERS, I LEARNED VIRTUALLY *NOTHING* ABOUT CHINA'S RICH HISTORY, CULTURE, OR LANGUAGE— *UNTIL* I STARTED FUELLING UP THE TIME MACHINE FOR VOLUME 9!!

AND NOW I'M *MAD!*

HOW CAN *SAN FRANCISCO* — WITH A HUGE CHINESE POPULATION THAT HELPED *BUILD* THE PLACE, WITH TOURISTS *FLOCKING* HERE TO SEE *CHINATOWN* — HOW CAN THIS CITY NOT HAVE *ONE STREET WITH A CHINESE NAME?* IT'S AN *OUTRAGE!* A *DISGRACE!* A *CRIME!*

AN ANNOYANCE!

AN ABSURDITY!

SO, AFTER YOU READ THIS BOOK, I HOPE YOU'LL DO WHAT I'M DOING— *WRITE THE MAYOR TO COMPLAIN...*

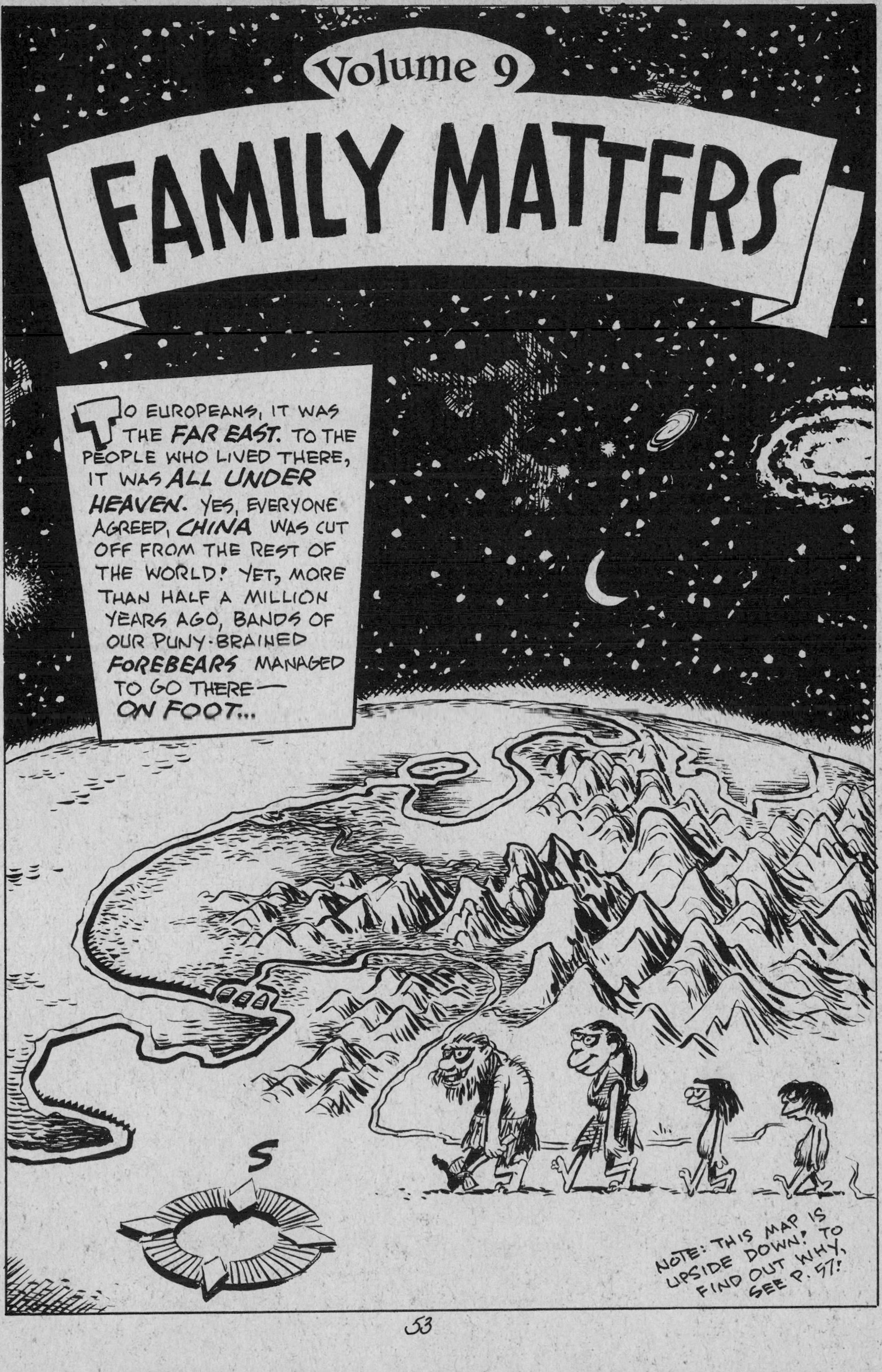

Volume 9
FAMILY MATTERS
TO EUROPEANS, IT WAS THE FAR EAST. TO THE PEOPLE WHO LIVED THERE, IT WAS ALL UNDER HEAVEN. YES, EVERYONE AGREED, CHINA WAS CUT OFF FROM THE REST OF THE WORLD! YET, MORE THAN HALF A MILLION YEARS AGO, BANDS OF OUR PUNY-BRAINED FOREBEARS MANAGED TO GO THERE— ON FOOT...
S
NOTE: THIS MAP IS UPSIDE DOWN! TO FIND OUT WHY, SEE P. 57!

SOME OF THESE PEOPLE BUILT THEIR FIRES IN THE *CHOU-KOU-TIEN* CAVES, NEAR BEIJING.

IMAGINE IF YOUR FAMILY LIVED IN THE SAME HOUSE FOR **200,000 YEARS!** THAT'S WHAT THESE GUYS DID, UNTIL THEY WERE SQUEEZED OUT BY THEIR OWN *ASH HEAP.*

IT'S BEEN *TOO FUNKY* FOR THE LAST 50,000 YEARS *AT LEAST!!*

A COUPLE THOUSAND CENTURIES LATER, MODERN HUMANS, EVE'S CHILDREN*, ARRIVED AND COMPLETELY *DISPLACED* THE ANCIENT NATIVES.

BY THE ANCESTORS, IT'S AN **INVASION!**

OH, *YOU* SAY INVASION, AND *I* SAY MIGRATION...

SINCE ALL THESE FOLKS CAME FROM *SOMEWHERE ELSE*, YOU HAVE TO WONDER HOW *ISOLATED* CHINA REALLY IS!

BORDERS LIKE A *SIEVE!*

SHH! WE'LL WALL IT OFF!

BY COMPARING HUMAN GENES FROM AROUND THE WORLD, SCIENTISTS HAVE REACHED A STARTLING RESULT: *EVERYONE ON EARTH* IS DESCENDED FROM *ONE WOMAN* WHO LIVED IN AFRICA NOT MORE THAN 200,000 YEARS AGO!

WOW

TRIBES OF HER DESCENDANTS THEN OVERRAN THE WORLD, DISPLACING MORE PRIMITIVE HUMANS — WITH VIRTUALLY NO INTERMARRIAGE.

WE'RE SMART! WE'RE HANDSOME! AND WE HAVEN'T INVENTED MORALITY YET!

SINCE "DISPLACE" IS A *EUPHE-MISM* FOR *STARVING* AND *KILLING*, MANY WELL-MEANING SCIENTISTS HAVE RESISTED THIS CHILLING CONCLUSION — *SCIENTIFICALLY*, OF COURSE!

ER... AHEM... YOU CAN SEE FROM THIS *LEGBONE* THAT PEOPLE ARE BASICALLY GOOD..

STONE-AGE CHINA SUFFERED THROUGH THE ICE AGES WITH THE REST OF THE WORLD...

...AND HAD THE SAME DISASTERS AS EVERYONE ELSE IN THE *BIG THAW* OF 10,000 B.C.

AS SNOW GAVE WAY TO RAIN, RIVERS COURSED THROUGH THE MOUNTAINS.

THE STREAMS SWEPT OUT ENOUGH *SILT* TO LAY DOWN AN EVER-WIDENING COASTAL PLAIN (FROM ZERO TO *300 MILES* IN 12,000 YEARS!).

TO THIS, ADD THE *YELLOW DUST*— "LOESS"—BLOWING IN FROM THE DRIED-OUT NORTH...

...AND YOU HAVE A GOOD SUPPLY OF *FERTILE TOPSOIL* FOR CHINA'S FARMERS TO TILL!

THEIR *LOESS* IS OUR *GAIN!*

IN THE YELLOW VALLEYS OF THE YELLOW RIVER, THEY BUILT THEIR HUTS... LEARNED TO FARM... TAMED THE WILD PIG... SANG THEIR SONGS... BEAT THEIR DRUMS, AND BOILED UP OFFERINGS TO THE *SPIRIT WORLD* IN THREE-LEGGED POTS, TRYING TO SEE WHERE ALL THE CHANGES WERE LEADING...

THOSE WERE DAYS OF GREAT **DISCOVERY** - AND ONE OF THE GREATEST DISCOVERIES WAS ALSO ONE OF THE **STRANGEST**. WHY WOULD ANYBODY BOIL **CATERPILLAR COCOONS**.??

HEY, MAN, I WAS **HUNGRY!**

THE CHEFS WERE SURPRISED TO SEE THAT EACH COCOON **UNWOUND** INTO A SINGLE STRAND **HUNDREDS** OF FEET LONG!

MOM! IS THIS **DIETARY FIBER**?

UM... I DON'T THINK SO...

THESE WOMEN WERE ALWAYS LOOKING FOR **NEW FIBERS!** SOON THEY WERE REELING IT UP THREE OR MORE STRANDS AT A TIME.

THEY BEGAN **FARMING** THE CATERPILLARS ON FRAMES COVERED WITH CHOPPED **MULBERRY LEAVES**. (THAT'S ALL THE BUGS WOULD EAT.)

THEY SELECTED THE CHOICEST COCOONS, LEFT A RESERVE FOR HATCHING THE NEXT GENERATION, REGULATED THE COOKING, CULTIVATED THE BEST VARIETIES OF MULBERRY BUSH, ETC. ETC. ETC....

THEN THEY WOVE THE FIBERS INTO **SILK**, THE FINEST FABRIC EVER MADE! IT WAS A BIT LIKE WEAVING CLOTHES OUT OF **COBWEBS**.

IN MY COUNTRY, WE USE WOOL FROM OUR FARM ANIMALS!

WOOL FROM PIGS?

SAGE AGE

ACCORDING TO LEGEND, THE SILK INDUSTRY WAS "INVENTED" BY A SAGE-QUEEN NAMED *LEI-ZU*.

ACTUALLY, I JUST GAVE THEM A PLACE TO WORK, TOLD THEM TO FIGURE OUT THE DETAILS, AND TOOK ALL THE CREDIT!

TRADITIONALLY, THIS WHOLE DAWN-OF-CIVILIZATION BUSINESS WAS SAID TO HAVE BEEN THE WORK OF A FEW GREAT *SAGES*.

AND OUR *PRESS* AGENTS!

LEI-ZU! LEI-ZU!

THE FIRST SAGE, *FU HSI*, COULD SEE THE FUTURE BY STARING AT A *TORTOISE*.

THE *TRIGRAMS* HE SAW THERE WERE *BINARY SYMBOLS* FOR COMMUNICATING WITH THE SPIRITS!!

STOP! THIS'LL WORK *SO MUCH* BETTER IF I *BOIL* YOU!!

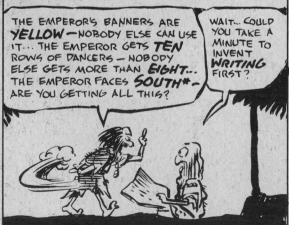

HUANG-TI, THE YELLOW EMPEROR, LEI-ZU'S HUSBAND, INVENTED COURT CEREMONY AND WARFARE.

THE EMPEROR'S BANNERS ARE *YELLOW* — NOBODY ELSE CAN USE IT... THE EMPEROR GETS *TEN* ROWS OF DANCERS — NOBODY ELSE GETS MORE THAN *EIGHT*... THE EMPEROR FACES *SOUTH** — ARE YOU GETTING ALL THIS?

WAIT... COULD YOU TAKE A MINUTE TO INVENT *WRITING* FIRST?

LEI-ZU SUPPOSEDLY INVENTED *SILK* AS A GIFT TO HUANG-TI, WHO WENT ON TO FATHER EVERY *ARISTOCRATIC FAMILY* OF CLASSICAL CHINA.

HEH!... THE HARDER I PULL, THE TIGHTER IT GETS... WOT *IS* THIS?

WOVEN SILK... AND IT'S NOT JUST FOR YOUR *FINGER*, HUANG BABY!

PASSING OVER THE INVENTORS OF *IRRIGATION* AND *FIRE*, WE COME TO TWO SAGE-KINGS WHO WERE VIEWED WITH REAL *NOSTALGIA* LATER: *YAO* AND *SHUN*.

KING YAO WAS FAMOUS FOR *NOT* CHOOSING HIS OWN *SON* TO SUCCEED HIM.

I WANNA KNOW WHO'S THE *BEST MAN* FOR THE JOB?

OBVIOUSLY, *YOU* ARE, SIRE!

WE ALREADY HAVE JOBS...

WELL, WHO *ELSE*, THEN?

WELL, THERE'S ALWAYS SHUN...

SHUN? SHUN, THE *SWINEHERD*?

YAO GAVE SHUN TWO OF HIS DAUGHTERS AS WIVES.

AND WHEN YAO DIED, SHUN BECAME *KING*.

HONEY, YOU CAN LET GO OF THE PIG NOW...

AS KING, SHUN WAS FAMOUS FOR THE SAME THING AS *YAO*.

SO — WHO'S THE BEST MAN FOR THE JOB?

OY.

WHO'S OY?

THE CHINESE WERE FIRST TO INVENT THE *COMPASS* AND HAVE ALWAYS THOUGHT OF IT AS POINTING *SOUTH*. (SEE MAP, P. 51.)

UM... HOW DO WE DECIDE WHICH ONE'S THE POINT?

FLIP A TORTOISE?

SOUTH BECAME A *SACRED DIRECTION*. IN MEETINGS AND CEREMONY, THE *KING* ALWAYS FACED SOUTH.

A LITTLE TO THE LEFT, YOUR MAJESTY!

THE CHINESE THEN IMPROVED THE INVENTION WITH A *SOUTH-POINTING CART*. WITH THE SEAT LINKED TO THE *STEERING MECHANISM*, THE PASSENGER AUTOMATICALLY SWIVELED AROUND, ALWAYS MAINTAINING A *SOUTHWARD ORIENTATION*.

HOW'S THE VIEW?

ALWAYS THE SAME.

When King Shun asked for names, the one that came up belonged to **BARON YÜ**, the tamer of floods. Yü was like the Chinese **NOAH** (of Bible fame) —but instead of **ESCAPING** in an **ARK**, Yü **ORGANIZED CHINA** to build dams and dikes, dredge and drain.

KEEP IT DRY! KEEP IT DRY! WATER'S HELL ON SILK!

Yü also spent years **SURVEYING** the realm, dividing it into nine provinces separated by mountain ranges...

☆◎#$!? HERE COMES CIVILIZATION!!

...and dividing it **POLITICALLY** into a huge **GRID**, with the king's personal space (100,000 sq. mi.) in the middle, and convicted criminals banished to the outer edge.

AFTER HIS WEDDING, YÜ SPENT ONLY *FOUR DAYS* WITH HIS WIFE —AND THEN BACK TO WORK!

GOTTA GO! NOT MY FAULT! ADDICTED TO FLOOD CONTROL!

KING SHUN OFFERED YÜ THE THRONE! YÜ'S REPLY WAS A PERFECT MODEL OF COURTLY DEPORTMENT.

MY VIRTUE IS NOT EQUAL TO THE POSITION. THE PEOPLE WILL NOT FOLLOW ME —BUT THERE IS KAO-YAO, MINISTER OF CRIME, WHOSE VIRTUE IS BELOVED BY ALL. CONSIDER HIS MERITS, O EMPEROR...

KAO YAO KEEPS HIS JOB!

COME ON, YÜ! I'M NOT GOING TO REPEAT MYSELF!

SUBMIT THE MERITORIOUS MINISTERS TO THE *DIVINATION:* CONSULT THE *TORTOISE* AND FOLLOW *ITS* RECOMMENDATION!

ALREADY DID IT!

PLEASE! I DON'T WANT THE JOB!

TSK!

BUT YÜ WASN'T JUST BEING POLITE! AS SOON AS HE BECAME KING, HE PUSHED THE THRONE ON HIS OLD FRIEND *YIH.*

I'M JUST TOO OLD AND *BURNED OUT*...

AND WHAT AM I?

YIH WAS AS TIRED AS YÜ...HE PASSED THE THRONE TO *YÜ'S SON.*

AS OFTEN AS I SAW THE OLD WORKAHOLIC, IT'S AMAZING HE *HAS* A SON...

...AND FROM THIS POINT ON, KINGSHIP PASSED FROM *SON* TO *SON.* THE GOLDEN AGE OF SAGE-KINGS HAD ENDED, AND CHINA HAD ITS FIRST *DYNASTY,* THE

HSIA

GESUNDHEIT.

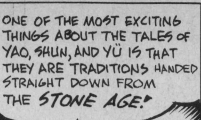
FAMILY MATTERS

ONE OF THE MOST EXCITING THINGS ABOUT THE TALES OF YAO, SHUN, AND YÜ IS THAT THEY ARE TRADITIONS HANDED STRAIGHT DOWN FROM THE *STONE AGE!*

DIGGING FOR RELICS OF THIS ERA (c. 2500 B.C.) TURNS UP LITTLE OF THE STUFF THAT MARKS THE BEGINNING OF *WESTERN* CIVILIZATION — SUCH AS *WRITING* OR *METAL* IN QUANTITY.

INSTEAD, ONE FINDS: *IMMENSE WALLS* OF *STAMPED EARTH* — A CLEAR SIGN OF LARGE-SCALE, IF LOW-TECH ORGANIZATION.

WE GET UP AT SUNRISE, WE REST AT SUNSET, WE DIG WELLS AND DRINK, TILL OUR FIELDS AND EAT, WHAT IS THE EMPEROR'S STRENGTH TO *US*?*

* PEASANT SONG FROM REIGN OF YAO.

THESE WALLS SURROUNDED *BIG HOUSES*. POWER WAS GROWING MORE CONCENTRATED AND UNEQUAL!

WHAT METAL THERE WAS, WAS MOSTLY *ARROWHEADS* — EVIDENCE OF ORGANIZED VIOLENCE DIRECTED *OUTWARD*.

...AND FINALLY — *LARGE-SCALE HUMAN SACRIFICE*: ORGANIZED VIOLENCE DIRECTED *INWARD*, SHOWING CLEARLY THE POWER OF *YAO, SHUN,* AND *YÜ*!!

ARE WE HAVING SHUN YET?

YAO!

WHEN YOU SEE THIS KIND OF POWER, YOU CAN BET IT'S IN THE HANDS OF **MEN** AT THE EXPENSE OF **WOMEN**...

WHY DON'T **WE** ORGANIZE AN ARMY?

WITH CHILD CARE?

ACCORDING TO LEGEND, **FU HSI** FOUNDED THE PATRIARCHY. HE BANNED MARRIAGES BETWEEN BOYS AND GIRLS RELATED THROUGH THEIR FATHERS.

WEIRD IDEA, FU! WHERE'D YOU GET IT?

A LITTLE TURTLE TOLD ME...

BUT TRACES OF THE OLD WAYS LINGERED ON...**YAO** AND **SHUN** BOTH TRACED THEIR ANCESTRY BACK TO THE YELLOW EMPEROR - THROUGH THEIR **MOTHERS**.

IT'S MORE **NOBLE**...

AND MORE **CERTAIN**...

THE REAL KEY TO THE STORY OF YAO AND SHUN IS THAT SHUN MARRIED YAO'S **DAUGHTER**. **QUEENSHIP**, NOT KINGSHIP, WAS HEREDITARY. AS IN ANCIENT EGYPT, THE KING HAD TO **MARRY INTO** THE ROYAL FAMILY.

REMEMBER - KINGS ARE **MADE** NOT BORN!

FINE BY ME!

IN ANCIENT EGYPT, THIS OFTEN LED AMBITIOUS PRINCES TO **MARRY THEIR OWN SISTERS**. SO, ONE HAS TO ASK, WHO WAS **YAO'S WIFE?** HISTORY IS SILENT!

SH!

BUT UNLIKE EGYPT, CHINA DROPPED HEREDITARY QUEENSHIP EARLY. BEGINNING AROUND 2200 B.C., A KING WAS NOTHING BUT **ANOTHER KING'S SON**...

SO THE **CHINESE FAMILY** HAS LASTED MORE THAN **4000 YEARS** — ONE OF THE TIGHTEST, MOST ENDURING INSTITUTIONS IN WORLD HISTORY...

IT'S BEEN HELD TOGETHER BY BONDS OF **REVERENCE** AND **OBEDIENCE:** WIFE OBEYS HUSBAND, SON OBEYS PARENTS, YOUNGER BROTHER OBEYS ELDER, DAUGHTER OBEYS MOM, DAD, AND BROTHERS, AND, FINALLY, **DAUGHTER-IN-LAW** OBEYS **EVERYBODY!**

WAIT... I AM DETECTING A **PATTERN** HERE...

THE OLDER YOU GOT, THE MORE **RESPECT** YOU GOT...

AND THE FEWER PEOPLE YOU HAVE TO RESPECT!

AND WHEN YOU **DIED?** THEN YOU WERE **WORSHIPPED!!**

PEOPLE GET WISER AS THEY GET OLDER...

WHY SHOULD BEING **DEAD** MAKE ANY DIFFERENCE?

AFTER A LIFETIME OF OBEDIENCE, IT MUST HAVE FELT **WEIRD** WHEN YOUR **FATHER** DIED. THE CUSTOMARY PERIOD OF MOURNING WAS **THREE YEARS.**

ONE OF A KING'S TITLES WAS **"THE LONELY ONE,"** PARTLY BECAUSE HE WAS PEERLESS, BUT ALSO BECAUSE HE WAS **FATHERLESS.**

SNIF

WHEN THE FIRST DYNASTY BEGAN, IT WAS JUST A CASE OF ONE PATRIARCHAL FAMILY HAVING THE LOYALTY OF OTHER PATRIARCHAL FAMILIES, INTIMIDATING STILL OTHER FAMILIES, ETC. ETC. ETC.

IT'S NOT EASY!

...WHICH EXPLAINS WHY THE PENALTY FOR *TREASON* WAS *DEATH* FOR THE TRAITOR'S *ENTIRE FAMILY!* ♣*

NEXT!

WOT ARE FAMILY VALUES?

WHEN ONE FAMILY IS MORE VALUABLE THAN ANOTHER FAMILY!

❋ SINCE ANCIENT TIMES, THE CHINESE CRIMINAL CODE SPECIFIED *FIVE PUNISHMENTS:* TATTOOING THE FACE, CUTTING OFF THE NOSE, CUTTING OFF THE FEET, CASTRATION, AND DEATH.

HEY, WOULD YOU RATHER LOSE YOUR NOSE, OR GO TO JAIL WITH A BUNCH OF AGGRESSIVE WEIGHT-LIFTERS?

EXECUTIONS TOOK PLACE IN THE MARKET SQUARE, POSSIBLY BECAUSE THEY STIMULATED THE ECONOMY...

WHAT ARE *YOU* SELLING?

NOSES 'N' THINGS.

AND SO, AROUND 2200 B.C., BEGAN THE CHINESE DYNASTIC AGE. BUT UNLIKE ANCIENT EGYPT, WHICH WENT THROUGH A DYNASTY EVERY CENTURY, CHINA HAD ONLY THREE DYNASTIES IN THE FIRST 1500 YEARS. THESE WERE THE HSIA, THE SHANG, AND THE ZHOU.

HOW DID YOU DO IT?

FAMILY VALUES.

THE HSIA, DESCENDED FROM THE GREAT YÜ, SET THE PATTERN FOR LATER DYNASTIES.

THERE'S A GREAT NOODLE PLACE IN SECTOR 17...

THE KING'S FAMILY AND FRIENDS WERE GIVEN FIEFS: PLOTS OF LAND, COMPLETE WITH THE PEASANTS WHO WORKED THERE.

PEASANTS FARM THE LAND, WE FARM THE PEASANTS!

THESE FIEFHOLDERS WERE VASSALS OF THE EMPEROR, BUT WERE FAIRLY FREE TO SQUABBLE AMONG THEMSELVES.

THIS HOVEL IS ON MY FIEF!!

MINE!

I KNOW! LET'S FIGHT OVER IT!

GOOD IDEA!

THIS SYSTEM, WHICH DIDN'T EVOLVE IN EUROPE UNTIL MUCH LATER, IS CALLED FEUDALISM.

HM! TOTALLY DESTROYED.

EXCELLENT COMPROMISE.

MEANWHILE, THE EMPEROR'S ABLE *MINISTERS* RAN THE DAILY BUSINESS OF THE STATE.

I REGULATE WEIGHTS AND MEASURES!

I REGULATE MUSIC!

I REGULATE THE CALENDAR!

I EAVESDROP ON PRIVATE CONVERSATIONS!

EVERYTHING WAS TAKEN CARE OF — SO WHAT WAS AN EMPEROR TO DO??

I INTEND TO *WALLOW IN PLEASURE!*

THE THIRD EMPEROR OF HSIA, *TAE-KANG,* WENT ON A *THREE-MONTH* HUNTING TRIP. THIS PROVOKED A PRINCE TO OVERTHROW HIM!

SORRY! I DIDN'T THINK I WAS NEEDED!

SOME YEARS LATER, THERE WAS A *SOLAR ECLIPSE,* AND TAE-KANG'S BROTHER *JUNG-KANG* SAW THE LIGHT!

YES. I NOW KNOW *WHO* IS TO BLAME FOR MY FAMILY'S WOES... IT'S THOSE ☆@#@** *ASTRONOMERS!*

HE RAISED AN ARMY AND SET OFF TO PUNISH *HE* AND *HO,* FAMILIES WHO HAD DONE THE STARS SINCE KING *YAO.*

"SUNK IN WINE IN THEIR PRIVATE CITIES, ETC. ETC..."*

*BOOK OF HISTORICAL DOCUMENTS

THE PENALTY FOR LETTING THE CALENDAR SLIP WAS *DEATH WITHOUT MERCY.*

AND MISSING AN ECLIPSE — AAAARGH!!

WHETHER JUNG-KANG WENT ON TO WIN BACK THE EMPIRE IS AS *OBSCURE* AS THE REST OF THE HSIA ERA, WHICH LASTED ANOTHER 300 YEARS BEFORE THE DYNASTY FELL...

THUD

The **SHANG** OPENED WITH A *BANG*, WHEN DUKE *TANG* LED A RELUCTANT ARMY AGAINST CHINA'S FIRST AND ONLY ROYAL FAMILY.

THEY'RE BAD! I'M JUST A HUMBLE PATRIOT WITH A GOOD SPEECH WRITER!

THE EMPEROR'S ARMY TURNED ON ITSELF, AND TANG TRIUMPHED.

HEY!

HEY!

AND THINGS WENT ON MUCH THE SAME AS BEFORE, BUT WITH A NEW SET OF COUSINS TO GET FIEFS.

OUT!

FROM THE SHANG ERA COME CHINA'S FIRST **BRONZES**. HOW THE CHINESE LEARNED TO SMELT AND CAST, WE DON'T KNOW, BUT THEY DID A MAGNIFICENT JOB *!!*

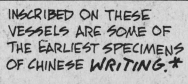

INSCRIBED ON THESE VESSELS ARE SOME OF THE EARLIEST SPECIMENS OF CHINESE **WRITING.***

THE OTHER EARLY SCRAPS OF SCRIPT ARE FOUND ON **TORTOISE SHELLS.**

IF YOU NEEDED ADVICE DURING THE SHANG DYNASTY, YOU ASKED A *DIVINER,* WHO "CONSULTED THE TORTOISE."

THE SEER HEATED THE SHELL AND CALLED ON THE SPIRITS.

HE **WROTE DOWN** THE ANSWER, LEAVING US VALUABLE INFORMATION ABOUT THE SHANG ERA!

IT'S A HARD TIME TO BE A TORTOISE!

"TIME FOR TURTLE SOUP"

LIKE ALL ANCIENT SCRIPTS, CHINESE WRITING WAS *PICTOGRAPHIC.* EACH CHARACTER REPRESENTED AN *IDEA,* A WHOLE WORD. OVER TIME, THESE IMAGES BECAME HIGHLY STYLIZED; BUT THE BASIC SYSTEM SURVIVES TO THIS DAY.

CORN

WEST

THIS COMPLEX SCRIPT HAS A SURPRISING *ADVANTAGE:* BECAUSE CHARACTERS ENCODE *MEANING,* CHINESE SPEAKING *DIFFERENT DIALECTS* CAN READ EACH OTHER'S MESSAGES, AND *ANCIENT TEXTS* ARE EASIER TO READ THAN IN THE WESTERN WORLD...

BEOWULF

WHEN EUROPEANS CAME TO CHINA IN THE 1600'S, THEY WANTED TO MAKE CHINESE *ALPHABETIC* — BUT THE CHINESE SUGGESTED THAT THE *EUROPEAN* LANGUAGES ADOPT *CHINESE SCRIPT* — SO EVERYONE COULD READ EVERYONE ELSE'S LANGUAGE!

WELL?

UH — WE PREFER TO BE MISUNDERSTOOD!

ANOTHER THING THE SHANG EMPERORS DID SEVERAL TIMES WAS *MOVE* THEIR *CAPITAL CITY*. THE BOOK OF HISTORY DOESN'T SAY WHY — DID THEY NEED BIGGER *PALACES*? BETTER *SANITATION*?

NOPE!

OR COULD IT HAVE BEEN BECAUSE OF THE *NORTHERN BARBARIANS*?

BUM BUM BUM BUM

GAH!

WHATEVER THE REASON, THE MOVE WAS MADE!!

AFTER THE FINAL MOVE, AROUND 1300 B.C., THE DYNASTY CHANGED ITS NAME FROM *SHANG* TO *YIN*.

MAYBE THEY WON'T RECOGNIZE US UNDER AN ASSUMED NAME...

AND ON IT WENT... KING FOLLOWED KING... SEASON FOLLOWED SEASON...

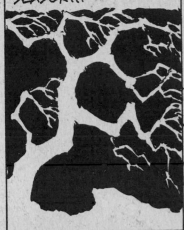

... UNTIL, AROUND *1150 B.C.*, THE IMMODERATE *JOU-SIN* TOOK THE THRONE. JOU-SIN SHOCKED EVERYONE, ESPECIALLY THE ELEPHANT COMMUNITY, BY USING *IVORY CHOPSTICKS*.

THESE CHOPSTICKS ARE DIRTY! KILL ANOTHER ELEPHANT.

HE BUILT A PLEASURE GARDEN FOR HIS FAVORITE CONCUBINE, THEN SHREDDED A MINISTER WHO DARED TO COMPLAIN.

WHAT DISH IS THIS, LORD, HONEY?

MINCED MINISTER WITH SNOW PEAS!

ANOTHER MINISTER, THE *CHIEF OF THE WEST*, JAILED FOR SYMPATHIZING WITH HIS CHOPPED COLLEAGUE, PASSED HIS TIME IN STIR WRITING THE *BOOK OF CHANGES.* *

OH, THERE'LL BE SOME CHANGES MADE, ALL RIGHT...

TO USE THE *I CHING*, OR BOOK OF CHANGES, ONE TOSSES COINS (OR, DOES SOMETHING ELSE RANDOM) TO DETERMINE A PAIR OF FU HSI'S *TRIGRAMS*, TOGETHER WITH THEIR "CHANGING LINES."

THE BOOK INTERPRETS THE SYMBOLS IN VAGUE, CRYPTIC, LANGUAGE THAT CAN BE AMAZINGLY HELPFUL IN ANALYZING THE PRESENT AND SUGGESTING WHAT TO DO NEXT.

"THIS HEXAGRAM INDICATES ADVANTAGE IN BEING FIRM AND CORRECT... THERE WILL BE GOOD FORTUNE IN RAISING A COW..."

O.K...

THE *I CHING* HAS BEEN IN PRINT LONGER THAN ANY OTHER BOOK, WHICH SEEMS TO PROVE THAT AUTHORS DON'T *HAVE* TO DO TALK SHOWS...

WHAT'S ON?

DWARFS WHO LOVE TOO MUCH, LESBIAN PLAYBOY CENTERFOLDS, AND SOME GUY WHO WROTE A BOOK...

ZHOU

AS WE'LL SEE OFTEN IN HISTORY, EMPIRES CAN SURVIVE PLENTY OF *GARDEN-VARIETY* DECADENCE... BUT THE SHANG COULDN'T SURVIVE THE *CHIEF OF THE WEST.*

THE CHIEF'S PEOPLE BRIBED HIS WAY OUT OF JAIL AND RAISED A REVOLT.

AK-URK-UNK. OOK.

BUT *I* HAVE THE MANDATE OF HEAVEN!

JOU-SIN RESPONDED TO ONE SAGE'S WARNING BY *CUTTING HIS HEART OUT.*

HM! THOUGHT SAGES HAD EXTRA VALVES OR SOMETHING...

AS HIS RELATIVES TOOK TO THE HILLS, THE LAST SHANG EMPEROR PERISHED IN FLAMES IN HIS PALACE...

...AND THE CHIEF OF THE WEST NAMED HIMSELF *WU,* THE FIRST EMPEROR OF *ZHOU.* *

FIEFS! GETCHA FIEFS HEAH!

AFTER WU TAMED THE EMPIRE, NEIGHBORING STATES AND TRIBES SENT HIM *PRESENTS.* THE ONE HE LIKED BEST WAS SOME *DOGS* WHO "KNEW THEIR MASTER'S MIND."

SIT!

THE KING WAS THRILLED — BUT HIS CHIEF MINISTER SAID TO *GIVE THE DOGS AWAY!*

WHY? IT'S SO *CUTE!*

THE REASON WAS PURE *POWER POLITICS:*

NEVER LET A BARBARIAN KNOW HE HAS SOMETHING YOU *WANT.* VALUE *NOTHING* THAT COMES FROM FAR AWAY!

THIS ATTITUDE TOWARDS ANYTHING *FOREIGN* BECAME OFFICIAL POLICY THROUGHOUT CHINESE IMPERIAL HISTORY!

NOW *THIS* IS A *REAL DOG!*

THE ZHOU WAS THE BIGGEST AND FINEST OF CHINA'S FIRST THREE EMPIRES... BUT EVEN THE *MIGHTY ZHOU* COULD NOT WITHSTAND — THE **NORTHERN BARBARIANS!!**

GAH!

IN 770 B.C., THE ZHOU KING ALSO MOVED HIS CAPITAL!!

'SCUSE!

PARDON!

SORRY!

AND GRADUALLY, THEIR POWER WANED... EMPERORS IN **NAME ONLY,** THE ZHOU KINGS KEPT FACING SOUTH, VAINLY HOPING FOR AN OCCASIONAL VISIT FROM THEIR SUPPOSED SUBJECTS... AND CHINESE HISTORY ENTERED A *NEW PERIOD.*

ANY VISITORS TODAY?

SPRING & AUTUMN (WE'LL EXPLAIN THIS NAME LATER!)

As ZHOU'S POWER WANED, THE NOBLES' DOMAINS DIVIDED LIKE AMOEBAS... AND CHINA SPLIT INTO A HEAP OF *PETTY STATES* — 1000 OF THEM, BY TRADITIONAL COUNT...

SIMPLE MATH SHOWS THAT, GIVEN 1000 STATES, THERE ARE $\frac{1}{2}(1000 \cdot 999) = 499,500$ POSSIBLE *PAIRS*. WHAT AN OPPORTUNITY FOR CONFLICT!

O.K., YOU FIGHT WITH HIM WHILE I FIGHT WITH HIM, THEN I'LL FIGHT WITH YOU, WHILE...

BUT *GOOD MANNERS* STILL COUNTED! IN 638 B.C., THE *DUKE OF SUNG* * REFUSED TO ATTACK AN ARMY THAT WAS *CROSSING A RIVER*.

IT WOULDN'T BE *SPORTING!*

* "I AM NOT THE DUKE OF SUNG." — MAO TSE-TUNG

AGAIN, IN 594, B.C., THE *KING OF CHU*, BESIEGING A CITY, SENT HIS WAR MINISTER TO *PEEK INSIDE*. AT THE WALL, HE MET AN MINISTER FROM THE *OPPOSITION*.

IN HERE, WE'RE EATING EACH OTHER'S CHILDREN! AND YOU?

ABOUT STARVING TO DEATH.

...SO THE ARMY OF CHU WENT HOME!

IF THEY WERE STARVING AND HONEST, SHOULDN'T WE BE?

OH, SHUT UP...

BUT ON THE FRINGES OF THE OLD EMPIRE WERE *NEW, UNCOUTH STATES*, LIKE *CHIN*, WHO IMPOLITELY GOBBLED UP THEIR NEIGHBORS!

WHAT'S THE RUSH? NOBODY KILLS THE WOUNDED. THAT'S *RUDE!*

AS COMPETITION HEATED UP AND STAKES GREW HIGHER, THE NICETIES BEGAN TO *DECAY*...

WELL... I'D PREFER NOT TO LIVE IN SUCH A PLACE, ANYWAY...

We SEE THE NEW STYLE OF WAR IN THE STORY OF THE MILITARY EXPERT **SUN WU**, SEEKING A JOB FROM KING HO·LU OF WU.

THE KING ASKED SUN WU TO SHOW OFF HIS TECHNIQUE — USING **WOMEN**.

NO PROBLEM!

THE KING ORDERED IN 180 CONCUBINES.

SUN WU DIVIDED THEM INTO TWO GROUPS, APPOINTED THE KING'S TWO FAVORITES AS OFFICERS, EXPLAINED "LEFT FACE," "RIGHT FACE," ETC... THEN HE BARKED AN **ORDER** — AND NOTHING HAPPENED.

WELL?

WHEN INSTRUCTIONS ARE NOT CLEAR, YOUR MAJESTY, THE **COMMANDER** IS AT FAULT!

SUN WU EXPLAINED EVERYTHING AGAIN; AGAIN HE BARKED HIS ORDERS; AND AGAIN NOTHING HAPPENED. NOW HE SAID:

WHEN ORDERS ARE CLEAR, BUT NOT CARRIED OUT, IT IS THE **OFFICERS'** FAULT!

OFF WITH THEIR HEADS.

WHEN THE KING SQUEALED IN PROTEST, SUN WU OFFERED HIS **THIRD** MAXIM:

A COMMANDER IN THE FIELD IS NOT ALWAYS BOUND BY HIS SOVEREIGN'S ORDERS!

BUT BUT BUT

WHIK WHIK

SUN WU APPOINTED NEW OFFICERS, AND THIS TIME...

ATTENTION.

SNAP

SUN WU GOT THE JOB... AND HIS CLASSIC "ON WAR" IS STILL IN PRINT.

THOSE WERE MY FAVORITES...

A FEW GENERATIONS LATER, IN 341 B.C., HIS DESCENDANT, GENERAL **SUN PIN** SET A FAMOUS **AMBUSH**: HE HID HIS ARCHERS ON EITHER SIDE OF A WOODED RAVINE, WHERE HE HAD WRITTEN ON A TREE, "PANG CHÜAN DIES UNDER THIS TREE."

THE ENEMY ARRIVED AT NIGHT... THEIR LEADER PANG CHÜAN SAW THE WRITING AND CALLED FOR A **LIGHT**.

THIS WAS THE SIGNAL FOR SUN PIN'S **10,000 BOWMEN** TO LET FLY!

MOST IMPOLITE!

ANOTHER NOVEL TACTIC CAME FROM THE KING OF YÜEH, WHOSE DESPERADOES OPENED A BATTLE BY **BEHEADING THEMSELVES**.

HA!

THIS WAS EFFECTIVE, THOUGH YOU WOULDN'T WANT TO DO IT OFTEN!

CHARGE!!

IN 1000 STATES, THERE ARE A MILLION STORIES, TOO — LIKE THE *DUCHESS* OF *CHING* WHO HATED HER FIRST SON, BECAUSE HIS BIRTH FRIGHTENED HER OUT OF A SOUND SLEEP!!

WHOA!

SO SHE FAVORED HER *SECOND* SON, CAUSING NO END OF FAMILY STRIFE!

NYA NYA NYA NYA NYAAAAH NYA!

THIS IS ALL *YOUR* FAULT, MOM!?!

DON'T SPEAK TO YOUR MOTHER THAT WAY!

THE FIRSTBORN, NOW DUKE, THREW HIS MOTHER IN JAIL AND VOWED NEVER TO SEE HER, UNTIL HE "WENT TO THE *UNDERWORLD*" (I.E., DIED).

OO! UNFILIAL!

STRICKEN WITH REMORSE, BUT BOUND BY HIS VOW, HE *TUNNELED UNDERGROUND* TO HER CELL, AND THEY LIVED HAPPILY EVER AFTER!

HSST! MOM! COMERE A SEC!?!

BUT BACK TO POLITICS... BY 450 B.C., *SEVEN STATES* HAD SWALLOWED UP THE REST: CHIN, CHU, CHAO, CHI, HANN, WEI, AND YÜEH. THEY BATTLED INCESSANTLY... BANDITS ROAMED... NO ONE FELT SAFE... AND EVERYONE WONDERED — WHICH *WAY OUT*??

UP, MAYBE?

THE WAY

Was it the troubled TIMES, or was it just TIME? Between 600 and 400 B.C., THALES and SOCRATES speculated in Greece, the BUDDHA bloomed in India, Israeli prophets preached, and in China, a HUNDRED SCHOOLS OF THOUGHT were searching for "THE WAY."

What was the way? In Chinese, the WAY, or TAO, just meant a path, but it also meant the way to LIVE, the way to GOVERN, and sometimes the mysterious, unknowable way of the COSMOS. To China's FIRST philosopher, the mystic poet LAO-TZU, all these ways were the SAME.

LAO-TZU'S RESPONSE TO THE EPIC CHAOS OF THE WARRING STATES WAS TO *GO WITH THE FLOW.* (THE TECHNICAL TERM IS *WU-WEI,* NON-ACTION).* DO NOTHING TO OPPOSE THE *TAO* ... CONTEMPLATE NATURE... SEEK A NON-VERBAL, MEDITATIVE STATE. LAO TZU'S *SOCIAL PHILOSOPHY,* IF YOU CAN CALL IT THAT, IS THAT *VIOLENCE* IS *WRONG,* AND THAT THE *BEST GOVERNMENT* IS NEITHER *KIND* NOR *HARSH,* BUT RATHER *BARELY DETECTABLE...*

A TAOIST MORAL APPEARS IN THE TALE OF *FAN LI,* WHO GREW RICH AS AIDE TO THE KING OF *YUEH* — UNTIL THE KING MADE HIM ONE *ROYAL OFFER:*

SHARE MY KINGDOM WITH ME — *PLEASE* SAY YES, OR I'LL *BISECT* YOU!

TIME TO SPLIT OR BE SPLIT!

FAN LI FLED, MADE ANOTHER FORTUNE, MOVED AGAIN, AND MADE ANOTHER ... AND THEN HIS SECOND SON WAS JAILED FOR *MURDER.* THERE WAS ONLY ONE THING TO DO — *BRIBE* HIS WAY OUT!

A RICH MAN'S SON DOES NOT DIE IN THE MARKETPLACE.*

* WHERE EXECUTIONS WERE PERFORMED

FAN LI WANTED TO SEND HIS *THIRD* SON ON THE ERRAND, BUT THE OLDEST SAID THIS WOULD BE *DISGRACEFUL!*

SEND *ME* OR I'LL KILL MYSELF, HONORABLE FATHER!

BETTER DO AS HE SAYS, OR WE'LL LOSE 2 OUT OF 3!

SO SON #1 WENT AND DELIVERED A BAG OF GOLD TO A CERTAIN MR. CHUANG.

MR. CHUANG PERSUADED THE KING TO *OPEN THE JAILS.*

THE STARS ARE WEIRD, SIRE! MAKE A NICE GESTURE!

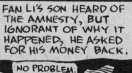

FAN LI'S SON HEARD OF THE AMNESTY, BUT IGNORANT OF WHY IT HAPPENED, HE ASKED FOR HIS MONEY BACK.

NO PROBLEM.

IRKED, MR. CHUANG SPOKE TO THE KING AGAIN:

PEOPLE ARE SAYING YOU'RE ONLY DOING THIS FOR FAN LI'S SON... BETTER KILL HIM FIRST, THEN OPEN THE JAILS!

AH!

WHEN THE ELDEST SON BROUGHT HOME THE CORPSE, FAN LI *LAUGHED.* "MY THIRD SON GREW UP RICH AND HAS NO IDEA OF THE VALUE OF MONEY. THIS IS WHY I WANTED TO SEND HIM. I KNEW MY OLDEST SON, WHO COUNTS EVERY PENNY, WOULD KILL HIS BROTHER. TRULY THIS IS *THE WAY* OF THE WORLD!"

HA HA HA HA

THIS IS ONE HILARIOUS PHILOSOPHY...

CONFUCIUS

(551-479 B.C.)

KUNG CHIU-TZU OR **MASTER KUNG** IS THE MOST IMPORTANT PHILOSOPHER, AND MAYBE THE MOST IMPORTANT **PERSON**, IN CHINESE HISTORY — A TOWERING FIGURE...

AND A TALL GUY!

UNLIKE LAO-TZU, KUNG'S IDEAS WERE **WORLDLY!** FOR HIM, THE **WAY** MEANT **DOING THINGS RIGHT.** EVEN AS A CHILD, HE LIKED MAKING **ARRANGEMENTS.**

HONEY! WHAT'S WRONG?

IT'S NOT PERFECT!

HE WAS BORN IN THE LITTLE STATE OF **LU,** WHICH BORDERED THE LARGER, MOSTLY FRIENDLY, BUT RATHER OVERBEARING STATE OF CHI.

JIN

CHI

BARBARIANS

WEI

LU

CHING

CHAO

CHU

ALTHOUGH LU HAD A DUKE, THE REAL POWER WAS IN THE HANDS OF A CLAN CALLED **CHI** (NO RELATION TO THE STATE). AS A YOUTH, CONFUCIUS WAS BARRED FROM A CHI FAMILY BANQUET.

SORRY! GENTLEMEN ONLY...

YOUNG KUNG CHIU GOT A JOB AS THE CHI FAMILY STABLE MANAGER. HE WAS EFFECTIVE, AND SO MET THE DUKE.

ONCE HE HAD THE DUKE'S EAR, KUNG CHIU URGED HIM TO INCREASE HIS OWN POWER AGAINST THE GRASPING CHI!

YOU HAVE A NICE HAT, BUT YOU'RE WEAK!

THIS MADE CONFUCIUS THE **ENEMY** OF THE CHI CLAN...

THE PRIME MINISTER CHI PING-TZU QUARRELED WITH THE DUKE (OVER A COCKFIGHT!) AND CHASED HIM OUT OF THE COUNTRY TO CHI, WITH CONFUCIUS IN TOW.

FASTER!

THIRTY-FIVE YEARS OLD...A PROMISING CAREER IN RUINS...LIVING IN A STRANGE LAND WITH NO OBVIOUS PROSPECTS...

EXCUSE ME, DO YOU KNOW ANYBODY NEEDING A PRIME MINISTER?

SO CONFUCIUS DID WHAT ANY UNEMPLOYED PERSON OF HIS CLASS AND EDUCATION WOULD DO — HE BECAME A *FREE-LANCE EDITOR.*

TAKE A FEW MUSIC LESSONS...

WHEN NOTHING WORKED OUT, CONFUCIUS RETURNED TO LU, TOOK PUPILS, PERFECTED THEIR BEHAVIOR, AND *AVOIDED POLITICS.*

POLITICS IN LU WERE IN CHAOS. THE OLD DUKE DIED, AND SO DID HIS EX-PRIME MINISTER. VARIOUS NOBLE FAMILIES BATTLED EACH OTHER... THE DUKE OF CHI ATTACKED LU... THE YOUNG DUKE OF LU MADE UP WITH THE EX-MINISTER'S SON... AND NAMED *CONFUCIUS* A JUDGE, THEN CHIEF JUSTICE, THEN *ACTING PRIME MINISTER*... THE SAGE WAS THEN 51 OR 52 YEARS OLD...

NOW MASTER KUNG COULD PUT HIS IDEAS INTO PRACTICE! AND WHAT **WERE** THOSE IDEAS?

FIRST, "RECTIFICATION OF TITLES." THIS MEANT FIXING THE **ORGANIZATIONAL CHART,** KNOWING EXACTLY WHO WAS OVER WHOM, TO MAINTAIN PERFECT ORDER AND GOOD MANNERS.*

SECOND, **PERFECT RITUAL:** CONFUCIUS CARED NOTHING FOR SPIRITUAL MATTERS, BUT HATED TO SEE **ANYTHING** DONE WRONG. SOME RITES WERE FOR KINGS, SOME FOR DUKES...

AND SOME ARE FOR UPSTART PARVENUS LIKE THE CHI CLAN!

AND THIRD, PERFECT **MUSIC** AND **DANCE:** CONFUCIUS PORED OVER ALL THE ANCIENT LORE TO DETERMINE WHICH SONGS TO SING WHEN!

BUNT

YOU DON'T **LIKE** "DUKE OF EARL?"

SOME EXAMPLES OF CONFUCIAN MANNERS (QUOTES FROM BOOK 10 OF THE ANALECTS):

"WHEN THE RULER SUMMONS HIM, A LOOK OF CONFUSION COMES OVER HIS FACE AND HIS LEGS SEEM TO GIVE WAY..."

"ON ENTERING THE PALACE GATE, HE SHRINKS..."

"WHEN ASCENDING THE AUDIENCE HALL, HE HOLDS UP HIS HEM AND HOLDS HIS BREATH."

"ON LEAVING, HIS EXPRESSION RELAXES INTO ONE OF SATISFACTION AND RELIEF."

"WHEN SALUTING HIS EQUALS, HE PASSES HIS RIGHT HAND TO HIS LEFT. HIS ATTITUDE IS ONE OF MAJESTIC DIGNITY."

"CONFRONTED WITH SOMETHING ESPECIALLY TASTY, HE MUST CHANGE HIS EXPRESSION AND RISE TO HIS FEET."

"IN BED, HE AVOIDS LYING IN THE POSITION OF A CORPSE."

AS THE STATE OF LU CALMED DOWN, THE DUKE OF CHI INVITED THE DUKE OF LU TO A PEACE CONFERENCE. CONFUCIUS WARNED HIS BOSS:

IN TIMES OF WAR, PREPARE FOR PEACE. IN TIMES OF PEACE, PREPARE FOR WAR! BETTER TAKE ALONG SOME BIG GUYS WITH WEAPONS!

THE MEETING BEGAN PLEASANTLY, WHEN THE DUKE OF CHI OFFERED SOME *MUSICAL ENTERTAINMENT.*

AS THE PLAYING BEGAN, CONFUCIUS LEAPED UP FURIOUSLY (BUT POLITELY!!).

THIS IS *PALACE* MUSIC! PLAYED HERE, THIS IS BARBARIC! THE BARBARIAN WHO ATTEMPTS TO BEGUILE HIS MASTER DESERVES TO *DIE!* I BEG THAT THE PUNISHMENT BE CARRIED OUT!

TREMBLE

TWITCH ♪ GNASH

83

THE DUKE OF CHI WAS DEEPLY EMBARRASSED BY HIS MUSICAL *GAFFE.*

WHOP BTAKK ETC...

THIS GUY *REALLY* CARES ABOUT MUSIC!

HE JUST *AGONIZED* OVER THE BEST WAY TO APOLOGIZE...

WOT CAN I *POSSIBLY* SAY?

ACTIONS SPEAK LOUDER THAN WORDS. KILL ME IF YOU DON'T LIKE HEARING THIS.

...AND EVENTUALLY GAVE BACK *THREE CITIES* TO LU. THE GRATEFUL DUKE OF LU PROMOTED CONFUCIUS TO *PRIME MINISTER,* AND HE WAS VISIBLY DELIGHTED!

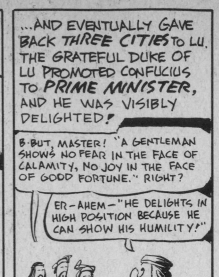

B-BUT, MASTER! "A GENTLEMAN SHOWS NO FEAR IN THE FACE OF CALAMITY, NO JOY IN THE FACE OF GOOD FORTUNE." RIGHT?

ER-AHEM—"HE DELIGHTS IN HIGH POSITION BECAUSE HE CAN SHOW HIS HUMILITY!"

BUT HE WAS TOO THIN-SKINNED FOR THE JOB. WHEN THE DUKE OF CHI SENT ANOTHER OFFERING OF *80 DANCING GIRLS* AND *120 HORSES,* THE COURT AT LU *SHUT DOWN* FOR THREE DAYS — SO CONFUCIUS QUIT!

"A WOMAN'S TONGUE CAN COST A MAN HIS POST; A WOMAN'S WORDS CAN COST A MAN HIS HEAD; WHY NOT RETIRE?"

LET'S GO!

AT AGE 56, HE LEFT LU AND BECAME A WANDERING TEACHER AND POLITICIAN, LOOKING FOR A PRINCE WHO WOULD RATHER LISTEN TO HIM THAN WATCH DANCING GIRLS...

SLAM

NEXT STATE!

FOR YEARS, THEY TRAVELED LIKE THIS, CONFUCIUS ALTERNATELY PROCLAIMING HIMSELF A *SIMPLE SCHOLAR*...

YESSIR... JUST BURY ME IN BOOKS AND I'M HAPPY!!

MASTER! THE STATE OF CHU IS LOOKING FOR A PRIME MINISTER!

...AND DESPERATELY SEEKING A *POST* OR A *FIEF!*

I'M GONE!

AT ONE POINT, HE SEEMED TO HAVE A SOLID OFFER FROM THE KING OF *CHU*, BUT CHU'S ENEMIES SENT TROOPS TO SURROUND CONFUCIUS AND HIS FOLLOWERS, WHO NEARLY STARVED TO DEATH...

MASTER, ARE WE POSSIBLY DOING SOMETHING *WRONG*?

I CAN'T THINK WHAT.

AFTER A FEW MORE NARROW ESCAPES, CONFUCIUS FINALLY RETURNED HOME TO LU...

SIGH...

...AND THERE HE DIED, DISAPPOINTED AND CRANKY...

WHERE THE ✱@# WERE *YOU*? DIDN'T YOU KNOW I WAS SICK?

ONLY HEAVEN UNDERSTANDS ME...

MY WAY IS UNPOPULAR...

ETC.

IN FAIRNESS TO OLD MASTER KUNG, THERE WAS MORE TO HIS PHILOSOPHY THAN CLOTHES, MANNERS, AND TUNES...

MORE? OY!

HOPE IT COSTS LESS THAN THESE *@# ROBES!

CONFUCIUS ALSO BELIEVED THAT ACTIONS AND POSES SHOULD REFLECT ONE'S *TRUE FEELINGS.*

YOU GOTTA BE *SINCERELY* POLITE!

IF POSSIBLE.

WELL, THERE'S A RELIEF. SOUNDS FREE.

BOSSES SHOULD BE *BENEVOLENT* AND *FAIR,* WHILE SUBORDINATES SHOULD BE *REVERENT* AND *OBEDIENT.*

WHAT IF YOUR BOSS IS *ARBITRARY, CRUEL, BESTIAL,* AND *ABUSIVE?*

I SAID, A SUBORDINATE IS REVERENT AND OBEDIENT!

SINCE THESE VALUES ARE LEARNED FROM INFANCY, CONFUCIUS TAUGHT THAT *ALL SOCIAL ORDER* WAS BASED ON RIGHT RELATIONS *WITHIN THE FAMILY.*

AH! A *REPUBLICAN!*

...WHICH MAKES IT ODD THAT HE NEVER MENTIONS HIS *OWN FAMILY* AND HAS NOTHING GOOD TO SAY ABOUT *WOMEN* (UNLIKE LAO-TZU, BY THE WAY).

♪ "THIS IS A MAN'S WORLD..." ♪

DESPITE THE MASTER'S WORLDLY FAILURES, HIS PUPILS GOT GOOD JOBS IN ALL THE WARRING STATES, SPREADING CONFUCIAN IDEALS!

BEND *LOW!* FEEL THE *HUMILITY!*

SO WHAT MADE CONFUCIUS SUCH A **BIG DEAL?** HOW DID THIS NOT-SO-SUCCESSFUL MINISTER OF A SMALL STATE BECOME A GUIDE TO COUNTLESS LATER GENERATIONS?

ONE REASON MUST HAVE BEEN YOUR **SUPERHUMAN SCHOLARSHIP:** IN YOUR **COPIOUS SPARE TIME,** YOU STUDIED ALL OF ANCIENT CHINESE MUSIC AND LITERATURE!

WHADDAYA MEAN, "COPIOUS SPARE TIME?"

:AHEM: YOU THEN COMPILED AND EDITED THE **AUTHORITATIVE VERSION** OF THE **CHINESE CLASSICS:** THE BOOKS OF **HISTORY, POETRY,** AND **RITES,** AND THE **SPRING AND AUTUMN ANNALS.**

EVEN IN YOUR BARBARIC TONGUE? YAO!

I'VE **RELIED** ON THESE BOOKS AS **SOURCES** — EVEN THOUGH YOU DID SOME **NOTORIOUS REWRITING** TO SUIT YOUR OWN OPINIONS.*

HEY! DON'T **YOU?**

NEVER!

HOW THESE BOOKS BECAME **ALL-IMPORTANT** IS A STORY WE'LL HAVE TO SAVE FOR VOLUME 10. SORRY!

I ACCEPT YOUR SINCERE APOLOGY.

* CONFUCIUS SINGLED OUT THE **SPRING AND AUTUMN ANNALS** AS THE BOOK THAT WOULD MAKE OR BREAK HIS REPUTATION. BUT READING THIS DRY, YEAR-BY-YEAR ACCOUNT OF OFFICIAL STATE BUSINESS, IT'S HARD TO SEE WHY HE THOUGHT SO!

"IN THE AUTUMN, HAIL FELL..."

HUH?

THESE "FACTS", IT TURNS OUT, WERE A BIT TWISTED: IN THE STORY OF THE DUKE OF CHING, FOR INSTANCE, (SEE P. 75), CONFUCIUS DEMOTED THE DUKE TO AN EARL, FAILS TO MENTION THAT HIS ENEMY WAS ALSO HIS BROTHER, LEAVES OUT THE MOTHER, ETC!!

WHY? WHY?

THIS WAS CONFUCIUS'S WAY OF PUNISHING THE DUKE FOR HIS LACK OF FAMILY FEELING!

NASTY BOY, SUFFER MY JUDGMENT!

AND SO, 2500 YEARS LATER, HIS TRANSLATOR WROTE OF CONFUCIUS:

HM... "NO REVERENCE FOR TRUTH... SHRANK FROM LOOKING TRUTH IN THE FACE... HAD MORE SYMPATHY WITH POWER THAN WITH WEAKNESS"

AWW... THEY STILL **CARE!**

AFTER CONFUCIUS HIMSELF, THE MOST IMPORTANT CONFUCIAN WAS **MENCIUS** (MENG-TZU). UNLIKE CONFUCIUS, WHO ALWAYS LUSTED AFTER POWER, MENCIUS WAS HAPPY TO TRAVEL AROUND WITH HIS NUMEROUS STUDENTS, VISITING PALACES, AND CRITICIZING HIS HOSTS (SO MUCH EASIER WHEN YOU'RE NOT *JOB·HUNTING!*).

LOVE YOUR INSULTS, MENG, BUT THE KITCHEN IS CLOSED!

ANOTHER CONFUCIAN WAS **HSÜN·TZU**, WHO WENT THE MASTER ONE BETTER BY DENYING THE *EXISTENCE OF THE SUPERNATURAL*.

HEAVEN KNOWS WHAT HEAVEN IS!!

BUT THE MOST SUCCESSFUL THINKER OF THE TIME WAS NO CONFUCIAN. THIS WAS **MO·TZU**, WHO PREACHED A DOCTRINE OF *UNIVERSAL LOVE.*

A CHRISTIAN MESSAGE, 400 YEARS B.C.!

WHAT?

THE MO-ISTS ALSO BELIEVED IN LIVING **SIMPLY** AND **FRUGALLY**, WHICH SPARKED ARGUMENTS WITH THE CEREMONIOUS CONFUCIANS!

THESE *FUNERALS* ARE A *WASTE* OF MONEY!

GASP!

I'M GONNA TELL YOUR ANCESTORS!

MO BUILT A BIG ORGANIZATION, BUT HAD TROUBLE GETTING OFFICIAL BACKING.

LOVE YOUR LOVE, MO, BUT I CAN'T RUN THE REALM ON IT!

COULDN'T YOU JUST PAY *LIPSERVICE* TO LOVE WHILE SLAUGHTERING MILLIONS?

OOK! BARBARIC THOUGHT...

HAN FEI-TZE HATED ALL THIS MUSHY MO-IST LOVE AND CONFUCIAN FILIAL PIETY...

UGH! PTUEY!

DON'T TAKE IT PERSONALLY. EVERYTHING DISGUSTS HAN FEI.

THE PROBLEM WITH FILIAL PIETY, HE SAID, WAS THAT PEOPLE WERE MORE LOYAL TO THEIR *FAMILIES* THAN TO THE *KING*. THEREFORE, A KING WAS *WASTING HIS TIME* TRYING TO MAKE PEOPLE *LIKE* HIM, AND SHOULD GOVERN WITH *STRICT LAWS* AND *HARSH PUNISHMENTS.*

LIKE DEATH BY 1000 CUTS, OR 1001 CUTS, OR 1002 CUTS, OR...

I'VE RARELY SEEN HIM SO ANIMATED!

HAN FEI WAS A MASTER OF *INVECTIVE** WHO APPEALED TO KINGS AND *FRIGHTENED* PHILOSOPHERS!

YOU GUYS BETTER WATCH OUT...

THEN THERE WERE COUNTLESS OTHER WANDERING POLITICIANS AND SPEAKERS, SOME OF WHOM WERE ALSO THINKERS...

THINGS CONSIST OF NOTHING BUT THEIR *ATTRIBUTES.* BUT *ATTRIBUTES* ARE NOT ATTRIBUTES IN AND OF *THEMSELVES.* THEREFORE, A WHITE HORSE IS NOT A HORSE!

HOW ABOUT A RED TOYOTA?

✳ THE CONFUCIANS BELIEVED THAT THE WAY TO RESTORE THE GLORIES OF THE PAST WAS TO REVIVE OLD *RITUALS:* WHAT WORKED ONCE SHOULD WORK AGAIN. HAN FEI SCOFFED AT THIS!

WOTTA BUNCH OF DUMMIES!

HE COMPARED THE CONFUCIANS TO A FARMER WHO ONCE HAPPENED TO SEE A RABBIT COLLIDE WITH A TREE STUMP, BREAKING THE RABBIT'S NECK.

WOW! LUNCH!

FOREVER AFTER, SAID HAN FEI, THE FARMER STOOD STARING AT THE STUMP, HOPING FOR ANOTHER RABBIT.

AH, THE GLORIOUS MEALS OF THE PAST!

AND, FINALLY, WE HAVE **CHUANG-TZU,** THE CARTOONIST'S PHILOSOPHER!! THE ONLY ONE WITH A SENSE OF HUMOR, HIS ATTITUDE CAN BEST BE SUMMARIZED IN **TWO WORDS —**

SO WHAT?

CHUANG-TZU MADE HIS POINTS WITH LITTLE **FABLES.** FOR EXAMPLE, A KING ADMIRES A **BUTCHER'S** TECHNIQUE. THE BUTCHER EXPLAINS: "WHEN I CUT, I DO NOT CUT. MY ART IS TO PUT AN EDGE OF **NO THICKNESS** INTO THE **SPACES BETWEEN** JOINTS. THAT'S WHY I HAVEN'T NEEDED A NEW KNIFE IN **19 YEARS...**"

WOW! REMIND ME TO TELL THIS TO THE **EXECUTIONER!**

OR: CHUANG-TZU VISITED CONFUCIUS'S HOME OF **LU.** THE DUKE SAID, "WE HAVE MANY **CONFUCIANS** HERE, BUT VERY FEW OF **YOUR** FOLLOWERS, SIR!"

CHUANG-TZU REPLIED —.

I SEE A LOT OF GENTLEMEN **DRESSED** LIKE CONFUCIANS, BUT ARE THEY **REALLY** CONFUCIANS??

90

WHY NOT ISSUE AN ORDER THAT EVERYONE WHO WEARS CONFUCIAN *CLOTHES* WITHOUT PRACTICING CONFUCIAN *DOCTRINE* SHALL BE *PUT TO DEATH?*

HEH HEH... I *LIKE* THAT...

THE DUKE ISSUED THE ORDER.

WITHIN FIVE DAYS, NO ONE WAS LEFT IN CONFUCIAN DRESS, EXCEPT A LONE OLD MAN...

...BUT HE COULD EXPOUND THE DOCTRINE LIKE A CHAMP!

BLAH BLAH BLAH BLAH

YOU SEE, DUKE? ONLY *ONE* CONFUCIAN IN LU!

HUI-TZU SAID TO CHUANG-TZU:

I HAVE A *BIG TREE.* ITS TRUNK IS *GNARLED,* AND ITS LIMBS ARE SO TWISTED, NO *CARPENTER* WOULD LOOK AT IT *TWICE.* IT REMINDS ME OF *YOUR WORDS:* *BIG* BUT *USELESS!!*

CHUANG-TZU REPLIED:

YOU HAVE THIS BIG TREE, AND YOU'RE UPSET BECAUSE IT'S *USELESS?* WHY NOT LIE DOWN IN ITS SHADE AND TAKE A *NAP?*

THESE STORIES ARE THE FORERUNNERS OF *ZEN...*

WHAT'S WRONG WITH BEING USELESS?

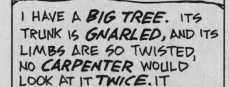

91

KINGMAKER, QUEENMAKER

IN 271 B.C., SOME TRAVELERS ENTERED THE **HAN·KU PASS**, GATEWAY TO THE MOUNTAINS OF **CHIN**. HIDING IN THE BAGGAGE WAS A FUGITIVE NAMED **FAN SUI**.

AS AIDE TO AN OFFICIAL IN THE STATE OF **WEI**, FAN SUI HAD FALLEN UNDER SUSPICION OF **TREASON**.

AT A DRUNKEN PARTY, HIS BOSS AND SOME OTHER GENTLEMEN BEAT HIM SENSELESS, KNOCKED OUT HIS TEETH, AND LEFT HIM FOR DEAD IN THE OUTHOUSE.

GENTLEMEN DO STRANGE THINGS UNDER THE INFLUENCE OF ALCOHOL.

HEY, EVERYBODY!? *PEE ON TH' CORPSE!?*

BUT FAN SUI ESCAPED TO CHIN. THERE HE WAITED IN POVERTY **TWO YEARS** FOR AN INTERVIEW WITH KING CHAO.

WHEN THE TIME FINALLY CAME FOR THE MEETING, FAN SUI PRETENDED TO HAVE WANDERED IN BY MISTAKE.

HSST! MOVE IT! HERE COMES THE **KING**!!

WHAT KING? CHIN HAS NO KING—ONLY THE QUEEN MOTHER AND HER BROTHERS!!

KING CHAO MUST HAVE WINCED AT THIS! IT WAS TRUE; THE KING'S MOTHER HAD GIVEN HER BROTHERS **HUGE FIEFS**, WHICH THEY ENLARGED BY WAGING PRIVATE WARS AGAINST THEIR NEIGHBORS. KING CHAO GREETED FAN SUI **COURTEOUSLY**.

TERRIBLY SORRY... I SHOULD HAVE SEEN YOU **AGES** AGO... BUT I'VE BEEN **SO** BUSY CONSULTING WITH **MOM**...

KING CHAO TOOK FAN SUI'S ADVICE TO HEART!

THOSE SKILLED AT ENRICHING THEIR **FAMILIES** DO SO AT THE EXPENSE OF THE **STATE**; THOSE SKILLED AT ENRICHING THE STATE DO SO AT THE EXPENSE OF **OTHER STATES**.

HE DEMOTED HIS UNCLES AND BANISHED THEM TO DISTANT FIEFS.

LOOK AT THEIR **BAGGAGE**!!

FAN SUI BECAME PRIME MINISTER; KING CHAO BECAME ALL-POWERFUL; CHIN BECAME THE TERROR OF THE WARRING STATES —AND FAN SUI MADE HIS OLD BOSS FROM **WEI** EAT STRAW AND BEANS LIKE A HORSE...

FAN SUI HAD THE GOOD SENSE TO *RETIRE* BEFORE MAKING *TOO* MANY MISTAKES, AND LIVED OUT HIS LIFE HEAPED WITH HONORS, WITH HIS HEAD STILL ATTACHED TO HIS NECK...

TAP TAP

BUT KING CHAO REIGNED ON AND ON... WHILE THE COURT WONDERED WHO WOULD FOLLOW HIM.

NEXT IN LINE WAS PRINCE *AN-KUO*, HIMSELF NO SPRING CHICKEN.

HE'S AN AUTUMN CHICKEN!

AN-KUO'S FAVORITE WIFE, THE LADY *HUA-YANG*, HAD NO SON.

THIS WAS SOMETHING TO WORRY ABOUT! WHAT IF SOME *OTHER* WIFE'S SON BECAME KING? WHAT WOULD BECOME OF LADY HUA-YANG AND HER FAMILY *THEN*?

NOTHING GOOD!?

ENTER *LU PU-WEI*, THE MOST AMAZING *ENTREPRENEUR* IN THE HISTORY OF THE UNIVERSE, LOOKING FOR INVESTMENT OPPORTUNITIES!

VISITING THE NEIGHBORING STATE OF *CHAO*, LU PU-WEI FOUND ONE OF THOSE SONS OF AN-KUO'S JUNIOR WIVES THAT THE LADY WAS *WORRIED* ABOUT!

JUST THROUGH THERE!

THIS WRETCH, *TZU-CHU*, WAS HELD IN CHAO AS A *HOSTAGE* TO GUARANTEE CHIN'S GOOD BEHAVIOR, AND HE DID NOT LIVE WELL!

OO! SQUALID!

LU PU-WEI PAID HIM A VISIT.

I BELIEVE I CAN *ENLARGE* YOUR GATE!

ARH... WHY DON'T YOU ENLARGE YOUR *OWN* ✿◉# GATE?

I INTEND TO ENLARGE *MINE* BY ENLARGING *YOURS*...

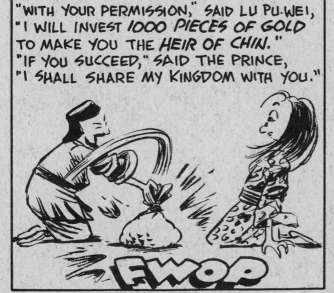

"WITH YOUR PERMISSION," SAID LU PU-WEI, "I WILL INVEST *1000 PIECES OF GOLD* TO MAKE YOU THE *HEIR OF CHIN.*"
"IF YOU SUCCEED," SAID THE PRINCE, "I SHALL SHARE MY KINGDOM WITH YOU."

FWOP

LU PU-WEI GAVE HALF THE MONEY TO TZU-CHU TO SPIFF HIMSELF UP AND WENT WEST WITH THE REST.

NOW FOR HEAVEN'S SAKE, GET SOME HANGERS-ON!!

BACK IN CHIN, LU PU-WEI BROUGHT PRESENTS TO LADY HUAYANG'S *OLDER SISTER*.

JUST A TOKEN OF *TZU-CHU'S* RESPECT!

TZU-*WHO*??

HE PRAISED THE HOSTAGE PRINCE TZU-CHU TO THE SKIES!

HE'S *SUCH* A NICE BOY, AND HE JUST *WORSHIPS* YOUR SISTER! DAY AND NIGHT HE *WEEPS* THINKING OF LADY HUA-YANG'S ≀AHEM≀ CHILDLESS CONDITION ...

NOW HERE'S MY PLAN...

A FRANK TALK BETWEEN SISTERS FOLLOWED!

I HAVE HEARD THAT FAVOR WON BY *BEAUTY* WILL CEASE WHEN BEAUTY *FADES*...

PRINCE AN-KUO LOVES YOU DEARLY, ALTHOUGH YOU ARE CHILDLESS. IF YOU ATTACH YOURSELF TO ONE OF HIS SONS, MAKING *HIM* THE HEIR AND *ADOPTING* HIM AS YOUR SON, AS LONG AS YOUR HUSBAND LIVES, YOU WILL BE *RESPECTED*, AND AFTER HIS DEATH, WHEN YOUR ADOPTED SON BECOMES KING, YOU WILL NOT LOSE YOUR *POWER*.

THIS IS CALLED "LASTING GAIN RESULTING FROM A SINGLE WORD."

96

WHILE YOU ARE BEAUTIFUL, YOU MUST PROVIDE FOR THE FUTURE, FOR ONCE YOUR BEAUTY HAS *FADED*, IT WILL BE *TOO LATE*.

TZU-CHU IS WORTHY, BUT AS A CONCUBINE'S SON, HE HAS NO CLAIM ON THE THRONE. IF YOU ADOPT HIM, HE WILL BE GRATEFUL AND LOYAL FOREVER!

YEH... BY THE WAY, WHERE'D YOU GET THE *CUTE* EARRINGS?

HERE WE SEE ANOTHER VIEW OF THE FAMILY: WOMEN WIELDED POWER AND GAINED SECURITY THROUGH THEIR *BEAUTY* OR THEIR *SONS*.

SO LADY HUAYANG ASKED HER HUSBAND...

HONEY... I'D LIKE TO ADOPT *TZU-CHU* WOULD YOU MAKE HIM YOUR HEIR? *PLEEASE...*

HEH! PERSUADE ME!

PRINCE AN-KUO AGREED AND GAVE LADY HUAYANG AN ENGRAVED JADE TOKEN AS HIS PLEDGE.

THE ROYAL COUPLE SENT LAVISH GIFTS TO *TZU-CHU* IN THE CARE OF *LU PU-WEI*, WHOM THEY NAMED ROYAL TUTOR.

BACK IN HAN TAN, CAPITAL OF CHAO!

SUCCESS!

HERE. BUY YOURSELF SOME NEW ARMOR!

SUDDENLY, LIFE WAS A *PARTY* — UNTIL, THAT IS, TZU CHU ADMIRED LU PU·WEI'S *MISTRESS*, THE HOTTEST DANCER IN HANTAN...

OH! MASTER LU! THIS RED-HOT LOTUS— *CAN I HAVE HER ??*

LU PU·WEI SWALLOWED HARD AND REFLECTED THAT HE HAD NEARLY BANKRUPTED HIMSELF TO GET THIS FAR

DON'T BLOW IT, DON'T BLOW IT, DON'T BLOW IT...

GWULP

SO THE PRINCE GOT WHAT HE WANTED—AND *MORE*: SHE WAS *PREGNANT.*

IN TIME, SHE BORE A SON—LU PU·WEI'S SON—AND TZU·CHU MARRIED HER.

WAS THAT *NINE MONTHS?* DIDN'T SEEM LIKE IT...

TIME FLIES WHEN YOU'RE IN A STUPOR!

UNFORTUNATELY, CHIN THEN ATTACKED CHAO... BUT THE HOSTAGE WAS NOW *RICH* ENOUGH TO BUY HIS FREEDOM. HE FLED FOR HOME!!

AT LAST, AFTER A 56·YEAR REIGN, THE KING OF CHIN WENT TO HIS ANCESTORS... CHAO RELEASED TZU·CHU'S WIFE AND CHILD, WHO RETURNED TO FIND AN·KUO KING, TZU·CHU CROWN PRINCE, AND LADY HUAYANG QUEEN MOTHER.

AND...AND *LU PU·WEI?*

SMILING LIKE A CAT!!

SUDDENLY, *AN·KUO* DIED, AND *TZU·CHU* WAS KING.

WE DID IT WE DID IT WE DID IT WE DID IT...

AS PROMISED, HE GAVE LU PU·WEI A FIEF OF *100,000 HOUSEHOLDS* AND NAMED HIM *ASSISTANT PRIME MINISTER.*

YOU EARNED IT, MASTER.. *COUGH*

AND THEN, JUST AS SUDDENLY, *TZU·CHU* ALSO DIED...

FWOP

99

THE LITTLE CHILD — *LU PU-WEI'S* CHILD — BECAME KING... LU PU-WEI WAS NOW *PRIME MINISTER*, WITH THE TITLE *"SECOND FATHER"*... HIS FORMER MISTRESS — OR *WAS* IT FORMER? — WAS QUEEN DOWAGER... COULD THIS PECULIAR FAMILY UNIT REALLY SUPPRESS THE OTHER *WARRING STATES*, RESTORE THE GLORIES OF THE *EMPIRE*, REVIVE THE RITUALS OF *YAO* AND *SHUN*..??

NOT TO MENTION THE *NORTHERN BARBARIANS*???!

NEXT: THE CRIMES OF *CHIN*

100

INTRODUCTION

IN THE LAST VOLUME, WE SAW THE FOUNDATIONS OF CHINESE CIVILIZATION... THE *LEGENDS*, THE *SILK*, THE *FAMILY*, THE *PHILOSOPHY*, THE POOR *TURTLES*...

IN THIS ONE, WE COVER THE STORY OF THE FIRST *CHINESE EMPIRES*—A WAR STORY, MOSTLY...

IMAGINE IF ROBIN HOOD HAD BECOME KING OF ENGLAND—SOMETHING LIKE THAT...

AT SOME POINT HERE, YOU MAY ASK YOURSELF, "WHY IS HE GIVING SO MUCH ATTENTION TO *ONE EPISODE*? HE JUST SPENT *20 PAGES ON 10 YEARS!*" I ASKED MYSELF THE SAME QUESTION...

WELL, THE ANSWER *MIGHT* BE THAT I WANT WESTERN READERS TO APPRECIATE THE *WEALTH* OF *DETAIL* PRESERVED BY CHINESE HISTORIANS... OR MAYBE I'M TRYING TO OVERCOME WESTERN *PREJUDICE* BY SHOWING THE CHINESE AS *INDIVIDUALS*...

I WANNA BE *POLITICALLY CORRECT*...

NAA·A·AH! THE *REAL* REASON IS—I *COULDN'T RESIST!* THE STORIES ARE JUST *TOO GOOD!!*

THUNK

SO BUCKLE YOUR SWASH, AND *LET'S GO*—TO THE *ROYAL PALACE* OF THE KINGDOM OF *CHIN*...

Volume 10
JADED PRINCES

LU PU-WEI, PRIME MINISTER OF THE STATE OF *CHIN*, HAS BEEN CARRYING ON A LOVE AFFAIR WITH THE *KING'S MOTHER*. NOW IT'S ABOUT *241 B.C.*, AND—

WE CAN'T GO ON LIKE THIS, DARLING!

OH, PUEY, WHY NOT? SOB!!

MY BLOSSOM, YOUR SON WAS A MERE **BOY** WHEN HE BECAME KING OF CHIN... HE CALLED ME —SNIF— **SECOND FATHER**. NOW HE APPROACHES MANHOOD...AND IF HE EVER FINDS OUT ABOUT US, I'M *1000 PIECES* OF *DEAD MEAT*...

YOU DON'T LOVE ME!

YES, I DO— AND I'LL **PROVE** IT!

BUT **HOW?**

I'VE **GOT** IT! I'LL FIND HER A **SUBSTITUTE!**

LU, YOU'RE A GENIUS!

SEEKING A **PINCH-HITTER**, LU PU-WEI FOUND **LAO AI**, WHO HAD A BIG BAT!!

HO! EVERYBODY ELSE, **DISMISSED!**

HE SHOWED OFF LAO AI AT A PARTY...

...AND MADE SURE THE QUEEN HEARD ABOUT IT!

I WILL **MEET** THIS LAO AI...

THE INTERVIEW WENT WELL!

AHEM!!

YOU **DO** LOVE ME, PUEY!

THEY HAD LAO AI'S *HAIR* AND *EYEBROWS* PLUCKED OUT, DISGUISED HIM AS A *EUNUCH*, AND MOVED HIM INTO THE QUEEN'S QUARTERS.

OO... THAT SEMI-SMOOTH FACE.. THIS IS REALLY *SICK*.. COME HERE, LAO AI...

THIS WAS LOVE! SOON THE QUEEN WAS *PREGNANT* AND MOVED TO THE COUNTRY TO HAVE THE "EUNUCH'S" BABIES.

SHE GAVE LAO AI HIS OWN *PALACE*, COMPLETE WITH HUNDREDS OF SERVANTS, GUARDS, GUESTS, AND HANGERS-ON.

HM... I DIDN'T KNOW YOU COULD RIDE ONE O' THEM THINGS THIS HIGH...

THE HAPPY COUPLE HAD TWO CHILDREN. INEVITABLY, THEY CONSIDERED THEIR *FUTURE*!

SUCH REGAL TODDLING! WHY SHOULDN'T *HE* BE KING, INSTEAD OF YOUR *CRUEL, PARANOID* LOUT OF AN ELDEST SON?

SUDDENLY, THE KING OF CHIN, WHO HAD BEEN TURNING A BLIND EYE TO THE WHOLE BUSINESS, TOOK AN INTEREST IN HIS MOM'S AFFAIRS!

THOSE *BASTARDS* THE HEIRS OF *MY* CHINNY CHIN CHIN??! I THINK *NOT*!!

THE KING CALLED FOR LAO AI'S ARREST... LAO AI USED THE QUEEN MOTHER'S CREDENTIALS TO CALL OUT TROOPS FOR HIMSELF...AND A BATTLE FOLLOWED.

WHEN IT WAS OVER, LAO AI'S **HEAD** HUNG IN THE MARKETPLACE, HIS **CHILDREN** WERE DEAD, THE **QUEEN MOTHER** WAS EXILED — AND **LU PU·WEI** WAS **NERVOUS.!!**

LUCKILY, CHIN'S MOST PERSUASIVE **ORATORS*** DEPENDED ON LU PU·WEI FOR BED AND BOARD.

MASTER LU'S **WISDOM** IS **UNFATHOMABLE!**

HIS **LOYALTY** IS **UNQUESTIONABLE!**

HIS **CHOW MEIN** IS **INEXHAUSTIBLE!**

O.K.! ALL **RIGHT!** I'LL GO EASY ON HIM...

AND OUR APPETITE IS UNBELIEVABLE!

THANKS TO THEM, HE MERELY LOST HIS **JOB,** NOT HIS **HEAD.**

OH, YOUR HIGHNESS, OUR **GRATITUDE** IS **INEXPRESSIBLE!**

MERE **WORDS** ARE **INADEQUATE.**

BUT, HEY, LEMME GIVE 'ER A TRY, ANYWAY...

¡AHEM! I AM JUST BEGINNING TO DISLIKE YOU PEOPLE...

A PATRON OF THE ARTS, LU PU·WEI HIRED THE BEST SCHOLARS MONEY COULD BUY TO COMPILE A **COMPLETE BOOK** OF LEARNING AND PHILOSOPHY.

EXCELLENT. NOW PUT MY NAME ON IT AND HELP YOURSELVES TO CHOW MEIN!

"THE ANNALS OF MASTER LU" WAS DISPLAYED IN THE MARKETPLACE, WITH A REWARD OF GOLD TO ANYONE WHO COULD ADD OR SUBTRACT A **SINGLE WORD.**

OF COURSE, YOU'LL HAVE TO **READ** IT FIRST!

THE BORING AND PEDANTIC BOOK SURVIVES TO THIS DAY, BUT WHAT BECAME OF THE GOLD NOBODY KNOWS...

SOME BOOKS IT JUST DOESN'T PAY TO READ...

106

BUT YOU DON'T STOP BEING THE **MOST IMPORTANT MAN** IN THE STATE JUST BECAUSE SOME TEENAGER SAYS SO!! LU PU-WEI STILL HAD WEALTH, CONNECTIONS, AND **TOO MANY VISITORS!!**

WHAT DO YOU MEAN, "SOME TEENAGER?"

THE KING WROTE TO MASTER LU, STRIPPING HIM OF HIS **FIEF** WITH THESE IRONIC WORDS:

WHAT HAVE YOU DONE FOR CHIN, SIR, TO DESERVE A FIEF OF 100,000 HOUSEHOLDS? WHAT RELATION ARE YOU TO CHIN THAT YOU SHOULD HAVE THE TITLE "SECOND FATHER?"

I'M DONE FOR!

SO LU PU-WEI PUT AN END TO HIS UNBELIEVABLE CAREER BY DRINKING POISON..

SO... THE CHOW MEIN—?

"LU PU-WEI WAS SURELY THE SORT OF MAN WHOM CONFUCIUS DESCRIBED AS ONE WHOSE GOOD REPUTATION BELIED HIS CONDUCT."

— SSUMA CHIEN

NO ONE WILL EVER KNOW IF THE QUEEN MOTHER TOLD HER SON THE WHOLE **TRUTH** ABOUT LU PU-WEI!

HE WAS YOUR FATHER!

A MERE RUMOR!

BUT SEVEN YEARS LATER, WHEN CHIN CONQUERED **CHAO**, HIS MOTHER'S BIRTHPLACE*, THE KING HAD ALL HER FAMILY'S ENEMIES **BURIED ALIVE**...

THIS OUGHTA PUT **THAT** STORY TO REST!

* SEE VOLUME 9.

AS *CHIN* ATTACKED *CHAO,* THE ROYAL FAMILY IN THE LITTLE STATE OF *YEN* WHICH WAS NEXT IN THE LINE OF FIRE, PACED NERVOUSLY.

IT'S CHIN OR US, IT'S CHIN OR US!

THE CROWN PRINCE SUMMONED AN AGING SWASHBUCKLER NAMED *TIEN KUANG* FOR ADVICE, BUT—

I AM *OLD,* BROKEN, AND PAST MY PRIME, YOUR HIGHNESS... BUT I HAVE A YOUNG FRIEND, *CHING KO,* WHO MIGHT HELP.

INTRODUCE ME!!

ON THE WAY OUT, THE PRINCE COMMITTED A *GAFFE:*

OH, BY THE WAY, *PLEASE* DON'T TELL *ANYONE* ABOUT OUR TALK—IT'S A MATTER OF *NATIONAL SECURITY...*

OF COURSE NOT...

TIEN KUANG FOUND HIS FRIEND IN THE MARKETPLACE, DRINKING WITH HIS FRIENDS, A MUSICIAN AND A VENDOR OF DOG FLESH...

A WORD WITH YOU, CHING KO?

CHING KO, THE CROWN PRINCE WANTS TO SEE *YOU...* I HOPE YOU'LL TAKE HIM A MESSAGE FROM ME...

EH? HIC... DROOL... WHAAA?

AS I WAS LEAVING, THE PRINCE SWORE ME TO *SECRECY,* SAYING THAT OUR TALK WAS VITAL TO NATIONAL SECURITY. BY DOING SO, HE SHOWED THAT HE *DOUBTS* ME...TO GIVE RISE TO SUSPICION IS A *SLUR* ON A MAN'S *HONOR!!*

PLEASE GO TO THE PRINCE AND TELL HIM I AM *DEAD*, SO I CAN'T POSSIBLY TALK!

EHHHH?

WITH THAT, TIEN KUANG SLIT HIS OWN THROAT AND DIED ON THE SPOT!

EEEAA-AAH!!

THIS WAS A LITTLE *MOTIVATIONAL PLOY* TO SPUR THE LAZY CHING-KO INTO ACTION...

COMING, MY PRINCE!

ZIP

THE PRINCE SENT HIM TO THE *COURT OF CHIN*, AND SOON CHING-KO FOUND HIMSELF FACE-TO-FACE WITH THE FEARSOME KING, BEARING A *MAP* (OF YEN), A *SEVERED HEAD* (OF ONE OF CHIN'S ENEMIES), AND A *POISONED DAGGER* (HIDDEN).

PLEASE BE SO GOOD AS TO HAND ME THE MAP, INSIGNIFICANT AS I AM...

JUST A SECOND— IT'S IN HERE...

SCRAPE A BIT...

HA! PREPARE TO DIE, TYRANT!

RIP

OOPS.

NONE OF THE KING'S ATTENDANTS WAS CARRYING A WEAPON — IT WAS *ILLEGAL* — BUT THE DOCTOR HAD HIS *MEDICINE BAG*...

FINALLY, THE KING THOUGHT TO DRAW HIS OWN SWORD.

:AHEM: OH, RIGHT!

THEN HE REMEMBERED TO CALL FOR THE *ARMED GUARDS,* WHO RUSHED IN AND FINISHED OFF CHING KO.

SO CHIN ATTACKED *YEN,* AND *EVERYONE* WHO EVER KNEW CHING KO WENT INTO *HIDING.*

CHING KO'S OLD FRIEND, THE MUSICIAN, STUFFED HIS INSTRUMENTS AND BECAME A WAITER.

WOTTA VOICE!

BUT HIS MASTER NOTICED HIS TALENT AND RECOMMENDED HIM TO THE KING OF CHIN.

SOMEONE RECOGNIZED HIM, SO THE KING HAD HIS EYES PUT OUT — AND THEN OFFERED HIM A JOB!

HOW'D YOU LIKE TO PLAY THE PALACE?

THE BLIND MUSICIAN PLAYED FOR THE KING, GETTING CLOSER AND CLOSER...

ONE DAY, HE BROUGHT IN A WEIGHTED INSTRUMENT AND TOOK A SWING — MISSING, OF COURSE!

TSK!

AFTER THIS, NOBODY FROM YEN COULD COME NEAR THE KING OF CHIN!

CAN YOU PLAY "FAR, FAR AWAY?"

NEW WORLD ORDER

PHEW! YOU CAN'T TRUST ANYONE!

BY THE TIME OF THE ASSASSINATION ATTEMPTS, THIS KING WAS NO MERE KING!

YES, HIGHNESS!

NO ONE, HIGHNESS!

EVER SINCE HIS CHILDHOOD, THE KING'S ARMIES HAD EXPANDED CHIN'S BORDERS... AND WHEN HE TOOK CONTROL FROM LU PU·WEI, CHIN'S *POWER* ONLY *INCREASED!!*

CHIN CONQUERED ALL THE OTHER WARRING STATES AND PUSHED BACK THE NORTHERN "BARBARIANS," UNTIL THE KING RULED MORE TERRITORY THAN ANY CHINESE KING BEFORE. IN THE YEAR 221 B.C., HE TOOK THE TITLE *SHIH HUANG·TI,* OR *FIRST EMPEROR.*

THE BLOODSHED OF THE LAST 500 YEARS WAS *SO* TIRESOME... LET'S *ORGANIZE* FOR *PEACE*... START BY ABOLISHING THESE NAMES AND KILLING THEIR KINGS...

YEN

CHAO

CHI

CHIN

HAN

LU

CHU

YUEH

HOW WAS THE NEW EMPIRE TO BE ORGANIZED? THE CONFUCIAN SCHOLARS URGED A RETURN TO THE GOOD OLD FEUDALISM OF THE ZHOU DYNASTY (SEE VOL. 9).

WE BEG YOU TO SET UP YOUR SONS AS PRINCES OF THE PROVINCES!!

YES! AND GIVE FIEFS* TO YOUR LOYAL GENERALS!

AND COUSINS!

AND UNCLES!

AND YOUNGER BROTHERS...

*GRANTS OF LAND, INCLUDING THE FARMERS WHO LIVED THERE.

EVERYONE AGREED, EXCEPT ONE— CHIEF JUSTICE LI SSU.

I HUMBLY BEG TO DIFFER.

RUSTLE
SWEAT
TREMBLE

THE KINGS OF ZHOU GAVE FIEFS TO THEIR RELATIVES... THEN, WHEN THE BARONS STARTED TO FIGHT AMONG THEMSELVES, THE KING WAS POWERLESS TO STOP THEM... NO, YOUR MAJESTY, FIEFS WERE THE DOWNFALL OF ZHOU...

B-BUT...THEN... HOW DO I REWARD MY FAMILY, MY LOYAL GENERALS, MY TOADIES AND FLATTERERS?

WHO, THEM? JUST KEEP 'EM HERE IN THE CAPITAL AND GIVE 'EM PENSIONS AND FANCY TITLES— THEY'LL BE EASY ENOUGH TO CONTROL!?

AND THE EMPEROR AGREED!

THE CHIEF JUSTICE IS RIGHT!? TIMES HAVE CHANGED...WE NEED SOMETHING NEW: A CENTRALIZED BUREAUCRACY CHOSEN ON MERIT!**

YES, YOUR MAJESTY !!

GROAN!

** NOT NECESSARILY HIS EXACT WORDS!

OUT FROM THE CAPITAL FLOWED THE STREAM OF *GOVERNMENT OFFICIALS*...*IN* FROM THE PROVINCES RUMBLED THE DELUGE OF *REPORTS, RECOMMENDATIONS, REQUESTS, STATISTICS,* ETC., ETC., ETC...

THE EMPEROR SET HIMSELF A DAILY QUOTA OF *120 POUNDS OF DOCUMENTS.*

SCALE!!

BUT *LI SSU,* THE CHIEF JUSTICE, WAS NO MERE *BUREAUCRAT*... HE WAS A *PHILOSOPHER,* A FOLLOWER OF *HAN FEI* AND THE *LEGALISTS* (SEE VOL. 9). THE LEGALISTS BELIEVED IN *STRICT LAWS* AND *HARSH PUNISHMENTS,* EVEN FOR PETTY CRIMES.

"ONLY AN INTELLIGENT RULER IS CAPABLE OF APPLYING HEAVY PUNISHMENTS TO LIGHT OFFENSES. IF LIGHT OFFENSES CARRY HEAVY PUNISHMENTS, ONE CAN IMAGINE WHAT WILL BE DONE AGAINST A SERIOUS OFFENSE. THUS THE PEOPLE WILL NOT DARE TO BREAK THE LAWS." —LI SSU

EVERYONE BECAME EQUAL UNDER THE *LAW.* ARISTO- CRATIC TITLES WERE ABOLISHED, AND ARISTOCRATS THEMSELVES EITHER *KILLED* OR PUT TO *WORK* LIKE EVERYONE ELSE!

HI, PRINCE!!

CRITICISING THE LAWS WAS PUNISHABLE BY *DEATH,* AND CITIZENS WERE EXPECTED TO *INFORM* ON THEIR NEIGHBORS.

AND SO THE EMPIRE WAS FINALLY AT *PEACE,* OF A KIND...

YEAH! NO ONE DARES TO SAY "PEEP!"

GUARDS!

WITH AN ENTIRE EMPIRE TO DRAW ON, THE EMPEROR WAS THINKING *BIG.* 700,000 MEN WORKED ON HIS *TOMB* ALONE —FOR *30 YEARS!*

FIRST THINGS FIRST!!

1000 DIVERS DIVED IN VAIN, LOOKING FOR SOME LOST TRIPOD OF ZHOU.

OH, WELL...

AN ARMY OF CONVICTS STRIPPED THE TREES OFF THE MOUNTAIN WHERE *YAO'S* DAUGHTER* WAS BURIED —TO PUNISH HER SPIRIT FOR AN INCONVENIENT SPELL OF *BAD WEATHER.*

AH! NOW I FEEL BETTER!!

*SEE VOL. 9.

COUNTLESS OTHERS MADE ROADS, DUG CANALS, LEVELLED HILLS, AND BUILT *PALACES* — OVER 700 OF THEM, INCLUDING A REPLICA OF EVERY ROYAL PALACE OF THE FORMER WARRING STATES.

A FEW OF US GET TO KEEP FARMING...

THOUSANDS MORE, INCLUDING CHILDREN, SAILED INTO THE PACIFIC, LOOKING FOR THE *LAND OF IMMORTALS.* (THEY MAY HAVE FOUND JAPAN.)

EXPLORERS WENT WEST, MEETING BARBARIANS WHO KNEW BARBARIANS WHO KNEW BARBARIANS NO ONE HAD EVER *HEARD OF* BEFORE.

QUO?

AND THE BIGGEST PROJECT OF ALL: DEALING WITH THE **NORTHERN BARBARIANS**, THE SHEEPHERDING **HSIUNG-NU** OF THE NORTHERN PLAINS. THE EMPEROR SENT ARMIES TO PUSH THE HSIUNG-NU BACK, MOVED SETTLERS INTO THE BARREN CONQUERED TERRITORIES, AND ORDERED 300,000 MEN TO BUILD A **GREAT WALL**, WHICH CONNECTED THE SMALL WALLS ALREADY THERE. THE GREAT WALL DID **DOUBLE DUTY**: IT KEPT THE HSIUNG-NU **OUT** AND THE CHINESE **IN**...

BUT SOME QUESTIONS REFUSED TO GO AWAY! IN 212 B.C., AT A BANQUET TO CELEBRATE THE EMPEROR'S 33 YEARS OF RULE, A SCHOLARLY GUEST BROUGHT UP THAT *FIEF* THING AGAIN!* *

SHANG AND ZHOU LASTED A THOUSAND YEARS BECAUSE THEY GRANTED *FIEFS* TO THE ROYAL SONS AND LOYAL OFFICIALS... I KNOW OF NOTHING *ENDURING* THAT IS NOT BASED ON *ANCIENT EXAMPLES!*

THIS WAS MOST *UNWISE!* BY SAYING THIS, HE HAD CRITICISED *LI SSU,* AS WELL AS REFERRING (OBLIQUELY) TO THE EMPEROR'S *DEATH...*

UM... YOUR HEALTH?

LI SSU RESPONDED:

THESE SCHOLARS LEARN ONLY FROM THE *OLD,* NOT FROM THE *NEW...* THEY DISCUSS EACH NEW DECREE, JUDGING IT ACCORDING TO THEIR OWN SCHOOLS OF THOUGHT, OPPOSING IT IN THEIR HEARTS, WHILE DISCUSSING IT OPENLY IN THE STREETS! *THIS MUST BE STOPPED!*

UNDER FEUDALISM, LAND WAS CONTROLLED BY THE GENTRY, AND FARMERS WERE TIED TO THEIR FARMS—BUT WHEN THE EMPEROR BANNED *FIEFS,* LAND BECAME A *COMMODITY* THAT COULD BE *BOUGHT* AND *SOLD.*

BUYING THE *EARTH?* ISN'T THAT LIKE SELLING THE *MOON* OR THE *STARS?*

NOW THE RICH COULD BEGIN TO OWN LARGE ESTATES, DRIVING OFF THE POOR OR CHARGING THEM RENT.

NO, REALLY... BUYING LAND IS SO MUCH EASIER THAN *FIGHTING* OVER IT!

SHOO!

SO, WHEN A SCHOLAR URGED A RETURN TO FEUDALISM, HE WAS RESPONDING TO NEW AND REAL PROBLEMS — *LANDLORDS, EVICTIONS,* AND *HOMELESSNESS.*

YOU'RE RIGHT... THIS MUST BE *PROGRESS!*

REVOLTING!

YES...AT THE FIRST OPPORTUNITY...

THERE'S ONLY ONE THING TO DO: **BURN ALL THE BOOKS** AND **EXECUTE** ANYONE WHO **QUOTES** THEM!!

HM! VERY IMAGINATIVE!

AND SO, AS SCHOOLCHILDREN CHEERED EVERYWHERE, EVERY **HISTORY BOOK** IN THE EMPIRE WENT UP IN FLAMES!! AND SO DID EVERY **OTHER** BOOK, EXCEPT FOR THE ONES ON **SCIENCE, MAGIC,** AND **FARMING**...

NOW THE EMPEROR BEGAN TO **CONCEAL** HIMSELF... DEMAND **IMMORTALITY DRUGS**... LISTEN CONSTANTLY TO SONGS ABOUT "**PURE BEINGS.**" HE TRUSTED NO ONE... BANISHED HIS SON THE CROWN PRINCE... HAD **400 SCHOLARS** BURIED ALIVE...

BURIED ALIVE? THIS IS **BAD**... I'M REPEATING MYSELF...

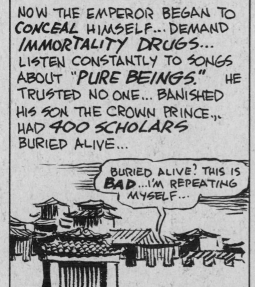

...AND THEN, ON A TOUR OF THE PROVINCES, FAR FROM HOME, HE DIED...

PERFECT BEING, PERFECT BEING...

LI SSU PUT HIS HEAD TOGETHER WITH **CHAO KAO**, THE CAPTAIN OF CHARIOTS.

THIS MUSTN'T GET OUT YET— NOW HERE'S MY PLAN...

THEY SENT IN **FOOD** AND **DOCUMENTS** TO THE RIPENING CORPSE AND LOADED A WAGON WITH **DRIED FISH** TO COVER THE SMELL!

MORE —GAG— DOCUMENTS, YOUR —HUALP— MAJESTY?

WITH THE EMPEROR'S **SECOND** SON **HU·HAI**, THEY FORGED THE IMPERIAL SIGNATURE ON A NOTE TO THE CROWN PRINCE, ORDERING HIM TO **COMMIT SUICIDE**.

BY THE TIME THEY REACHED THE CAPITAL TWO MONTHS LATER, THEY FELT SAFE ENOUGH TO MAKE THE **ANNOUNCEMENT**.

UM—THE PERFECT BEING IS A TRIFLE UNDER THE WEATHER...

WE'LL JUST COVER HIM OVER UNTIL HE **RIPENS**...

SHIH HUANG·TI WAS BURIED IN HIS INCREDIBLE TOMB, ALONG WITH ALL HIS WIVES WHO HAD NO **SONS**, AND THE TOMB WAS THEN DISGUISED TO LOOK LIKE AN ORDINARY **HILL**.

HU·HAI BECAME **SECOND** EMPEROR, WITH **CHAO KAO** AS PRIME MINISTER. HE TRIED HARD TO THINK OF SOME **BIG PROJECTS**, BUT THEY HAD ALL BEEN DONE ALREADY...

MM...LACQUER THE CITY WALLS?

RIGHT! WHERE YOU GON FIND A DRYING SHED BIG ENOUGH?

CHAN, JESTER TO SEVERAL EMPERORS

WHEW!

AT ABOUT THE SAME TIME, IN THE FORMER STATE OF CHU, A PLATOON OF DRAFTEES SAT STUCK IN THE MUD.

WHAT'S THE PENALTY FOR BEING *LATE*?

DEATH.

WHAT'S THE PENALTY FOR *REBELLION*?

DEATH.

WELL, GUESS WHAT? WE'RE *LATE!*

THEY MURDERED THEIR OFFICERS AND ATTACKED THE OLD CAPITAL OF CHU.

SOON, THEIR LEADER, *CHEN SHEH*, SAT IN A PALACE AS *KING OF CHU!* IT WAS TOO EASY!!

WHEW! EVEN CHEN SHEH CAN BE KING!*

*THIS BECAME A PROVERB.

SUDDENLY, THE EMPIRE'S WEAKNESS WAS OBVIOUS! OTHERS DESERTED OR REVOLTED, UNTIL THE SWAMPS SWARMED WITH BANDITS...

IN ANOTHER PART OF CHU, THE LOCAL GOVERNOR SUMMONED *HSIANG LIANG*, WHO CAME FROM AN ANCIENT MILITARY FAMILY.

IN TIMES LIKE THESE, HSIANG LIANG, IT PAYS TO STRIKE *FIRST!* I WANT TO RAISE AN ARMY, WITH *YOU* AND *HUAN CHU* AS MY GENERALS!

BUT HUAN CHU IS AN *OUTLAW* IN THE SWAMP...

...AND NOBODY KNOWS WHERE HE IS — EXCEPT FOR MY *NEPHEW*, HSIANG YU!

THEN PLEASE BE SO GOOD AS TO SUMMON HSIANG YU...

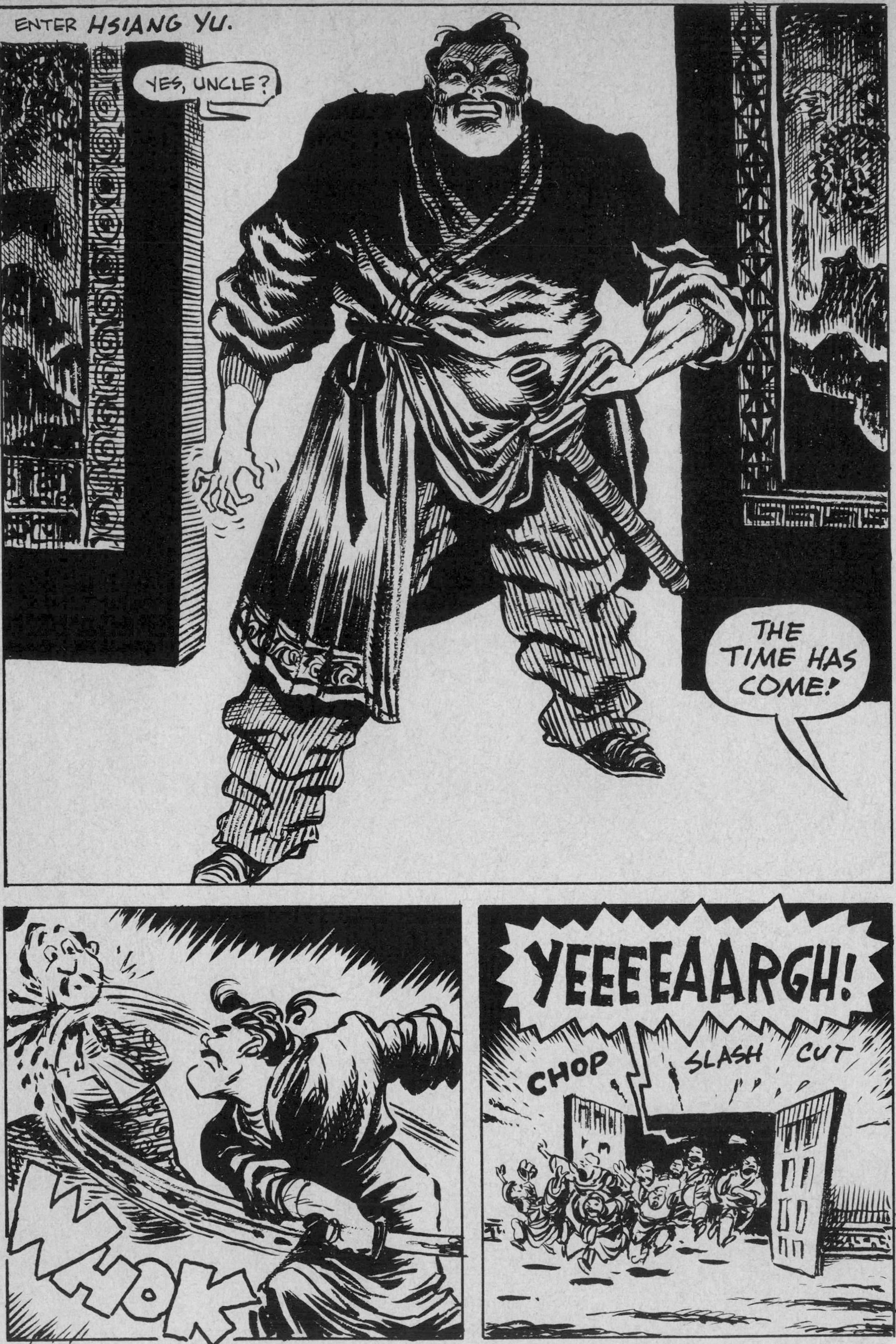
ENTER HSIANG YU.
YES, UNCLE?
THE TIME HAS COME!
WHOK
YEEEEAARGH!
CHOP
SLASH
CUT

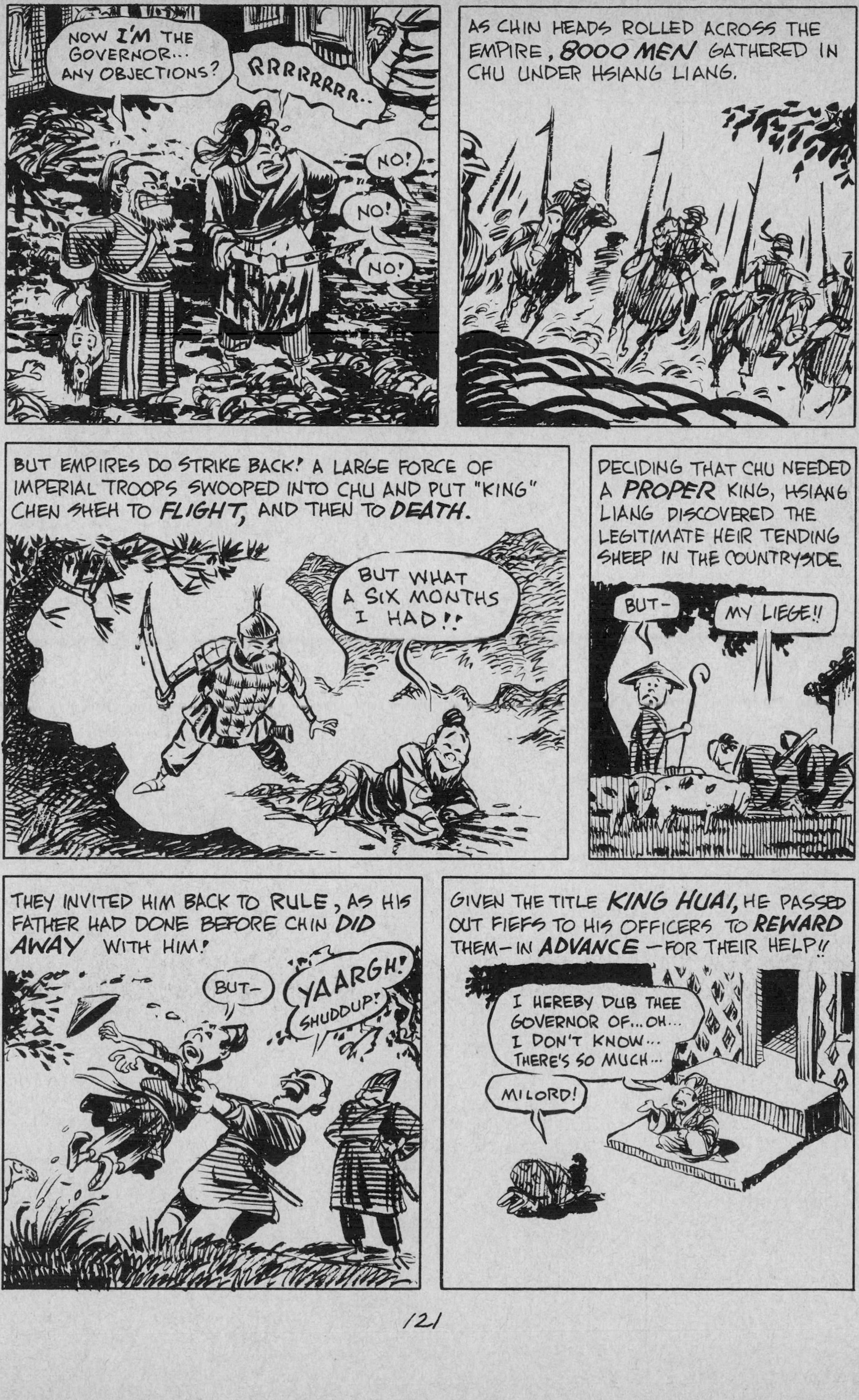
NOW I'M THE GOVERNOR... ANY OBJECTIONS?
RRRRRRRRR..
NO!
NO!
NO!
AS CHIN HEADS ROLLED ACROSS THE EMPIRE, 8000 MEN GATHERED IN CHU UNDER HSIANG LIANG.
BUT EMPIRES DO STRIKE BACK! A LARGE FORCE OF IMPERIAL TROOPS SWOOPED INTO CHU AND PUT "KING" CHEN SHEH TO FLIGHT, AND THEN TO DEATH.
BUT WHAT A SIX MONTHS I HAD!!
DECIDING THAT CHU NEEDED A PROPER KING, HSIANG LIANG DISCOVERED THE LEGITIMATE HEIR TENDING SHEEP IN THE COUNTRYSIDE.
BUT-
MY LIEGE!!
THEY INVITED HIM BACK TO RULE, AS HIS FATHER HAD DONE BEFORE CHIN DID AWAY WITH HIM!
BUT-
YAARGH! SHUDDUP!
GIVEN THE TITLE KING HUAI, HE PASSED OUT FIEFS TO HIS OFFICERS TO REWARD THEM—IN ADVANCE—FOR THEIR HELP!!
I HEREBY DUB THEE GOVERNOR OF... OH... I DON'T KNOW... THERE'S SO MUCH...
MILORD!

WITH THIS INSPIRING LEADERSHIP, THE CHU ARMIES WON SEVERAL VICTORIES— BEFORE BEING **OVERWHELMED** BY THE **IMPERIAL TROOPS**... IN THE BATTLE, **HSIANG LIANG** WAS KILLED.

BUT THE FEROCIOUS NEPHEW **YU** WASN'T THERE! HE HAD BEEN SENT OFF TO PILLAGE AND SLAUGHTER WITH ANOTHER YOUNG LEADER **LIU PANG**.

YEARRRGH!

THIS GUY IS OVER THE ★@# EDGE...

HSIANG YU AND LIU PANG RETURNED TO A SCENE OF DEVASTATION.

SHALL I INSPIRE THE TROOPS BY YELLING SOME MORE, PANG?

MAYBE NOT RIGHT NOW...

THEY DECIDED TO **CALM** THEIR TREMBLING TROOPS BY PULLING BACK AND REJOINING KING **HUAI**.

WHEN THE ARMIES REGROUPED, THE OFFICERS MADE AN **AGREEMENT**: THE **FIRST ONE** TO LEAD HIS TROOPS THROUGH THE **HAN-KU PASS** INTO **CHIN** WOULD BECOME ITS **KING**, CONTROLLING THE WEALTH OF AN EMPIRE (IF HE LIVED)!

AND WHEN THE TIME CAME TO CHOOSE THE LUCKY GUY, KING HUAI PICKED NOT **HSIANG YU**— BUT **LIU PANG**!!

SO LONG, PAL! AND GOOD LUCK BRINGING UP THE REAR!

NGRRR...

STILL SMOLDERING, HSIANG YU MARCHED WITH THE REST OF THE CHU ARMY TO *CHAO*... WHERE THEY SAT IN CAMP FOR A *MONTH*, STARVING AND WAITING FOR THE *"RIGHT TIME"* TO MAKE THEIR MOVE.

C'MON C'MON C'MON

IN A FIT OF *IMPATIENCE*, HSIANG YU BEHEADED HIS OWN COMMANDER-IN-CHIEF.

GOOD MORNING, HSIANG-YURK!

...WHICH IS HOW *HSIANG YU* BECAME *COMMANDING GENERAL* OF CHU!!!?

ARGH?

ULP...IN VIEW OF YOUR FAMILY'S SERVICES TO OUR STATE...

HE HEADED FOR THE NEAREST ARMED CHINS... LED HIS MEN ACROSS A RIVER, AND ORDERED THEM TO BURN THEIR *BOATS* AND *BAGGAGE*.

THERE'S NO GOING BACK!

AS OTHER REBEL BANDS WATCHED FROM THE HILLS, HSIANG YU LED HIS MEN INTO *NINE BATTLES* WITH THE ARMY OF CHIN, DESTROYING IT COMPLETELY!

WOTTA VOICE!

YEEEEAAAAH

ALL THE REBEL LEADERS APPROACHED HSIANG YU *ON THEIR KNEES*.

WITH HIS HUGE, NEW ARMY, HSIANG YU WANTED TO HURRY ON TO **CHIN.** ONLY ONE THING WAS STOPPING HIM: CHIN'S **MAIN ARMY.**

OOPS!

FOR A CHANGE, HSIANG YU USED STRATEGY! HE SENT A LETTER TO THE CHIN GENERAL, CHANG HAN.

"YOUR MASTER, PRIME MINISTER **CHAO KAO*** IS JEALOUS OF OTHERS' SUCCESS. IF YOU LOSE, HE WILL HAVE YOUR HEAD... IF YOU WIN, AND GAIN FAME, HE WILL ACCUSE YOU OF SOME CRIME, AND YOU WILL LOSE YOUR HEAD ANYWAY... WHY NOT COME OVER TO US?"

SIGH...

*SEE P.116

SO CHANG HAN SURRENDERED HIS ARMY WITHOUT A FIGHT.

BUT HSIANG YU **MISTRUSTED** THIS ARMY OF CHIN... SO, THAT NIGHT, THE REBELS FELL ON THEM AND MASSACRED **200,000 MEN** IN COLD BLOOD...

NOW THEY WERE READY TO SWEEP THROUGH THE **HAN-KU PASS** INTO CHIN—

I'M GONNA BE **EMPEROR!** WOW!

EXCEPT FOR **ONE MORE SURPRISE:** THE PASS WAS **BLOCKED** AND GUARDED BY FOLLOWERS OF **LIU PANG!**

YAAAAH!

SWORD DANCE

AS *LIU PANG* LED HIS MEN INTO THE CHIN HIGHLANDS, HE MAY WELL HAVE REFLECTED ON THE CHAIN OF EVENTS THAT BROUGHT HIM THERE...

WHAT THE ✦❊#@ YOU TALKIN'? I NEVER DID?!

IT'S ONLY A TIRED LITERARY DEVICE, GENERAL...

AS A YOUTH, HIS *PERSONAL MAGNETISM* WAS FAMOUS. BARTENDERS USED TO POUR HIM FREE DRINKS, HE WAS SO GOOD FOR BUSINESS.

HE CHARMED THE RICH MR. *LU* INTO GIVING HIM HIS DAUGHTER TO MARRY—OVER MRS. LU'S OBJECTIONS!

HE'S ARROGANT! A DRUNK! FOUL-MOUTHED! A BOOR! A WOMANIZER! A SELF-PROMOTER!

YES... A BORN *POLITICIAN*...

CHOSEN HEAD MAN OF HIS TOWN, HE LED A GANG OF DRAFTEES TO WORK ON THE EMPEROR'S TOMB. ONE BY ONE, THE MEN SLIPPED AWAY...

12, 13... OY! I'M A *DEAD HEAD MAN!*

...SO HE CUT THE REST LOOSE.

GOOD-BYE! GET LOST!? I'M GONNA HAVE A *DRINK* AND *DISAPPEAR!*

SEVERAL OF THEM FOLLOWED HIM INTO THE SWAMP!

YOU SEE, MEN...? HIC! THIS'S WOT COMES OF ALL THIS *DEATH PENALTY* ✦#@❊!!

WHEN THE REVOLT BROKE OUT, LIU PANG EMERGED, AND JOINED FORCES WITH HSIANG LIANG.

HIS MANNERS WERE *NOTORIOUS*—HE ONCE RECEIVED A CONFUCIAN SCHOLAR WHILE *WASHING HIS FEET*—BUT HE COULD TAKE CRITICISM!

IF YOU AIM TO RULE THE WORLD, YOU'LL HAVE TO DO BETTER!

SORRY

BECAUSE OF LIU PANG'S MERITS, THE KING OF CHU CHOSE HIM TO LEAD THE INVASION OF CHIN.

SUCH A NICE BOY...

LIU PANG'S ARMY BATTLED INTO CHIN, SURROUNDED A CITY, AND OFFERED **MERCY** TO ITS PEOPLE AND **FIEFS** TO ITS LEADERS, IF THEY SURRENDERED.

MERCY? FIEFS?

TEN MORE CITIES IMMEDIATELY CAME OVER WITHOUT A FIGHT!

WE GIVE UP!
WE GIVE UP!
WE GIVE UP!
WE GIVE UP!
WE GIVE UP!
WE GIVE UP!

BUT LIU PANG WASN'T ALWAYS SO **NICE!** HE ALSO USED **HSIANG YU'S** TACTIC OF LULLING THE ENEMY GENERALS WITH **BRIBES,** AND THEN SLAUGHTERING THEIR ARMIES...

WHATEVER WORKS!

IN THE CAPITAL, EVERYONE BLAMED **EVERYONE ELSE** FOR THE DISASTER... PRIME MINISTER **CHAO KAO** EXECUTED THE **SECOND** EMPEROR... THE **THIRD** EMPEROR EXECUTED CHAO KAO... AND FINALLY, IN **206 B.C.** THE LAST KING OF CHIN **SURRENDERED** TO LIU PANG.

HOW TH' ★#@‡ DO YA LIKE **THIS?**

IT'S YOUR FAULT!
YOURS!
QUIET

IN LATER YEARS, SCHOLARS ASKED THEMSELVES WHAT WENT WRONG WITH THE CHIN DYNASTY.

UM....THE MAN WAS **NOT NICE** TO HIS MOTHER!

HOW NOT NICE? HE BURIED HER ENEMIES ALIVE...

SOMETHING ELSE, THEN!

THEY CAME UP WITH **TEN CRIMES OF CHIN:** 1. ABOLITION OF FEUDALISM. 2. BUILDING THE GREAT WALL. 3. MELTING DOWN THE PEOPLE'S WEAPONS. 4. BUILDING THE IMPERIAL PALACE. 5. BURNING BOOKS. 6. BURYING SCHOLARS ALIVE. 7. BUILDING THE EMPEROR'S TOMB. 8. SEEKING IMMORTALITY DRUGS. 9. BANISHING THE CROWN PRINCE. 10. INFLICTING CRUEL PUNISHMENTS.

THE CURRENT (COMMUNIST) GOVERNMENT OF CHINA, HOWEVER, SEES THESE NOT AS CRIMES, BUT AS **PROGRESSIVE, NATION-BUILDING ACHIEVEMENTS!**

EVEN -ULP- KILLING SCHOLARS?

YOU CAN'T MAKE AN OMELET WITHOUT BREAKING EGGHEADS!

AT LAST, THE INVADERS ENTERED *HSIEN-YANG*, THE IMPERIAL CAPITAL, WITH ITS LAVISH PALACES, BULGING STOREHOUSES, CROWDED HAREMS —AND *MERCILESS TRADITIONS*. WHAT COULD THE CITIZENS EXPECT?

OH, MAN, LOOK AT *THIS*!? LET'S BRUSH OFF THE DUST AND *WALLOW* AWHILE!?

:AHEM!:

BUT —AFTER LISTENING TO HIS FRIENDS, LIU PANG *TOUCHED NOTHING*, SEALED THE PALACES, AND TOOK HIS MEN BACK OUT OF TOWN TO THEIR *TENTS!*

TAKE THE *LONG VIEW*... GENERAL ... SHOW 'EM YOU'RE A *GOOD GUY*... THEY'VE BEEN PILLAGED ENOUGH BY THE LAST DYNASTY..

SIGH..

HE SUMMONED THE LEADING CITIZENS TO HIS CAMP AND ANNOUNCED:

YOU HAVE TOO ★#@& MANY *LAWS!* FROM NOW ON, ONLY *THREE LAWS:* DON'T *MURDER*... DON'T *INJURE*... AND DON'T *STEAL!?* ALL OTHER LAWS ARE *ABOLISHED!?!?*

JUST AS THE ENTIRE KINGDOM OF CHIN WAS SIGHING WITH RELIEF, A MESSENGER ARRIVED WITH SOME NEWS: *HSIANG YU*, WITH *100,000 MEN*, WAS STORMING THE HAN-KU PASS!!

UM...DID HE LOOK *UPSET*?

THE MESSENGER WAS *HSIANG PO*, HSIANG YU'S BROTHER, AND A FRIEND OF LIU PANG'S ADVISER *CHANG LIANG*...

CHANG LIANG, SAVE YOURSELF! HSIANG YU IS COMING, AND HE'S GRUMPY!

NO... I'M LOYAL TO THE BOSS... BUT MAYBE WE CAN STILL PATCH THINGS UP... HMMM...

CHANG LIANG BROUGHT HSIANG PO TO LIU PANG, WHO TURNED ON THE CHARISMA.

WELCOME TO CHIN! SAY, LOOK, I HAVEN'T TOUCHED A *THING* SINCE I ARRIVED... I'VE BEEN SAVING IT ALL FOR *HSIANG YU!* REALLY, I CAN'T STOP THINKING ABOUT THAT WONDERFUL GUY... HOW'S HIS HEALTH?

CARE FOR A DRINK?

HSIANG PO STAGGERED BACK TO SOFTEN UP HIS BROTHER.

WHAT A CHARMING, CHARMING, MAN!

THE NEXT DAY, LIU PANG, WITH 100 HORSEMEN, RODE TO HSIANG YU'S CAMP.

AAARGHROWWL?

HEY, IT'S GREAT TO SEE YOU AGAIN! SORRY ABOUT THE, AH, MISUNDERSTANDING AT THE PASS... REALLY! SAY, WHAT TOOK YOU SO LONG? GOT ANYTHING TO DRINK AROUND HERE?

HSIANG YU INVITED LIU PANG IN FOR DRINKS WITH HSIANG PO, CHANG LIANG, AND HSIANG YU'S STRATEGIC ADVISER *FAN TSENG*.

AS THE DRINKS WENT DOWN, FAN TSENG KEPT SIGNALLING HSIANG YU TO DO AWAY WITH HIS GUEST...

YEAH, WHERE ELSE WOULD ANYONE WANT TO BE, EXCEPT *RIGHT HERE*? HEH! SAY, THE HONORABLE SAGE IS MIGHTY TWITCHY TONIGHT...

NUDGE GESTURE HINT

...BUT HSIANG YU IGNORED HIM!

EXCUSE ME!

OUTSIDE, FAN TSENG FOUND ANOTHER ONE OF HSIANG YU'S RELATIVES...

HSIANG CHUANG! YOU'VE GOT TO *OFF* THAT LOUDMOUTH! GO IN, AND ASK TO DO THE SWORD DANCE...THEN, *WHACK!*

TWITCHY GUY LIKE THAT NEEDS ACUPUNCTURE... BLAH BLAH...

IN THEY WENT!

LET ME *APOLOGIZE* FOR THE LACK OF *ENTERTAINMENT* HERE... WILL YOU PERMIT ME TO PERFORM A *SWORD DANCE?*

PROCEED.

DRAWING HIS SWORD, HE BEGAN — BUT *HSIANG PO* JUMPED UP AND *ALSO* DANCED — KEEPING HIMSELF BETWEEN THE SWORDSMAN AND LIU PANG.!'

UM... EXCUSE ME!

NOW *CHANG LIANG* STEPPED OUTSIDE.

HOW'S IT GOIN' IN THERE?

TOUCH AND GO... SWORDS ARE STARTIN' TO SWING...

LIU PANG'S CHARIOTEER BURST IN!'

RRROWWL! WHO'S THIS?

GENERAL LIU'S CARRIAGE ATTENDANT...

BRAVE GUY! GIVE HIM SOME PORK!

So LIU PANG SLIPPED AWAY, LEAVING CHANG LIANG TO APOLOGIZE AND FAN TSENG TO FUME!

FOR THE SECOND TIME IN LESS THAN A MONTH, A CONQUERING ARMY ENTERED HSIEN-YANG... BUT THIS TIME, *HSIANG YU* WAS IN CHARGE...

THE FIRES THEY SET TOOK *THREE MONTHS* TO DIE OUT COMPLETELY...

FINALLY, HSIANG YU ANNOUNCED THAT HE WAS GOING *HOME*, LEAVING CHIN, WITH ITS STRATEGIC POSITION, FERTILE SOIL, AND IRON MINES...NO, *HIS* CAPITAL WOULD BE IN THE PESTILENTIAL SOUTHERN SWAMPS OF *CHU!* AS HE PUT IT —

TO BECOME RICH AND FAMOUS WITHOUT GOING HOME IS LIKE PUTTING ON A BEAUTIFUL ROBE AND TAKING A WALK AT NIGHT. WHO'S TO KNOW ABOUT IT??

THESE MEN OF CHU ARE NOTHING BUT APES WEARING HATS!

BOILED ALIVE FOR SAYING THIS

AND *LIU PANG?* DESPITE THE PACT THEY HAD MADE, THAT THE FIRST WHO ENTERED THE PASS WOULD RULE CHIN, HSIANG YU MADE LIU PANG KING OF *HAN*, ON CHINA'S FAR WESTERN BORDER.

JUST UP THE GORGE THERE, BROTHER!

LIU PANG SWALLOWED HARD AND LED WHAT WAS LEFT OF HIS ARMY ALONG THE WOODEN ROAD TO HAN, TEARING IT UP BEHIND THEM...

UM...YOU RIDE ON THE OUTSIDE...

131

HAN WAS A DUMP!

GAH   UGH   ECH   URP

BUT IT HAD A DISTINCT ADVANTAGE: *HSIANG YU* WASN'T THERE... SOON THE PLACE WAS CRAWLING WITH THE LOUD ONE'S ENEMIES, ALL LOOKING TO LIU PANG FOR HELP!!

HSIANG YU HAS TAKEN AWAY OUR LANDS TO REWARD HIS FRIENDS!

HE KILLED THE KING OF CHU!

WHAT? THAT'S WONDERF— I MEAN, HORRIBLE, IT'S HORRIBLE!!

WE WANT *YOU* TO LEAD US!

WITHIN MONTHS, THEY MARCHED BACK OUT OF THE MOUNTAINS AND QUICKLY RECONQUERED *CHIN.*

LIU PANG TURNED ALL THE FORMER IMPERIAL PARKS AND PONDS BACK TO THE PEOPLE FOR FARMING, THEN MARCHED ON.

WOTTA GUY!!

HALF A MILLION MEN FLOCKED TO HIS BANNER AND MARCHED STRAIGHT THROUGH CHU INTO HSIANG YU'S CAPITAL...

BUT OF COURSE, HSIANG YU WAS *OUT OF TOWN* AT THE TIME...

HM... WONDER WHERE HE WENT...?

HE WAS ELSEWHERE IN THE KINGDOM, PUTTING DOWN REVOLTS, BUT WHEN HE CAME *BACK*—

YAAAAAAAA

WAA—I FORGOT THAT *VOICE*!!

SO MANY OF LIU PANG'S MEN WERE KILLED, THEY *DAMMED* A *RIVER*. THE SURVIVORS TOOK TO THE HILLS!!

WITH HIS ATTENDANT *FAN KUAI* (THE ONE WHO ATE HSIANG YU'S PORK), LIU PANG FLED TO HIS HOME TOWN TO RESCUE HIS FAMILY. ALL HE COULD FIND WERE TWO OF HIS *CHILDREN*...

BUT WHEN THE *PURSUIT* GOT *HOT*, HE TRIED TO KICK THEM *OUT OF THE CARRIAGE!*

YER SLOWIN' US DOWN!

MASTER! NO!

FATHER!

AT LAST, THEY MADE IT BACK TO HAN — ONLY TO HEAR THAT LIU PANG'S *WIFE* AND *PARENTS* WERE *PRISONERS* OF HSIANG YU...

THE NEXT YEAR, LIU PANG RAISED ANOTHER ARMY AND MARCHED OUT AGAIN...

HOW DID HE "RAISE" YOU? WITH THAT LEGENDARY CHARM?

NO...WITH THAT OFFER OF FOOD IF I JOINED, COMBINED WITH DEATH IF I DIDN'T..

OOPS! HOLED UP AND SURROUNDED!

HEY, YU!! LET'S TALK!!

FAN TSENG WAS STILL ADVISING HSIANG YU...

YOU MISSED YOUR CHANCE ONCE TO GET RID OF THIS GUY... NOW THE EMPIRE IS IN FLAMES... WE MUST SAVE OUR STRENGTH...INSTEAD OF STORMING THE CITY, WHY NOT TALK TO LIU PANG, COME TO TERMS, AND *THEN* KILL HIM?

SIGH.. ALL RIGHT... I'LL SEND SOMEONE.

LIU PANG AND HIS PALS NOW COOKED UP THE FOLLOWING *PLOY*: THEY LAID OUT A LAVISH *BANQUET* FOR HSIANG YU'S EMISSARY, THEN...

I COME FROM HSIANG DROOL—I MEAN, YU!!

OH! *YOU* COME FROM *HSIANG YU!*

WE'RE SORRY! WE THOUGHT YOU CAME FROM FAN TSENG!!

GET RID OF THE SUMPTUOUS REPAST, AND *BRING ON TH' SLOPS!*

WHEN HSIANG YU HEARD THIS, HE BEGAN EYEING FAN TSENG *SUSPICIOUSLY*...

SO FAN TSENG RESIGNED.

I BEG LEAVE TO RETIRE ON ACCOUNT OF ILL HEALTH

GRANTED!

FROM NOW ON, HSIANG YU HAD TO RELY ON HIS *OWN* WITS. TOO BAD! LIU PANG DRESSED 2000 *WOMEN* AS SOLDIERS AND HAD THEM CHARGE OUT OF THE MAIN CITY GATE, WHILE HE SLIPPED OUT THE *BACK*...!

EEK SCREEK YARGH ETC.

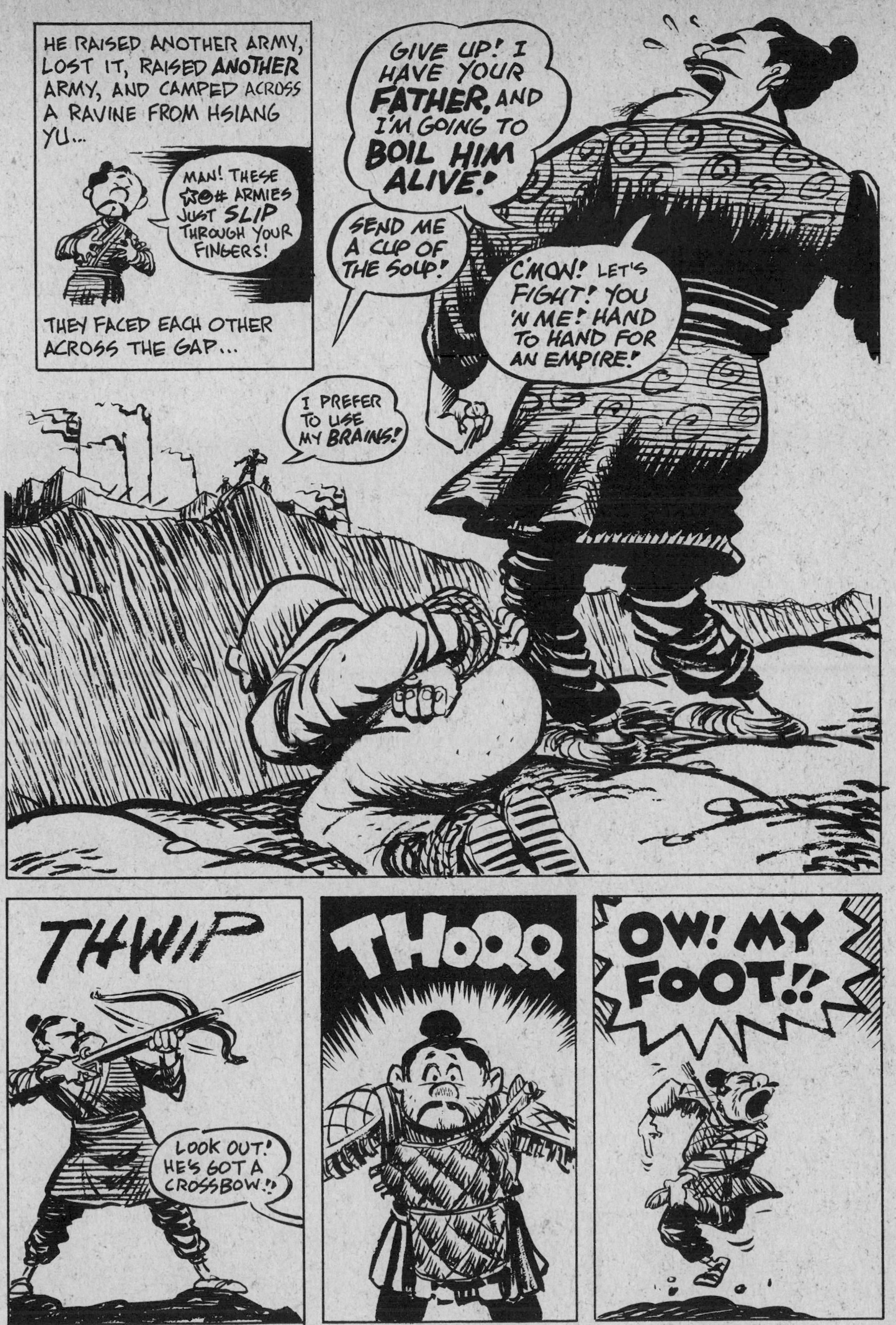
HE RAISED ANOTHER ARMY, LOST IT, RAISED ANOTHER ARMY, AND CAMPED ACROSS A RAVINE FROM HSIANG YU...
MAN! THESE ☆@# ARMIES JUST SLIP THROUGH YOUR FINGERS!
THEY FACED EACH OTHER ACROSS THE GAP...
GIVE UP! I HAVE YOUR FATHER, AND I'M GOING TO BOIL HIM ALIVE!
SEND ME A CUP OF THE SOUP!
C'MON! LET'S FIGHT! YOU 'N ME! HAND TO HAND FOR AN EMPIRE!
I PREFER TO USE MY BRAINS!
THWIP
LOOK OUT! HE'S GOT A CROSSBOW!!
THOQQ
OW! MY FOOT!!

AS LIU PANG RECOVERED, THE TIDE TURNED TOWARD *HAN*... THE CHU ARMY WAS RUNNING OUT OF *FOOD** AND HSIANG YU RODE OFF TO SOLVE THE PROBLEM *PERSONALLY*...

DON'T DO A *THING* UNTIL I GET BACK!

*I WISH I HAD SPACE TO EXPLAIN WHY!

THE HAN ARMY *TAUNTED* THE CHUS, DARING THEM TO COME OUT AND FIGHT WHILE THE BOSS WAS AWAY.

YOU'RE NOTHIN' BUT A BUNCHA *WOMEN!*

OO!

OUCH! THAT HURTS!

WAIT... I *LIKE* WOMEN... WHAT'S WRONG WITH WOMEN?

WELL... THEY'RE... UM, Y'KNOW, TOO... EH.. ARTICULATE...

THE CHUS UNWISELY TOOK THE BAIT!!

HOW DARE THEY IMPLY THAT WE'RE NURTURING, CARING BEINGS WITH A TENDENCY TO TALK ABOUT OUR PROBLEMS?

KILL 'EM

THE FORCES OF HAN WON THE BATTLE...

HA! THEY DON'T HAVE "*THE VOICE!!*"

YARGH?

YARGH?

... AND HSIANG YU RETURNED TO FIND ALL THE TREASURES OF CHU IN *LIU PANG'S* HANDS.!!!

YARGH!

THE TWO LEADERS MADE PEACE... THEY AGREED TO *DIVIDE* THE EMPIRE... LIU PANG'S FAMILY RETURNED... THE ARMIES CHEERED...

"CUP OF THE SOUP," *INDEED!!*

BUT—LIU PANG NOW SUMMONED EVERY WARLORD HE KNEW, HANDED OUT *FIEFS*, AND ORDERED THEM TO *DESTROY* HSIANG YU — WITH AN EXTRA FIEF TO THE MAN WHO BROUGHT IN THE *BODY*.

GUESS WE CHEERED TOO SOON...

SH!

HIS ARMY SURROUNDED, HSIANG YU PICKED A HUNDRED HORSEMEN AND BROKE THROUGH THE LINES...

CHASED INTO A SWAMP, WOUNDED DOZENS OF TIMES, HSIANG YU SAW SOMEONE HE KNEW AMONG THE HAN CAVALRY..

IS THAT MY OLD FRIEND LU MA-TUNG? I HEAR THE KING OF HAN HAS OFFERED A REWARD FOR ME ...SO... LET ME DO YOU A FAVOR...

IT'S HSIANG YU!

...AND HE SLIT HIS OWN THROAT.

IT'S HSIANG YU!

HSIANG YU!

HSIANG YU!

THE REWARD HAD TO BE DIVIDED *FIVE WAYS!*

MAN! I'VE HEARD THAT TWO PEOPLE CAN GROW *APART*... BUT I NEVER KNEW A BODY COULD DO IT ALL BY *HIMSELF*!

GROWING A DYNASTY

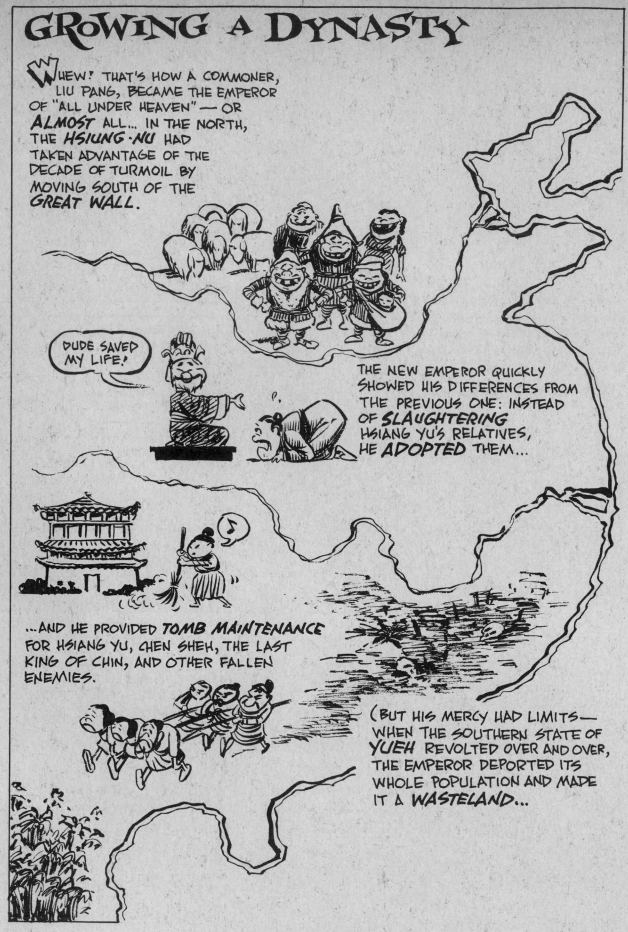

WHEW! THAT'S HOW A COMMONER, LIU PANG, BECAME THE EMPEROR OF "ALL UNDER HEAVEN" — OR *ALMOST* ALL... IN THE NORTH, THE *HSIUNG·NU* HAD TAKEN ADVANTAGE OF THE DECADE OF TURMOIL BY MOVING SOUTH OF THE *GREAT WALL*.

DUDE SAVED MY LIFE!

THE NEW EMPEROR QUICKLY SHOWED HIS DIFFERENCES FROM THE PREVIOUS ONE: INSTEAD OF *SLAUGHTERING* HSIANG YU'S RELATIVES, HE *ADOPTED* THEM...

...AND HE PROVIDED *TOMB MAINTENANCE* FOR HSIANG YU, CHEN SHEH, THE LAST KING OF CHIN, AND OTHER FALLEN ENEMIES.

(BUT HIS MERCY HAD LIMITS— WHEN THE SOUTHERN STATE OF *YUEH* REVOLTED OVER AND OVER, THE EMPEROR DEPORTED ITS WHOLE POPULATION AND MADE IT A *WASTELAND*...

HE INVITED "MEN OF WISDOM AND ABILITY" TO JOIN THE GOVERNMENT.*

COME ON OUT! I'LL MAKE YOU FAMOUS!

*FROM A DECREE OF 196 B.C.

THE PERSECUTED SCHOLARS EMERGED AND TRIED TO PIECE TOGETHER THE KNOWLEDGE LOST IN THE FLAMES...

HEY, HERE'S THAT LU PU-WEI THING IN ONE PIECE!

FILE IT!

INSIDE THE WALLS OF A SCHOLAR'S HOUSE, A TROVE OF CONFUCIAN CLASSICS WERE DISCOVERED.

THIS HELPS TO ANSWER A QUESTION WE ASKED LAST VOLUME: WHY DID CONFUCIUS WIELD SO MUCH INFLUENCE ON LATER GENERATIONS? IN PART, IT WAS PURE LUCK! MOST OF CONFUCIUS'S BOOKS SURVIVED!

HEY! DON'T FORGET THAT I ALSO HAD INTRINSIC MERIT... OR THAT THE HAN DYNASTY MADE ME THEIR OFFICIAL PHILOSOPHER!!

O.K. O.K. O.K.!

THE GOVERNMENT MOVED TO REVIVE THE ECONOMY BY CUTTING TAXES, SIMPLIFYING THE LAWS, SUBSIDIZING FARMERS, AND REDUCING BUREAUCRACY.

BECAUSE THE PEOPLE ARE STARVING?

WELL, MAYBE...BUT MAINLY, I CAN'T FIND FOUR HORSES THE SAME COLOR TO PULL ME AROUND!

AND SO BEGAN THE HAN DYNASTY. IT LASTED 400 YEARS AND ESTABLISHED THE MODEL FOR ALL LATER CHINESE GOVERNMENT!

AND NOW, SOME FAMILY BUSINESS!

OOP!

THE EMPRESS *LU*, KAO-TZU'S FIRST WIFE, HAD TO SHARE THE WOMEN'S QUARTERS WITH *LADY CHI*, THE EMPEROR'S NEW FAVORITE. LADY CHI HAD A SON, *JU·I*.

EMPRESS LU WAS *NOT HAPPY* ABOUT THIS...

BITCH.

SHE WORRIED THAT JU·I WOULD DISPLACE HER OWN SON — THE FUTURE EMPEROR *HUI* * — AS CROWN PRINCE. SHE TURNED TO *CHANG LIANG* FOR ADVICE.

YOU KNOW THE EMPEROR... WHAT CAN WE *DO*?

SIGH... THIS ISN'T MY SPECIALTY... BUT...

* THE ONE LIU PANG TRIED TO KICK OUT OF THE CARRIAGE.

"THERE ARE THREE SCHOLARS *HIDING* IN THE HILLS... THEY THINK THE EMPEROR IS *TOO RUDE*... IF *THEY* WILL SPEAK UP FOR YOUR SON, THEN MAYBE... "

EMPRESS LU PERSUADED THE THREE SAGES TO APPEAR AT COURT.

HEY! WHO THE *#@ ARE *THOSE GUYS*?!

PSSTSSTSST

NO! BRING 'EM HERE!!

THE EMPEROR WAS AWESTRUCK!

WHERE TH' ☆#@% HAVE YOU BEEN?

WE STAYED AWAY FROM COURT BECAUSE YOUR MAJESTY'S MANNERS ARE SO ATROCIOUS... BUT YOUR SON HUI IS SUCH A NICE YOUNG MAN... WE CAME FOR HIS SAKE...

HA! I GET IT! THIS IS LADY LU'S *WORK!* WOTTA WOMAN! I AM IMPRESSED!

SO EMPRESS LU'S SON REMAINED HEIR TO THE EMPIRE!

SORRY, HONEY, BUT SHE *GOT* YOU WITH THOSE OLD GEEZERS — I MEAN VENERABLE SAGES!!

BUT FUTURE EMPEROR HUI HAD LITTLE INTEREST IN STATECRAFT AND WAR... HE PREFERRED TO IDLE IN THE PLEASURE GARDENS WITH A BOY NAMED *HUNG*.

"ALL THE PALACE ATTENDANTS...OF EMPEROR HUI TOOK TO WEARING... GAUDY FEATHERS AND SASHES OF SEASHELLS AND TO PAINTING THEIR FACES, TRANSFORMING THEMSELVES INTO A VERITABLE HOST OF... HUNGS," SAYS SSUMA CHIEN.

AND NO *JESSE HELMS!*

WHEN WAR BROKE OUT WITH THE *HSIUNG·NU* THE EMPRESS BEGGED HER HUSBAND NOT TO SEND HUI...

PLEASE... HE'S SO DELICATE...

I GUESS I'VE GOT TO DO EVERYTHING MYSELF!!

SO LIU PANG LED THE ARMY — INTO NEAR *DISASTER*. SURROUNDED AND FREEZING, THE EMPEROR WROTE A *SECRET LETTER* TO THE *QUEEN* OF THE HSIUNG·NU... AND THE HAN WERE LET GO... WHAT DID THAT LETTER *SAY*? NO ONE WILL EVER KNOW!!

JUST NEVER MIND!!

SIGH... WHIPPED BY THE HSIUNG·NU... MY WIVES WANT TO KILL EACH OTHER... THE PRINCE WEARS ROUGE... WAS IT *WORTH* IT??

141

AT LAST, ON JUNE 1, 195 B.C., THE EMPEROR DIED. NO MORE NARROW ESCAPES FOR LIU PANG...

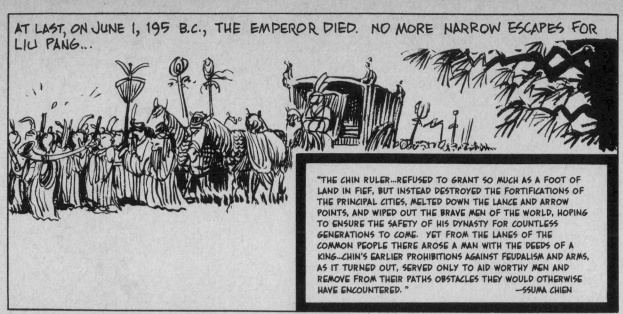

"THE CHIN RULER...REFUSED TO GRANT SO MUCH AS A FOOT OF LAND IN FIEF, BUT INSTEAD DESTROYED THE FORTIFICATIONS OF THE PRINCIPAL CITIES, MELTED DOWN THE LANCE AND ARROW POINTS, AND WIPED OUT THE BRAVE MEN OF THE WORLD, HOPING TO ENSURE THE SAFETY OF HIS DYNASTY FOR COUNTLESS GENERATIONS TO COME. YET FROM THE LANES OF THE COMMON PEOPLE THERE AROSE A MAN WITH THE DEEDS OF A KING...CHIN'S EARLIER PROHIBITIONS AGAINST FEUDALISM AND ARMS, AS IT TURNED OUT, SERVED ONLY TO AID WORTHY MEN AND REMOVE FROM THEIR PATHS OBSTACLES THEY WOULD OTHERWISE HAVE ENCOUNTERED."
—SSUMA CHIEN

BUT THE EMPRESS LU WAS STILL *TROUBLED* BY LADY *CHI* AND HER BOY... SO SHE HAD THE BOY POISONED...

OHH-- *MOTHER!*

REALLY...

THEN SHE (OR HER SERVANTS) CHOPPED OFF LADY CHI'S HANDS AND FEET, PUT OUT HER EYES, THREW HER INTO THE OUTHOUSE (WHERE THE PIGS DINED), AND SHOWED HER OFF TO *HUI*, THE NEW EMPEROR.

LOOK, SON: THE "HUMAN PIG!"

MOTHER— YOU'RE... YOU'RE *INHUMAN!!*

ANOTHER ANIMAL COULD THINK OF THIS?

SNORF SNUFL

SINKING INTO DRINK AND DESPAIR, EMPEROR HUI DECLINED QUICKLY AND DIED...

TSK! TRY AND DO SOMEBODY A *FAVOR!*

AT HUI'S FUNERAL, IT WAS NOTED THAT EMPRESS LU SHED NO *TEARS*.. THIS MADE EVERYONE NERVOUS...

WHY IZZAT?

GULP!

CHANG PI-CHIANG, THE 15-YEAR-OLD SON OF CHANG LIANG, SUGGESTED—

SINCE EMPEROR HUI HAS NO GROWN SONS TO PROTECT HER, SHE IS *AFRAID* OF YOU MINISTERS. WHY NOT MAKE HER BROTHERS GENERALS AND LET THE *LU* FAMILY INTO THE GOVERNMENT? THEN SHE CAN *RELAX*— AND SO CAN :AHEM: *WE!!*

BRIGHT LAD!

THIS WAS DONE—AND *THEN* THE EMPRESS WEPT...

SOB!

WHEW!

FOR THE NEXT EIGHT YEARS, EMPRESS LU RULED THE EMPIRE PERSONALLY, RUTHLESSLY DOING AWAY WITH ANYONE WHO QUARRELED WITH THE LU CLAN...

EEK!

OW!

OO!

...AND IT WAS AMAZING HOW LITTLE DIFFERENCE IT MADE "ON THE GROUND!!"

LU, LIU — WHAT DIFFERENCE DOES IT MAKE?

WHEN SHE DIED, IN 180 B.C., THOSE SAME HIGH OFFICIALS TOOK BACK THE GOVERNMENT, *ASSASSINATING* EVERYONE IN THE *LU* FAMILY THEY COULD FIND, AND INSTALLED LIU PANG'S OLDEST LIVING SON (BY ANOTHER WIFE) AS *EMPEROR WEN.*

EEP!

DID YOU HEAR SOMETHING?

In some ways, Emperor Wen was an *IDEAL RULER*: He let the bureaucracy run the government, and his wife's family had no ambition!

Wot's my job then?

Just *BE* there...

Unlike the Chin, the Han emperors handed out *FIEFS* — this was the ancient way, after all.

Ah, Marquis, how do you do?

Fine, Marquis, how you?

But whenever a lord got too *UPPITY*, the emperor would accuse him of some *CRIME* and take the fief *AWAY!* This kept the empire *STRONG*...

What did they nail you for, former Marquis?

I was seen talkin' to *YOU!*

The government encouraged *FARMING* by taxing farmers lightly...

Drought, flood, locusts... at last, the government is off the list of natural disasters!

MERCHANTS and *TRADERS*, however, were tightly controlled.

Got your permits, stamps, forms, records, variances, seals, and environmental impact statements?

Why do you *DO* this to me?

Because you produce nothing *EDIBLE*, and you're a greed-driven *SCUM*..

Ah! Just asking...

IN TIMES OF PLENTY, WHEN PRICES DROPPED, THE GOVERNMENT HELPED FARMERS BY **BUYING SURPLUS GRAIN.**

WHY NOT JUST PAY US **NOT** TO GROW IT?

SEE NEXT PANEL!

IN TIMES OF SHORTAGE, THE GOVERNMENT PROTECTED CONSUMERS BY OPENING ITS GRAIN WAREHOUSES. THIS PRACTICE WAS CALLED "THE BALANCED STANDARD."

THIS IS **SO** UNFAIR TO SPECULATORS!

BY THE YEAR **140 B.C.,** FARMERS THRIVED, THE IMPERIAL WAREHOUSES BULGED WITH GRAIN, AND THE TREASURIES WERE HEAPED WITH CASH BEYOND COUNTING...*

AND THESE **HORSES**!! YOW!

SAY, ISN'T THE BALANCED STANDARD THE SAME AS **BUYING CHEAP** AND **SELLING DEAR** LIKE A COMMON MERCHANT?

SH!

 THE EARLIEST CHINESE MONEY MUST HAVE BEEN SEASHELLS AND TOOLS, BECAUSE THE FIRST COINS WERE BRONZE MODELS OF THESE ITEMS OF VALUE.

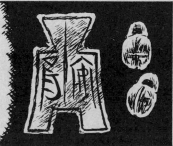

THE CHIN ISSUED THE FIRST OF THE SQUARE-HOLED COINS, WHICH COULD BE STRUNG TOGETHER LIKE BEADS.

THE HAN DYNASTY CONTINUED THESE COINS — BUT WHEN SHORT OF **CASH,** THE HAN LOOKED FOR DIFFERENT MATERIALS FOR MONEY.

UM...HOW ABOUT **AIR**?

IT ALREADY **HAS** HOLES...

THE MOST LAVISH WERE WHITE DEERSKIN SQUARES, EACH WORTH 400,000 COINS. THE EMPEROR ORDERED ALL CASH GIFTS TO HIMSELF CARRIED ON ONE OF THESE.

HIS HIGHNESS IS UNCLEAR ON THE CONCEPT OF POVERTY!

145

IN 140 B.C., ARRIVED EMPEROR **WU**, MORE OF A **HANDS·ON** EMPEROR.

JUST LET ME GET MY **HANDS ON** THIS TREASURE!

WU MEANS *"MILITARY"...* IN HIS LONG REIGN, WU·TI CONQUERED IN EVERY DIRECTION!

I JUST **LOVE** BIG PROJECTS!

HE DRAFTED WORKERS TO BUILD ROADS IN THE **WILD WEST** AND SOLDIERS TO GUARD THEM.

AND TO **FEED** THEM—?

FEED THEM... YES... WELL...

THESE ROADS WERE SO REMOTE THAT **90%** OF THE GRAIN SHIPPED TO THE WORKERS **DISAPPEARED** EN ROUTE.

WHERE DID IT GO??!

UM...LET ME THINK... *BURP!*

THANKS TO ALL THE GRAND SCHEMES HE LAUNCHED WITHOUT COST CONTROL, THE IMPERIAL BANK BALANCE SHRANK TO **ZERO.**

NOW WHAT?

TAKE IT OUT OF THE AGRICULTURE DEPARTMENT BUDGET...

IT WAS DONE!

SO THE EMPEROR BEGAN **SELLING TITLES** AND **GOVERNMENT JOBS...**

I THOUGHT YOU **DISSED** BUSINESSMEN!

YES...BUT **NOW** YOU'RE AN **OFFICIAL** OF **30TH RANK!**

BROKE OR NO, EMPEROR WU PRESSED ON WITH HIS *COSTLIEST* PROJECT: FIGHTING THE *NORTHERN BARBARIANS*, OR *HSIUNG·NU*. EVER SINCE THE COLLAPSE OF CHIN, THE HSIUNG·NU HAD RAIDED NORTH CHINA AT WILL.

THE HAN EMPERORS WERE ABLE TO DO NOTHING—EXCEPT TO *SEND PRESENTS* AND *BEG* (IN DIPLOMATIC LANGUAGE!).

"OUR TWO GREAT NATIONS, THE HAN AND THE HSIUNG-NU, STAND SIDE BY SIDE. SINCE THE HSIUNG-NU DWELL IN THE NORTH, WHERE THE LAND IS COLD AND THE KILLING FROSTS COME EARLY, WE HAVE DECREED THAT OUR OFFICIALS SHALL SEND TO THE *KHAN* EACH YEAR A FIXED QUANTITY OF MILLET, LEAVEN, GOLD, SILK CLOTH, THREAD, FLOSS, AND OTHER ARTICLES.

"NOW THE WORLD ENJOYS PROFOUND PEACE AND THE PEOPLE ARE AT REST. WE AND THE *KHAN* MUST BE AS PARENTS TO THEM. WHEN WE CONSIDER PAST AFFAIRS, WE REALIZE THAT IT IS ONLY BECAUSE OF PETTY MATTERS AND TRIFLING REASONS THAT THE PLANS OF OUR MINISTERS HAVE FAILED. NO SUCH MATTERS ARE WORTHY TO DISRUPT THE HARMONY THAT EXISTS BETWEEN BROTHERS..."

DURING THE REIGN OF *EMPRESS LU*, THE HSIUNG·NU *KHAN* (LEADER) DARED TO WRITE HER AN *INTIMATE LETTER* WHICH BECAME A SYMBOL OF CHINESE HUMILIATION!

"WE ARE BOTH OLD... MAYBE WE COULD GET TOGETHER AND CONSOLE EACH OTHER..."

GUARDS!! DISMEMBER THIS MESSENGER SLOWLY!

EMPEROR WU, THE MARTIAL EMPEROR, DECIDED THE HSIUNG·NU HAD GONE *TOO FAR*.

I'M YOUNG AND PROUD.

HE SENT SEVERAL EXPEDITIONS INTO THE NORTH TO BATTLE THE BARBARIANS...

GONG BOOM
TWEEDLE

BUT THE NOMADIC HSIUNG·NU COULD BE HARD TO *FIND*...

HM... MAYBE WE SHOULD HAVE TONED DOWN THE GONGS...

THEN THEY STRUCK LIKE *LIGHTNING!*

GAH!

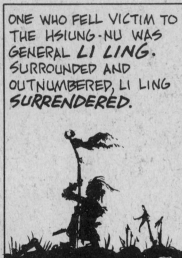

ONE WHO FELL VICTIM TO THE HSIUNG·NU WAS GENERAL *LI LING.* SURROUNDED AND OUTNUMBERED, LI LING *SURRENDERED.*

THIS WAS *DISGRACEFUL!* A CAPTURED GENERAL WAS SUPPOSED TO *COMMIT SUICIDE!!!*

SORRY.

EMPEROR WU, LIKE THE CHIN EMPEROR BEFORE HIM, SUPPORTED A HOST OF *DIVINERS, OMEN·READERS,* AND *MAGICIANS* WHO USED THEIR ARTS TO GUIDE HIS PLANS.

I WILL NOW PERFORM MYSTERIOUS PROCEDURES REQUIRING EXPERT INTERPRETATION IN AN ARCANE JARGON!

GO FOR IT.

AMONG THEIR RIDICULOUS-SOUNDING PROJECTS WAS THE SEARCH FOR AN *"IMMORTALITY FUNGUS."* EAT IT, AND YOU WOULD LIVE FOREVER!

AHEM! STILL IN PROCESS!

SOUNDS RIDICULOUS... BUT MODERN RESEARCH SHOWS THAT THE EDIBLE CHINESE FUNGUS KNOWN AS *"CLOUD EARS"* REDUCES CHOLESTEROL AND HEART DISEASE!* SO ASK YOURSELF — WHAT WAS THE DIFFERENCE BETWEEN *MAGIC* AND *SCIENCE?*

ABRACADABRA! RESULTS!

WHEN THE NEWS REACHED EMPEROR WU, HE FURIOUSLY SENTENCED LI LING'S WHOLE FAMILY — MOTHER, WIFE, CHILDREN — TO *DEATH!*

I *REALLY* CARE ABOUT THIS HSIUNG-NU STUFF!

NO ONE DARED TO OBJECT — WELL, *ALMOST* NO ONE...

FUME TREMBLE GNASH

UM... EXCUSE ME? YOUR MAJESTY?

THIS WAS *SSUMA CHIEN,* COURT HISTORIAN AND ASTRONOMER.

WELL?

WELL... UM... 'SCUSE ME... BUT... ER... GENERAL LI LING WAS... UM... A *NICE GUY*... AND A REALLY *GOOD GENERAL*... AND... HE'S PROBABLY HOPING TO... UM... WIN *MORE* BATTLES FOR YOUR MAJESTY... SO HE... DIDN'T... YOU KNOW...

OFF WITH HIS—

HMM... WAIT... OFF WITH HIS *WHAT?*

GLEEP!

LUCKILY FOR US, IT WASN'T HIS *HEAD*... SSUMA CHIEN WAS TRIED, CONVICTED OF *DECEIVING* THE *EMPEROR*, IMPRISONED, TORTURED, AND FINALLY CASTRATED... LIKE GENERAL LI LING, SSUMA CHIEN SUBMITTED TO THIS DISGRACE WITHOUT COMMITTING SUICIDE...

HE SURVIVED TO FINISH ONE OF THE GREATEST HISTORIES EVER WRITTEN — THE ENCYCLOPEDIC *SHIH CHI*, FROM WHICH EVERYTHING IN THIS VOLUME HAS BEEN ADAPTED!

149

THE HAN EVENTUALLY DID PUSH BACK THE HSIUNG-NU, BUT THE COST OF WAR RUINED THE EMPIRE...

MEANING—A FEW LIKE *ME* AND MANY LIKE THEM!

IN 9 A.D., A REBEL NAMED *WANG MANG* WON CONTROL OF THE REALM, INTERRUPTING THE LIU FAMILY'S CONTROL FOR SEVERAL YEARS..

LET'S GET TO WORK!

WANG MANG'S CURE FOR THE AILING ECONOMY WAS TO PULL *ALL GOLD* OUT OF CIRCULATION.

IT'S THE ROOT OF ALL *EVIL*— OF *COURSE* THE GOVERNMENT SHOULD HAVE IT!

GRAB

ONE LITTLE PROBLEM: SUDDENLY CHINA COULD NO LONGER *TRADE* WITH THE OUTSIDE WORLD!

UM.... WILL YOU TAKE *TEA?*

NOT ON THIS CAMEL...

THIS SENT ECONOMIC *SHOCK WAVES* ACROSS TWO CONTINENTS!

BY JUPITER, SATURN, NEPTUNE, AND *PLUTO!!* WHERE'S ALL THE *GOLD?*

NEXT! ROME

150

INTRODUCTION

IN THE LAST VOLUME WE SAW *CHINA* CONQUER THE FIRST GREAT EMPIRE IN EAST ASIA... NOW WE MOVE ON TO SEE THE *ROMANS* DO THE SAME TO *WESTERN EUROPE!*

THE ROMANS WERE FAMOUS *BUILDERS.* THEIR FINE ENGINEERING—AND THEIR RECIPE FOR *CONCRETE*—ENABLED THEM TO BUILD *BRIDGES, AQUEDUCTS,* AND EVEN *SEWERS* THAT HAVE LASTED TO THIS DAY!

THEIR *LANGUAGE* STILL PEPPERS THE VOCABULARY OF *LAW, SCIENCE, MEDICINE,* AND THE *ROMAN CATHOLIC CHURCH!*

THE FOUNDERS OF THE *U.S.A.* USED ROME'S *SYSTEM OF GOVERNMENT* AS A *MODEL.* HERE, TOO, THE LATIN LANGUAGE LIVES: *SENATE, QUORUM, VETO, ET CETERA...*

"WE LIVE IN A REPUBLIC, NOT A DEMOCRACY," MY OLD CIVICS TEACHER USED TO SAY...

WHATEVER THAT MEANS!

BUT THE ROMANS ALSO LEFT A MODEL OF WHAT HAPPENS WHEN THE *RICH* PUSH THE *POOR TOO FAR:* IN ROME, THE POOR TURNED TO A *DICTATOR* TO "PROTECT" THEMSELVES...

OOPS!

AND WHEN *THAT* HAPPENS, YOU'RE... UM... STUCK...

SWIM?

THE CARTOON HISTORY OF THE UNIVERSE

Volume 11

REPUBLICANS

Our story about Rome begins in *Babylon* on June 23, 323 B.C.

ALEXANDER'S AFTERMATH

ON THAT DAY, IN AN ANCIENT BABYLONIAN PALACE, ALEXANDER THE GREAT LAY DYING.

WHEN WE LEFT ALEXANDER IN VOLUME 8, HIS EXHAUSTED ARMY HAD TURNED BACK FROM *INDIA*.

BUNCHA WIMPS...

MORE THAN ONCE ON THE WAY HOME, HIS MEN WERE READY TO LIE DOWN AND DIE, BUT ALEXANDER CHARGED ON...

HUP!

OW!!

OY... OOG...

HOW EMBARRASSING...

154

IN 324 THEY ARRIVED IN PERSIA (THEIR HQ), AND ALEXANDER SPRANG INTO ACTION AGAIN!

HUP! OW! COUGH!

HIS GOAL WAS TO BLEND TWO CIVILIZATIONS INTO A WORLD-CLASS *GRECO-PERSIAN CULTURE.*

WEAR PERSIAN CLOTHES!

PUT YOUR FACE ON THE FLOOR!

MAKE ME A GOD!!

AND BRING ME SOME MORE LAMB WITH APRICOTS!

HE HELD A *MASS WEDDING*: 10,000 SOLDIERS MARRIED THEIR ASIAN CONCUBINES; WHILE ALEXANDER HIMSELF MARRIED THE PERSIAN PRINCESS *BARSINE*.

ACTUALLY, ALEXANDER ALREADY HAD A PERSIAN WIFE, *ROXANE*, BUT IN REALITY, THE GREAT ONE CARED FOR NO WOMAN (EXCEPT HIS MOTHER).

O.K... HERE'S YOUR ROOM... ROXANE WILL INTRODUCE YOU TO THE EUNUCHS... I'LL BE BACK... SOMETIME...

NO... NO PATERNITY SUITS DOGGED ALEXANDER. THE LOVE OF *HIS* LIFE WAS A *MAN*, HIS SIDEKICK, *HEPHAESTION*...

ALEXANDER PROMOTED HEPHAESTION TO *GENERAL*, THEN *SECOND-IN-COMMAND*, AND FINALLY *GRAND VIZIER*, OR PRIME MINISTER.

HE HAS THE PERFECT QUALIFICATION: COMPLETE DEVOTION TO *ME*...

BUT AFTER THE INDIA TRIP, HEPH DIED, POISONED EITHER BY DISGRUNTLED GENERALS OR HEAVY DRINKING... ALEX LAY WITH THE BODY *TWO DAYS*...

SOME WAY TO FOUND A DYNASTY...

156

HE ORDERED UP AN *IMMENSE* FUNERAL PYRE... IT TOOK WEEKS TO BUILD AND A DAY TO BURN.

ANYBODY GOT A LIGHT?

WITHIN A YEAR, ALEXANDER HIMSELF COLLAPSED AFTER ONE OF HIS FAMOUS ALL-NIGHTERS.

IMAGINE! HE CONQUERED THE WORLD BOMBED OUT OF HIS MIND!

HE DIED IN BABYLON ON JUNE 13, 323 B.C., AGED 33 YEARS.

:OOF!: "THE GREAT" IS RIGHT...

A GOLDEN COFFIN, HOUSED IN A ROLLING SILVER TEMPLE PULLED BY 64 MULES, CARTED THE CONQUEROR'S CORPSE TOWARDS MACEDON FOR BURIAL.

SO... FOR THE ALEXANDER *COIN*, DO YOU FAVOR THE GLAMOROUS YOUNG CONQUEROR OR THE PUFFY OLD FATSO?

BUT NOTHING WENT ACCORDING TO PLAN... ALEXANDER'S BODY WAS *HIJACKED TO EGYPT* AND BURIED THERE... *ROXANE* MURDERED HER RIVAL *BARSINE* AND WAS MURDERED IN TURN, ALONG WITH ALEXANDER'S ONLY SON. WITH NO LEGITIMATE HEIR, THE EMPIRE WAS CARVED UP BY WARLORDS... FOR DECADES, CHAOS REIGNED... BY AROUND 300 B.C., THE EMPIRE HAD BROKEN INTO *THREE PARTS—EGYPT, SYRIA,* AND *MACEDONIA*—ALL RULED BY MACEDONIAN GENERALS OR THEIR HEIRS.

GAULS, OR *CELTS* (SAME THING; "CELT" HAS A HARD C), OCCUPIED WESTERN EUROPE, WHILE IN THE EAST, *GERMANS* FILLED THE FORESTS.

IN THE WESTERN MEDITERRANEAN AND BEYOND, THE PHOENICIAN CITY OF *KAR-HADASHT,* OR *CARTHAGE,* CONTROLLED ALL THE BUSINESS.

CARTHAGE, FOUNDED AROUND 700 B.C. BY LEBANESE REFUGEES FLEEING THE ASSYRIAN EMPIRE, WAS RULED BY A COUNCIL OF ELDERS, WHO WORSHIPPED BAAL AND PRACTICED *CHILD SACRIFICE.*

IN EGYPT, *PTOLEMY I,* WHO HIJACKED ALEXANDER'S COFFIN, FOUNDED A MACEDONIAN DYNASTY OF PTOLEMIES. THEY BUILT A GREAT *LIBRARY* AND *UNIVERSITY,* WHERE *EUCLID* TORMENTED *GEOMETRY* STUDENTS, AND *ERATOSTHENES* MEASURED THE *EARTH'S GIRTH,* ACCURATE TO WITHIN *100 MILES.*

GAUL

SPAIN

ROME

SICILY

CARTHAGE

MACEDONIA

ATHENS

RHODES

ALEXANDRIA

EGYPT

Sahara Desert

THIS BEGAN THE *HELLENISTIC AGE*... GREEK CULTURE COVERED THE MAP...
GREEK ART, WHICH COULDN'T GET ANY BETTER, GREW *BIGGER*: THE *COLOSSUS
OF RHODES*, THE *MAUSOLEUM*, THE *LIGHTHOUSE OF ALEXANDRIA*—THESE
WERE *WONDERS OF THE WORLD*. SCIENCE AND MATH FLOURISHED, AND
ENGINEERS DEVELOPED *LEVERS*, *PULLEYS*, *SCREWS*, AND *CRANKS* INTO
POWERFUL NEW *MACHINES*. SHIPS GREW IMMENSE... WARFARE MORE DEADLY...

ACROSS THESE VAST STEPPES,
COUNTLESS SHEEPHERDING
NOMADS WANDERED.

IN CHINA, THE ERA OF THE
CHIN DYNASTY AND THE
GREAT WALL WAS BEGINNING.

CASPIAN SEA

BLACK SEA

ALEXANDRIA

ARMENIA

GREEK CITIES, FOUNDED BY ALEXANDER,
PEPPERED WESTERN ASIA, BUT A
NATIVE PEOPLE CALLED THE *PARTHIANS*
WERE ON THE RISE.

ALEXANDRIA

MAUSOLEUM

SYRIA WAS RULED BY ANOTHER
MACEDONIAN DYNASTY, THE
SELEUCIDS, DESCENDED FROM
ALEXANDER'S GENERAL SELEUCUS
AND HIS PERSIAN BRIDE.

ALEXANDRIA

ALEXANDRIA

SYRIA

JERUSALEM

BABYLON

PARTHIAN
ARMORED
KNIGHTS

IN INDIA, *ASHOKA*
WON HIS EMPIRE.

AND *ROME*, THE SMALL TOWN ON THE
WEST COAST OF ITALY, SEEMED OF *NO
IMPORTANCE WHATSOEVER*...

159

GUYS AND BIRDS

THE EARLIEST DAYS OF ROME ARE MURKY AT BEST... OUR SHOVELS ASSURE US THAT VILLAGES DOTTED THE ROMAN HILLS AS LONG AGO AS *800 B.C...* BUT EVERYTHING ELSE IS THE STUFF OF *LEGEND...*

ONCE UPON A TIME—BEGINS THE LEGEND—TWIN BROTHERS NAMED *ROMULUS* AND *REMUS* WERE ABANDONED BY THEIR PARENTS...

THE BOYS WERE RAISED BY EITHER A *SHE-WOLF* OR A *PROSTITUTE* (SAME WORD IN LATIN)...

BRONZE WOLF, c. 500 B.C., WITH BRONZE BABIES ADDED 2000 YEARS LATER.

WHEN THEY GREW UP, THE TWINS DECIDED TO *FOUND A CITY*...

WE'LL NEED—CURSE THESE FLEAS—ARCHITECTS, PLUMBERS, COOKS, ACCOUNTANTS—ANYTHING ELSE?

GRRR—NO BATHS!

BY ALL ACCOUNTS, THE FOLLOWERS THEY GATHERED WERE AN ODD LOT.

YOU! WE'RE FOUNDING A CITY! DO YOU HAVE ANY SKILLS?

UM...I CAN READ THE *FUTURE* FROM CHICKENS!

IT'LL DO...

WHEN THEY FOUND A GOOD SPOT, THEY *CONSULTED THE BIRDS** AND THE SIGNS WERE GOOD.

BUT SOON A FIGHT BROKE OUT AND ROMULUS *MURDERED* REMUS.

DOES THIS MEAN IT WON'T BE CALLED "REM?"

✳ IN ANCIENT ROME, NO SERIOUS DECISION WAS EVER MADE WITHOUT CONSULTING THE FORTUNE-TELLERS, OR *AUGURS*, WHO READ THE FUTURE FROM BIRDS.

RAIN! THIS MEANS RAIN!

ANY UNUSUAL BIRD ACTION, FROM THE ODD GOOSE HONK TO A STRAY EAGLE, COULD BRING ALL STATE BUSINESS TO A SCREECHING (OR HONKING) HALT.

BUT THIS DIDN'T STOP ROMAN *GOURMETS* FROM DEVELOPING A TASTE FOR *PEACOCK* AND *FLAMINGO*.

FLAMINGO STUFFED WITH CANARIES AND BLUEBIRDS?

MM... IN ROME, THE BIRDS ARE FOR US, AND VICE VERSA...

THE FLEDGLING ROMANS SOON NOTICED THE LACK OF AN *ESSENTIAL INGREDIENT* FOR AN ETERNAL CITY: *WOMEN.*

MUST... HUMP... SOMETHING...

HANDS OFF... WE'RE ROMANS, NOT GREEKS...

ROMULUS INVITED THE NEIGHBORING SABINE TRIBE TO A GRAND TRACK MEET.

BIG FUN! WE'LL EAT LIKE *HOGS* AND RUN THE *100-YARD DASH!!* BRING THE WHOLE FAMILY! 'SPECIALLY THE —AHEM— *WOMEN!*

THE SABINES ACCEPTED... THE RACE WAS ABOUT TO BEGIN... AND THEN—

TOGA PARTY!

THE ROMANS POUNCED ON THE SABINE WOMEN AND *DRAGGED THEM AWAY!*

BY THE TIME THE SABINE *MEN* DECLARED *WAR,* THE SABINE *WOMEN* ALREADY HAD *ROMAN BABIES,* AND THE WAR NEVER HAPPENED.

CONGRATULATIONS. YOU ARE NOW THE PROUD ANCESTOR OF ROME'S MOST NOBLE FAMILIES. DON'T SCREW THINGS UP.

BY THE WAY, WHAT TOOK YOU SO LONG?

UNDER ROMULUS, ROMANS MADE WAR ALL THE TIME, UNTIL THEY HAD OVERPOWERED ALL THEIR NEAREST NEIGHBORS.

AT LAST, ROMULUS DIED, UNDER MYSTERIOUS CIRCUMSTANCES: ACCORDING TO LEGEND, THE BODY *VANISHED.*

IS HE UNDER HERE?

;PHEW; LET'S QUIT LOOKIN'...

THE NEW KING, *NUMA POMPILIUS,* CALLED FOR PEACE, BUT THEN WORRIED HOW TO CONTROL HIS OWN ROMANS, SO ACCUSTOMED TO *RAPINE* AND *PILLAGE.*

YEAH! WE NEED AN *EMOTIONAL OUTLET!*

HEY! WHO STABBED MY BUTT?

NUMA SOUGHT ADVICE FROM A "WOODLAND NYMPH." (SEE VOL 4 FOR ANOTHER EXAMPLE OF A LAWGIVER'S CONSULTANT.)

THEY'RE *INCORRIGIBLE!*

MY FEE WILL BE $175 AN HOUR...

SHE POINTED OUT THE ADVANTAGES OF *LOTS OF RELIGION.*

OBEDIENCE TO THE GODS INSTILS REVERENCE FOR AUTHORITY... PERFORMING RITUALS BUILDS GOOD HABITS; AND IT'LL *KEEP 'EM BUSY...*

SO NUMA INVENTED SO MANY SACRED *LAWS, CEREMONIES,* AND *FESTIVALS,* THAT ROME GOT THE REPUTATION AS ITALY'S *MOST PIOUS CITY...*

O.K. RITUAL'S OVER... *NOW* CAN WE FIGHT?

NOPE! TIME FOR THE *NEXT RITUAL!!*

WOMAN RAPED; REPUBLIC BORN!

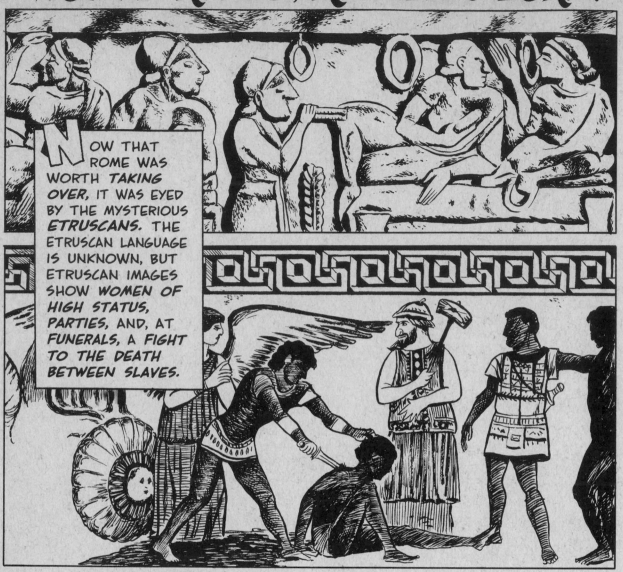

NOW THAT ROME WAS WORTH *TAKING OVER*, IT WAS EYED BY THE MYSTERIOUS *ETRUSCANS*. THE ETRUSCAN LANGUAGE IS UNKNOWN, BUT ETRUSCAN IMAGES SHOW *WOMEN OF HIGH STATUS*, PARTIES, AND, AT *FUNERALS*, A FIGHT TO THE DEATH BETWEEN SLAVES.

IN MANY ANCIENT CULTURES, SERVANTS BECAME *HUMAN SACRIFICES* WHEN THEIR MASTERS DIED. SOME ETRUSCAN HAD THE IDEA OF MAKING TWO OF THE SLAVES FIGHT TO THE DEATH.

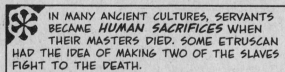

WHY DO THEY KILL US WHEN MASTER DIES?

SO WE'LL TAKE GOOD CARE OF HIM WHEN HE'S ALIVE!!

THE ROMANS BORROWED THIS ETRUSCAN CUSTOM OF *GLADIATORS*, AND TURNED IT INTO A *PROFESSIONAL SPORT*. (JULIUS CAESAR WAS ONE OF THE FIRST BIG SPONSORS.)

EVENTUALLY, IT BECAME A *BIG BUSINESS*, WITH HUGE ARENAS AND *STAR STATUS* FOR THE BEST FIGHTERS, MUCH TO THE DISGUST OF MORE CIVILIZED PEOPLE, LIKE THE GREEKS.

BARBARIC!

WHY CAN'T THEY BE LIKE GREEKS AND ADMIRE RUNNING FAST, NAKED?

GLADIATORIAL COMBAT WAS SO POPULAR IN ROME THAT IT CONTINUED WELL INTO THE REIGNS OF THE *CHRISTIAN EMPERORS*.

YES...UM...IT'S UNCHRISTIAN, BUT SO ARE CHRISTMAS TREES...

164

AROUND 550 B.C., A COUPLE HEADED FOR ROME: *TANAQUIL*, AN ETRUSCAN LADY AND PSYCHIC, AND HER HUSBAND *TARQUIN*, A PHOENICIAN BUSINESSMAN.

ON THE WAY, AN *EAGLE* SNATCHED TARQUIN'S HAT: A CLEAR *OMEN!*

IT'S A *GOOD* SIGN! TRUST ME — I'M NOT JUST A PSYCHIC, I'M ALSO AN *OPTIMIST!*

THEN IT PUT THE HAT BACK—EVEN CLEARER!!

CROWNED BY AN EAGLE!

IN ROME, TARQUIN BEGAN *RUNNING FOR KING,* THE FIRST PERSON IN ROME TO *CAMPAIGN FOR OFFICE.*

HI, I'M TARQUIN, I'M RICH, I'M HONEST, I HAVE A MAGIC HAT, ETC ETC ETC BLAH BLAH...

HE WON, AND RULED LONG AND WELL, ROME'S FIRST ETRUSCAN KING.

WELL, MY *WIFE'S* ETRUSCAN, ANYWAY...

BUT WHO WOULD SUCCEED HIM? TANAQUIL SAW FLAMES SHOOTING OUT OF THE HEAD OF A SERVANT, *SERVIUS TULLIUS.*

GROOMED BY TANAQUIL, SERVIUS TULLIUS BECAME KING, TO THE ENVY OF TARQUIN'S *BIOLOGICAL* SONS!

BETRAYED—BY OUR OWN *MOM!* RG!

EVEN MORE THAN I'M ANGRY, I'M *HURT*...

FINALLY, *LUCIUS TARQUIN* COULD STAND IT NO MORE AND HEAVED SERVIUS DOWN THE SENATE STEPS.

IN THE CHAOS, LUCIUS'S WIFE—SERVIUS'S DAUGHTER—DROVE OVER HER *OWN FATHER'S BODY*, AS SHE HURRIED TO HER HUSBAND'S SIDE...

EASY, DRIVER!

AND LUCIUS TARQUIN BECAME *TARQUIN THE PROUD*, ROME'S WORST AND FINAL KING.

OH, *DARLING!?* ARE YOU *ALL RIGHT??!*

TARQUIN KILLED HIS ENEMIES, GRABBED THEIR WEALTH, MADE WAR, DUG A SEWER, AND BUILT ROME'S FIRST *GIANT MONUMENT*: A TEMPLE TO JUPITER *TWICE* THE SIZE OF ATHENS' PARTHENON!!

TARQUIN THE PROUD WAS A TRUE TYRANT, SURROUNDED BY *TOADIES* AND *YES-MEN*, AND HIS SONS WERE NEARLY AS BAD!

ONE OF THESE LADS, INFLAMED BY THE BEAUTY OF HIS FRIEND'S WIFE *LUCRETIA*, BROKE INTO HER CHAMBER...

NO!

... AND DID AS HE PLEASED WITH HER.

NO! NO! NO!

DON'T BLAME ME! I NEVER HEARD THIS WORD BEFORE...

TO PRESERVE THE FAMILY HONOR, LUCRETIA TOLD ALL AND THEN *STABBED HERSELF.*

B-BUT WHY, DAUGHTER?

TO PRESERVE THE HONOR OF THE *PATRIARCHAL FAMILY!*

A FAMILY FRIEND, TARQUIN'S NEPHEW *JUNIUS BRUTUS*, PULLED OUT THE KNIFE, VOWING REVENGE.

WELL, ALL RIGHT, SINCE YOU PUT IT THAT WAY...

COME ON, MEN!

BRUTUS, WHO UNTIL THEN HAD BEEN KNOWN AS *"THE DULLARD,"* DISPLAYED THE CORPSE IN TOWN TO INFLAME EVERYONE, THEN LED A *REVOLT* AGAINST THE TARQUINS.

HOW DARE THOSE TARQUINS INTERFERE WITH *OUR* REPRODUCTIVE BIOLOGY?

DOWN WITH KINGS!

WHEN IT WAS OVER (507 B.C.), KINGS WERE *OUT,* AND ROME HAD BECOME A

REPUBLIC,

WITH BRUTUS AS ITS FIRST CHIEF EXECUTIVE.

SO ROME WAS NOW A REPUBLIC. WHAT DID *THAT* MEAN? WELL, ACCORDING TO *TRADITION*...

START WITH THE UPPER-CLASS BOYS' CLUB, OR *SENATE*. SENATORS, THE SONS OF ROME'S OLDEST, NOBLEST FAMILIES, HELD A *LIFETIME TERM* IN THIS LAWMAKING BODY. SENATORS WERE ELECTED—BY THE SENATE.

EACH YEAR THE SENATE CHOSE TWO *CONSULS*, CHIEF EXECUTIVES WITH KINGLY AUTHORITY FOR ONE YEAR.

AND AFTER THE YEAR'S UP?

CONSULTING... LOBBYING...

FASCES, THE EMBLEM OF KINGLY POWER, HELD BY ONLY ONE CONSUL AT A TIME. THE FASCES WAS A BUNDLE OF REEDS, SYMBOLIZING *STRENGTH IN UNITY*. (ONE REED BREAKS, A BUNDLE DOESN'T.)

THE CONSULS HAD AN ARMED GUARD OF *LICTORS*, WHO ALSO ACTED AS POLICE.

THE GOOD LICTOR AND THE BAD LICTOR!

SO AT FIRST, ROME WAS RULED BY THE OLD, NOBLE FAMILIES, OR *PATRICIANS*.

OR AT LEAST BY THE *SONS* OF THE OLD, NOBLE FAMILIES...

HRRMPH!

THE REST OF THE CITIZENS WERE THE *PLEBEIANS*, OR JUST PLAIN PLEBS.

TRIBUNES

THE PATRICIANS MAY WELL HAVE HAD ONLY THE GOOD OF THE STATE AT HEART AT ALL TIMES...

YES...THAT'S WHY WE WANT TO HELP YOU "LITTLE PEOPLE!"

SO... WHILE THE PLEBS WERE OFF AT WAR—WHICH WAS *OFTEN*—THE PATRICIANS HELPED OUT THEIR FAMILIES WITH *LOANS*.

ANYT'ING YOU NEED WHILE THE MAN'S AWAY—JUST NAME IT!

THANK YOU, GODFATHER!!

AND LOANS MUST BE *REPAID!*

SOB...WE *CAN'T* RIGHT NOW...BUT I KNOW HOW YOU FEEL ABOUT THE *GOOD OF THE STATE...*

AHEM... ENFORCING LOAN PAYMENTS *IS* THE STATE...

AND IF THE FOOT-SOLDIER, WHO BASICALLY LIVED OFF *PLUNDER*, HAD FAILED TO LOOT ADEQUATELY, HE NOW FACED LOSING HIS *SAVINGS*, HIS *LAND*, AND EVEN HIS *FREEDOM*.

AFTER THE NOBLE LENDERS HAD *BEGGARED, BEATEN, ENSLAVED, AND MURDERED* ENOUGH DEBTORS, THE PLEBS DEMANDED A *CHANGE.*

DEBT RELIEF! DEBT RELIEF!

THE SENATE WENT INTO A STALL...

I REMAIN HOPEFUL THAT THE PLEBS WILL COME TO THEIR SENSES WITHIN... OH... A YEAR... OR TWO...

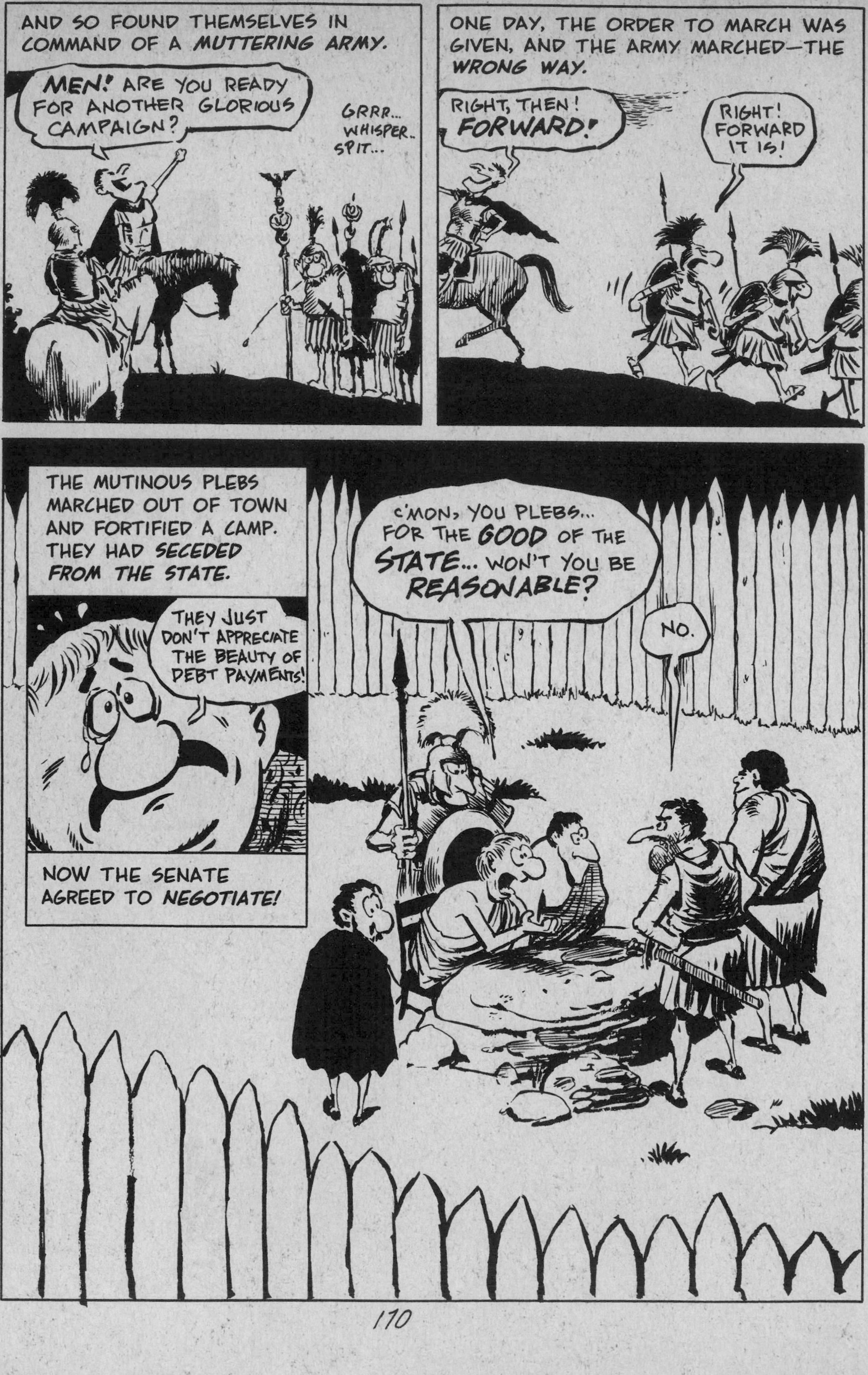
AND SO FOUND THEMSELVES IN COMMAND OF A *MUTTERING ARMY.*
MEN! ARE YOU READY FOR ANOTHER GLORIOUS CAMPAIGN?
GRRR... WHISPER.. SPIT...
ONE DAY, THE ORDER TO MARCH WAS GIVEN, AND THE ARMY MARCHED—THE *WRONG WAY.*
RIGHT, THEN! *FORWARD!*
RIGHT! FORWARD IT IS!
THE MUTINOUS PLEBS MARCHED OUT OF TOWN AND FORTIFIED A CAMP. THEY HAD *SECEDED FROM THE STATE.*
THEY JUST DON'T APPRECIATE THE BEAUTY OF DEBT PAYMENTS!
NOW THE SENATE AGREED TO *NEGOTIATE!*
C'MON, YOU PLEBS... FOR THE *GOOD* OF THE *STATE*... WON'T YOU BE *REASONABLE?*
NO.

THE LEADER OF THIS MUTINY, *SICINIUS*, IS BARELY REMEMBERED, EVEN THOUGH HE ACCOMPLISHED ONE OF THE *GREATEST FEATS* IN ROMAN HISTORY:

MUTINIED AND SURVIVED!

PLEBS AND SENATE CREATED A *NEW OFFICE* IN THE ROMAN GOVERNMENT, DESIGNED STRICTLY TO PROTECT THE PLEBS: *TRIBUNE OF THE PEOPLE.*

MEN! WE HAVE *INSTITUTIONAL CHANGE!!*

WHY COULDN'T WE JUST KILL THEM?

UM... BECAUSE WE PROMISED NOT TO, I THINK...

ELECTED BY THE TRIBES, TRIBUNES WERE *PERSONALLY INVIOLATE,* I.E., IT WAS ILLEGAL TO LAY HANDS ON THEM.

AAARGH—

TUT TUT! NO TOUCHY!!

DURING THE SECESSION, FIVE TRIBUNES WERE CHOSEN—INCLUDING *SICINIUS.*

MY FELLOW CITIZEN!

TRIBUNES HAD THE POWER TO *VETO ANY LAW PASSED BY THE SENATE.* FOR CENTURIES, ROME RANG WITH THEIR VETOES!

VETO! VETO! VETO! VETO! VITO!

EXCUSE ME... ARE YOU A TRIBUNE?

NO... I'M LOOKING FOR MY BOY, *VITO!*

SOME PATRICIANS REBELLED, E.G., *CORIOLANUS*... (YOU CAN FIND THE DETAILS IN SHAKESPEARE.)

YOU'RE A **BAD BOY!**

OTHERS RESPONDED BY TRYING TO **COOPT THE PLEBS**...

WHAT CAN I GET YOU, TRIBUNE? LAND? HORSES? MARRY MY DAUGHTER?

FOR THE NEXT 60 YEARS, THE STRUGGLE BETWEEN THE CLASSES SEESAWED...

WITH A BRIEF INTERRUPTION AROUND **390 B.C.**, WHEN THE **GAULS** INVADED ITALY.

IN THE IMMENSE BATTLE, THE SCREAMING GALLIC HORDE SLAUGHTERED THE WELL-TRAINED, DISCIPLINED ROMANS.

PAF

AS THE NORTHERN WARRIORS APPROACHED ROME, IT'S SAID, THE **CAPITOL GEESE** WERE THE FIRST TO NOTICE.

UH-OH... LOOKS BAD...

IN 387, THE GAULS SWEPT INTO ROME AND *BURNED IT DOWN*. ALL HISTORICAL RECORDS WENT UP IN SMOKE, WHICH EXPLAINS WHY EVERYTHING EARLIER THAN 387 BELONGS TO THE *REALM OF LEGEND...*

THEN, FOR REASONS THAT REMAIN VAGUE, THE GAULS LEFT.

CONCORD

FOR ROME, THE FIRE MARKS THE END OF LEGEND AND THE BEGINNING OF *HISTORY*... MANY DOCUMENTS WRITTEN AFTER 387 HAVE SURVIVED... WHICH, IN A WAY, ONLY MAKES THE STORY *MURKIER*...

LEGENDS AT LEAST ARE CLEAR...

FALSE, BUT CLEAR...

THE NEXT 20 YEARS WERE UNSTABLE... *EXTERNALLY*, THE ARMY UNDER THE PATRICIAN *CAMILLUS* HAD TO BATTLE THE GAULS AND OTHERS...

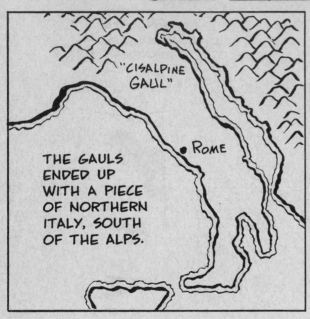

"CISALPINE GAUL"

• ROME

THE GAULS ENDED UP WITH A PIECE OF NORTHERN ITALY, SOUTH OF THE ALPS.

INTERNALLY, ROME SAW PLEBEIAN REVOLTS, RIOTS, SHAKY GOVERNMENTS, SOMETIMES *NO* GOVERNMENT...

UNTIL THE YEAR *367 B.C.*, WHEN THE PLEBEIAN TRIBUNES *LICINIUS* AND *SEXTUS* PUSHED THROUGH A PROGRAM THAT BECAME THE BASIS OF THE REPUBLIC'S CLASSIC CONSTITUTION: BESIDES RELIEVING DEBTORS, THEIR LAWS OPENED ALL *STATE OFFICES* TO PLEBEIANS.

SURE HOPE THIS WORKS!!

174

IN THAT SAME YEAR, THE OLD WARHORSE *CAMILLUS* DEDICATED A TEMPLE OF CONCORD TO SYMBOLIZE THE HARMONY BETWEEN THE CLASSES.

ALTHOUGH IT WAS THE TWO TRIBUNES WHO HAD REFORMED THE LAWS, *CAMILLUS* WAS THE ONE WHO BECAME KNOWN AS THE *SECOND FATHER OF HIS COUNTRY.*

:SIGH: GENERALS GET *ALL* THE CREDIT...

LIKE ROME, CONCORD WASN'T BUILT IN A DAY! FOR THE NEXT *40 YEARS,* THERE WERE MORE REFORMS, GOVERNMENT COMMITTEES, RIOTS...

UNTIL 326, WHEN *ENSLAVEMENT FOR DEBT* WAS FINALLY *ABOLISHED.* NEVER AGAIN COULD ROMAN ENSLAVE ROMAN!

WE CAN RELAX AT LAST...

THIS PRESENTED THE ROMAN RICH WITH A *NEW CHALLENGE:*

WHOM WE GONNA ENSLAVE *NOW?*

BEFORE EXPLORING THE ANSWER, LET'S NOTE THAT WE'VE NOW ABOUT REACHED THE YEAR OF *ALEXANDER THE GREAT'S* DEATH, THE BEGINNING OF THE HELLENISTIC AGE, AND THE POLITICAL FRAGMENTATION THAT GAVE ROME SOME *NEW OPPOR- TUNITIES...*

LET'S HAVE ANOTHER LOOK AT THIS ROMAN GOVERNMENT, NOW THAT THE PLEBS WERE MORE INVOLVED.

BESIDES THE SENATE, CONSULS, AND TRIBUNES, ROME NOW SPROUTED *MORE OFFICERS: PRAETORS, QUAESTORS,* AND *CENSORS,* EACH WITH HIS DUTIES...

SIMPLE: THE PRAETOR'S LIKE A MAYOR... QUAESTORS ARE JUDGES... AND THE CENSOR DOES THE CENSUS AND BANS SMUT...

THERE WAS ALSO A *POPULAR* ORGAN OF GOVERNMENT, THE *TRIBAL ASSEMBLY.* ("TRIBUNE" AND "TRIBUTE" BOTH COME FROM "TRIBE.")

BUT UNLIKE SOME POPULAR ASSEMBLIES, THIS ONE DID *NOT* OPERATE ON THE PRINCIPLE OF *ONE MAN, ONE VOTE.*

WHAT PRINCIPLE *DOES* IT FOLLOW?

ONE WOMAN, NO VOTE...

FOR VOTING PURPOSES, EVERY ROMAN WAS ASSIGNED TO A *TRIBE,* AND EACH TRIBE HAD *ONE VOTE.*

BUT WHAT IF *OUR* TRIBE IS *BIGGER* THAN *YOUR* TRIBE?

THEN I'M A HAPPY GUY!!

DESPITE THE LARGE PLEBEIAN MAJORITY IN THE ROMAN POPULATION, *LESS THAN HALF THE TRIBES WERE PLEBEIAN.* THIS UNDERREPRESENTATION PROTECTED THE INTERESTS OF THE UPPER CLASSES.

"CHECKS AND BALANCES," CHUMS!

NOW THAT THE CLASSES HAD QUIT BASHING *EACH OTHER*, THEY SET OUT TO BASH *EVERYONE ELSE*.

WHY BE CHOOSY?

BEGINNING IN 290, THEY PUSHED SOUTH, AGAINST THE *SAMNITES*.

WHEN THIS IS OVER, WE GOTTA PUT A *ROAD* THROUGH HERE!

ECH!

(THERE WAS A BRIEF INTERRUPTION IN THE 280S WHEN THE GREEK *PYRRHUS* INVADED ITALY...

PYRRHUS WON BATTLE AFTER BATTLE, BUT LOST SO MANY MEN THAT HE HAD TO QUIT, AND THE PHRASE *"PYRRHIC VICTORY"* ENTERED THE LANGUAGE...)

CONGRATULATIONS, MEN! GLORIOUS JOB! LET'S GO HOME!

ROME RESUMED THE *SAMNITE WARS*, AND BY THE YEAR *260 B.C.* HAD MASTERED ALL OF ITALY, FROM THE *PO* TO THE *TOE*.

PHEW!

DIRECTED BY **APPIUS CLAUDIUS**, CONSUL AND ENGINEER, ROMANS BUILT THEIR FIRST *MILITARY ROAD*, THE *APPIAN WAY*, AS WELL AS AN *AQUEDUCT*, TO BRING WATER, AND THE *CIRCUS MAXIMUS*, FOR CHARIOT RACES.

GURGLE GURGLE

WELL, WE MAY NOT DO *PHILOSOPHY*, BUT WE SURE ARE GOOD AT *WAR* AND *CONSTRUCTION!* WHAT DOES THIS *MEAN??*

UM...UM... UH...EH... AH....?

APPIUS DESIGNED HIS *WAY* TO GO MORE OR LESS STRAIGHT FROM POINT A TO POINT B, EVEN IF IT MEANT SOME PRETTY STEEP GRADES NOW AND THEN...

SLOW DOWN SLOW DOWN SLOW DOWN...

LATER ROMAN ENGINEERS DID MORE *SURVEYING* AND *EARTH MOVING*, AND THEIR ROADS WERE A LITTLE EASIER ON THE LEGS.

BUT ALL OF THEM USED *DURABLE MATERIALS*, *DEEP FOUNDATIONS*, AND *GOOD DRAINAGE*, WHICH IS WHY SO MANY ROMAN ROADS SURVIVE TO THE PRESENT DAY.

"INFRASTRUCTURE"— ISN'T THAT LATIN FOR SOMETHING-OR-OTHER?

WAR AGAINST PUNS

AT THE END OF THE SAMNITE WARS, A BAND OF SAMNITES FLED TO *SICILY*, SWORE AN OATH TO THE WAR GOD *MAMERS* (OR MARS), ATTACKED A TOWN, SLAUGHTERED THE MEN, MARRIED THE WOMEN, AND BEGAN LIVING OFF PIRACY...

ATTACKED BY THEIR NEIGHBORS, THESE *MAMERTINE* CORSAIRS ASKED FOR HELP FROM THE NEAREST *GREAT POWERS*: *ROME* AND *CARTHAGE* (SEE P. 154).

MEN OF CARTHAGE! PROTECT US AND GAIN A **STRATEGIC POSITION** IN *SICILY!*

MEN OF ROME! LIKE HE SAID!

IN ROME, DEBATE WAS HOT: THIS WOULD BE ROME'S FIRST *OVERSEAS* ADVENTURE.

ITALY IS ENOUGH FOR US, AND ANYWAY, THESE GUYS ARE *THUGS!*

HEY, BUT THEIR *WEDDING CUSTOMS* ARE SO *ROMAN...*

THE VOTE WAS TO SEND MEN...

WHEN THEY ARRIVED, THERE WERE THE CARTHAGINIANS, ALSO "HELPING OUT."

GO HOME!!

THEY CLASHED, SETTING OFF THE *FIRST PUNIC WAR* ("PUNIC" BECAUSE CARTHAGE WAS *PHOENICIAN*).

NO, **YOU** GO HOME!

YOU!

CARTHAGE RULED THE WESTERN SEAS, WITH A COMPLETE MONOPOLY ON SHIPPING IN THE WESTERN MEDITERRANEAN.

I DON'T THINK WE CAN WADE OUT THAT FAR...

BUT THE LANDLUBBERLY ROMANS BUILT A *NAVY*, EQUIPPED WITH A NEW TYPE OF GRAPPLING IRON CALLED THE *"RAVEN."*

WHEN DROPPED, THE RAVEN BECAME A BRIDGE TO THE ENEMY SHIP, TURNING A SEA BATTLE INTO AN *INFANTRY ENGAGEMENT*.

BRUNCH

BUT RAVENS WERE HEAVY, NOT WHAT YOU'D WANT UP YOUR MAST IN HIGH SEAS!

GLEEP!

THE RAVEN WAS SCRUBBED... THE SIDES WERE EVENLY MATCHED... THE WAR DRAGGED ON, MOSTLY IN SICILY, FOR *25 YEARS*... AND EVENTUALLY, CARTHAGE WAS THE FIRST TO GIVE OUT, AND GIVE UP...

GIVE UP?

NO.

I DO.

CARTHAGE PAID A GREAT SUM OF MONEY, AND ROME NOW CONTROLLED SICILY AND SARDINIA.

SPAIN

ROME

SARDINIA

SICILY

CARTHAGE

FOR ROME, THIS WAR BROUGHT SOME *FIRSTS*: THE FIRST ROMAN *NAVY*, THE FIRST *OVERSEAS PROVINCES*, AND THE FIRST TIME ROME HAD *ENSLAVED* WHOLE CITIES AT A TIME...

BUT NOT THE LAST!

ONE OF THE MOST PUZZLING PUNIC CUSTOMS WAS *CHILD SACRIFICE*: IN TIMES OF STRESS, THE CHIEF FAMILIES OF CARTHAGE WOULD SACRIFICE THEIR OWN CHILDREN IN A RITUAL KNOWN AS *MOLOCH*.

QUIET! OR YOU'RE NEXT!

SCHOLARS HAVE SUGGESTED MANY THEORIES TO EXPLAIN THE CUSTOM:

OBVIOUSLY A FORM OF *POPULATION CONTROL*...

A DRUG-INDUCED ABBERATION!

A CULTURAL PERVERSION THAT LED TO THEIR DOWNFALL!

BY WEEDING OUT UGLY BABIES, THEY MADE THE RACE PRETTIER!

ONE IDEA I HAVEN'T SEEN IS THIS: IN A SOCIETY LIKE CARTHAGE'S, RULED BY A *GROUP OF ELITE FAMILIES* WITH NO KING, THE LEADERS NEEDED TO FEEL THAT EACH FAMILY WAS *SACRIFICING EQUALLY*...

SHOULDER TO SHOULDER, WE'RE LOOKING OVER EACH OTHER'S SHOULDER...

BUT CARTHAGE BOUNCED BACK, THANKS TO THE PUNIC GENERAL *HAMILCAR BARCA* ("LIGHTNING HAMILCAR"), WHO INVADED *SPAIN*, SEIZING ITS RICH MINES AND POOR CITIZENS FOR HIS ARMY.

MINE! ALL MINE!

IN *221*, HAMILCAR'S DARING GRANDSON *HANNIBAL* BEGAN MARCHING ON ROME FROM THE *REAR*—FROM SPAIN, THROUGH GAUL, OVER THE ALPS, INTO ITALY.

THE ALPS WEREN'T EASY: ELEPHANTS FROZE; MEN PLUNGED INTO CREVASSES; THE SWISS GAVE BAD DIRECTIONS...

WHAT DID THEY MEAN, "YO-DE-LAY-HE-HOO?"

TWO THIRDS OF THE PUNS PERISHED, BUT HANNIBAL WAS AN *OPTIMIST!*

ONE THIRD SURVIVED! *FORWARD!*

IN ITALY, HORDES OF GAULS FLOCKED TO HANNIBAL'S BANNER, ONLY TOO READY TO RAVAGE THE ROMANS...*

I KNEW THOSE ROMANS HAD PLENTY OF ENEMIES!

*BECAUSE ROMAN VETERANS OF THE PREVIOUS PUNIC WAR HAD SETTLED ON GALLIC LANDS.

BUT HANNIBAL WOULD HEAD NO HORDES! A TACTICAL MASTER, HE TRAINED HIS TROOPS CAREFULLY.

HUT! HUT!

IF WE LOSE, WE CAN STILL PUT ON A GREAT HALFTIME SHOW AT THE CIRCUS...

NO ROMAN COULD MATCH HIM... AFTER SEVERAL MEDIUM DEFEATS, THE ROMANS SUFFERED A *BIG ONE*: THE BATTLE OF *CANNAE (216)*, WHERE TENS OF THOUSANDS FELL TO HANNIBAL'S COORDINATED CAVALRY CHARGES.

AND THEN, A *BLUNDER*: AFTER CANNAE, HANNIBAL COULD HAVE MARCHED ON ROME—BUT HE DIDN'T!

AN ARMY HAS TO EAT... THE ROMANS BURNED EVERY FIELD AROUND, AND JUST TRY GETTING A TABLE FOR 50,000...

INSTEAD, HE WENT SOUTH AND SPENT *FOURTEEN* AIMLESS YEARS WITHOUT SETTLING ANYTHING.

SIGH....

SO THE WAR WAS DECIDED ELSEWHERE: IN *SICILY*, WHERE THE ROMANS TOOK SYRACUSE, DESPITE ITS AMAZING DEFENSE ENGINES...

YAAAH

AND IN *SPAIN*, WHERE ROME'S *SCIPIO AFRICANUS* LED A NEAR-MIRACULOUS ASSAULT ON THE PUNIC STRONGHOLD OF *NEW CARTHAGE*.

AT THE SPANISH NEWS, HANNIBAL HURRIED HOME TO AFRICA.

I'VE FAILED!

SCIPIO GAVE CHASE, AND THEY MET AT THE BATTLE OF *ZAMA* IN *202*.

CARTHAGE SURRENDERED... THE WAR WAS OVER.. AND HANNIBAL SET SAIL FOR MORE ADVENTURES IN THE EAST, FAR FROM ROME...

✿ SYRACUSE'S DEFENSES WERE DESIGNED BY THE GREEK *ARCHIMEDES* (287-212 B.C.), THE GREATEST MATH GENIUS OF ANCIENT TIMES. (HE'S MOST FAMOUS FOR LEAPING OUT OF HIS BATH AND STREAKING THROUGH THE STREETS, INSPIRED BY HIS DISCOVERY OF BUOYANCY.)

EUREKA!

WHEN THE ROMANS ENTERED SYRACUSE IN 212, ARCHIMEDES WAS DOODLING OUT SOME MATH PROBLEM IN THE SAND... A ROMAN SOLDIER ORDERED HIM TO MOVE ALONG...

MM? YESYES... JUST A MINUTE...

ARCHIMEDES WASN'T QUICK ENOUGH... THE ROMAN KILLED HIM... AND LATER GENERATIONS TOLD THE STORY TO CONTRAST THE GREEKS' *HIGH-MINDEDNESS* WITH ROMAN *HAMHANDEDNESS*.

WHOK

BUT IT MAY NOT BE SO *SIMPLE*... REMEMBER, ARCHIMEDES ALSO DESIGNED THE *WAR ENGINES* THAT HAD KILLED THOUSANDS OF ROMANS!!

GUY WAS A ☆@#☆ WAR CRIMINAL!

NOT VERY NICE

TO ROME, THIS VICTORY HAD A HEADY SCENT... AND WHERE ROMAN NOSES LED, ROMAN ARMS FOLLOWED... IN SHORT, SENATE-SENT ARMIES NOW PROJECTED ROMAN POWER INTO *SPAIN*... *GREECE*... *ILLYRIA*... *ASIA MINOR*... *AFRICA*...

ITALY

ROME

ILLYRIUM

ASIA MINOR

GREECE

AFRICA

EGYPT

AND IN THE PROCESS, THE ROMANS DID A FEW THINGS THAT MIGHT SEEM A TRIFLE *HARSH*, EVEN TO A PERSON OF THE 20TH CENTURY... FOR EXAMPLE:

IN *SPAIN*, 4000 SPANISH REBELS SURRENDERED AFTER THE ROMAN GOVERNOR PROMISED TO SPARE THEM... AND THEN WERE SLAUGHTERED ON ORDERS OF THE *SENATE*.

CAN'T THE SENATE *RECONSIDER*?

MAYBE AFTER THE NEXT ELECTION...

AFTER A *THIRD* PUNIC WAR, ROME TORE CARTHAGE TO THE GROUND AND SALTED ITS FIELDS (146 B.C.).

IN GREECE, ROME *DECIMATED* ATHENS (I.E., KILLED EVERY TENTH PERSON), RAZED CORINTH, SLAUGHTERED INTELLECTUALS AND DEMOCRATS, AND STOLE ALL THAT GOOD *ART*.

AND REMEMBER, IF THE BOAT SINKS, MY *INSURANCE* GUARANTEES ME REPLACEMENT ART OF EQUAL VALUE. *

*SUPPOSEDLY A GENUINE QUOTE

FARTHER EAST, ROMAN WARS, SLAVE RAIDS, AND TAXES RUINED WHOLE NATIONS.

HOW MANY LANGUAGES EVEN *HAVE* A WORD FOR "KILLED EVERY 10TH PERSON?"

THE ISLAND OF *DELOS* BECAME ROME'S GREAT HUMAN CLEARING HOUSE, ABLE TO MOVE UP TO *10,000 SLAVES A DAY*...

IN *ITALY* AND *SICILY* THESE WRETCHES WENT TO WORK ON GREAT PLANTATIONS. SICILY NOW GREW THE GRAIN THAT MADE ROMES BREAD.

AND WHAT HAPPENS TO US FREE SICILIAN FARMERS?

SMALL FARMERS WERE PUSHED OFF THE LAND BY THE SENATORIAL SLAVE-MASTERS.

THIS IS *YOUR* OPPORTUNITY TO STRIKE IT RICH IN THE *BIG CITY*...

THE LANDLESS FLOCKED TO *ROME*, RUBBING ELBOWS WITH THE NEWLY RICH WHO PROFITED FROM THE WARS... HOUSING WAS *CROWDED*, FIRES *FREQUENT*, FOOD SOMETIMES *EXPENSIVE*...

IN *136 B.C.*, THE SLAVES OF SICILY ROSE IN REVOLT. THE UPRISING, WHICH INTERRUPTED ROME'S VITAL GRAIN SUPPLIES, TOOK YEARS TO PUT DOWN, WITH IMMENSE LOSS OF LIFE ON BOTH SIDES...

WOA! BUMMER!

IS ANTIQUITY *RELEVANT?* TRY THIS: AFTER THE PUNIC WARS, THE ROMANS LEVELED CARTHAGE FAIRLY FLAT, BUT ONE THING THEY *PRESERVED:* A LATIN TRANSLATION OF THE CARTHAGINIAN *SLAVE-OWNER'S MANUAL.*

EVERY CULTURE HAS *SOMETHING* OF VALUE!

THIS BOOK WENT THROUGH COUNTLESS EDITIONS FOR MANY CENTURIES, BEING READ BOTH IN *MEDIEVAL EUROPE* AND THE *ARAB CIVILIZATIONS* THAT BEGAN THE AFRICAN SLAVE TRADE...

"WORK 'EM HARD... PAY 'EM LITTLE... TELL POSTERITY THAT YOU TREAT 'EM GENTLY..."

AND SO THE PUNIC PRINCIPLES WERE PASSED STRAIGHT TO AMERICA'S LATIN-EDUCATED *FOUNDING FATHERS.* RELEVANT? COULD BE...

IF I SEEM *SORE*, IT'S BECAUSE I HAVE *GIANTS* STANDING ON MY SHOULDERS...

WITH APOLOGIES TO OL' ISAAC NEWTON!

WHO'S THE BOSS?

FOR MANY IN ROME, THE REVOLT WAS A **WAKE-UP CALL!** IF CITIZENS NO LONGER OWNED *LAND*, IF THE CITY DEPENDED FOR FOOD ON OVERSEAS *SLAVE PLANTATIONS*, WHAT WOULD BECOME OF THE REPUBLIC?

SOME SENATOR TOOK MY LAND, AND NOW HE WANTS ME TO FIGHT FOR "OUR" COUNTRY!!

IN 133 B.C., THE PEOPLE ELECTED A RADICAL TRIBUNE, *TIBERIUS GRACCHUS.*

GRACCHUS PROPOSED A BILL TO GIVE *LAND TO THE LANDLESS.* WHEN THE OTHER TRIBUNE VETOED, GRACCHUS HAD HIM *THROWN OUT* BODILY.

HEY! YOU DON'T TOUCH THE TRIBUNE!

THE SENATE, FULL OF LANDLORDS, DETESTED T. GRACCHUS, BUT COULDN'T LEGALLY BLOCK HIS LAWS...

IT'S SO FRUSTRATING!

SO THEY ACCUSED HIM OF TREASON, GATHERED A MOB, AND ATTACKED THE TRIBUNE WITH FURNITURE FRAGMENTS.

TOUCH THAT TRIBUNE!!

GRACCHUS AND 300 OF HIS PARTY WERE **BEATEN TO DEATH** AND PITCHED IN THE RIVER.

BUT TIBERIUS HAD A BRAVE YOUNGER BROTHER, AND IN 126, *GAIUS GRACCHUS* WAS ELECTED TRIBUNE.

NOT ONLY DID HE PASS A LAND REFORM BILL, BUT UNTIL 122 HE WAS THE VIRTUAL *BOSS* OF *ROME.*

TRIBUNE THREE YEARS IN A ROW? HE'S UNCONSTITUTIONAL! UNCONSCIENABLE!

AND SOON TO BE UNCONSCIOUS...

AGAIN THE SENATE SENT ITS MOB, AND GAIUS GRACCHUS WENT THE WAY OF HIS BROTHER.

TERM LIMITS! TERM LIMITS!!

DESPITE THEIR DEATHS, THE GRACCHI'S PROGRAM WENT FORWARD, AND MANY POOR ROMANS WENT BACK TO THE LAND... BUT PEOPLE HAD TO WONDER: DID CROSSING THE SENATE NOW GUARANTEE ASSASSINATION?

A FINE DETERRENT!

TO THE NEWLY ELECTED (107 B.C.) CONSUL *GAIUS MARIUS*, THE ANSWER WAS:

NOT IF YOU HAVE YOUR OWN ARMY!!

MARIUS OPENED THE ARMY TO *ALL*, DRILLED IT WELL, AND WON MANY VICTORIES ABROAD.

ALTHOUGH MARIUS HIMSELF WAS *UNTOUCHABLE*, HIS LIBERAL FRIENDS KEPT GETTING MURDERED, EVEN IN *MARIUS'S OWN HOUSE*.

PELTED TO DEATH WITH ROOF TILES, FOR EXAMPLE...

SO MARIUS LEFT ROME UNDER A CLOUD, AND IN A HUFF.

THIS PLACE IS GETTING IMPOSSIBLE, EVEN IF YOU *DO* HAVE YOUR OWN ARMY...

MEANWHILE, ROME'S NON-ROMAN *ITALIAN* NEIGHBORS WERE STEAMING... THE LAND REFORM PROGRAM WAS PUTTING ROMANS ON *ITALIAN-OWNED LAND*.

BUT LOOK! I GOT DEEDS! TITLES! PINK SLIPS! VOUCHERS!

AH, BUT I GOT ROMAN CITIZENSHIP!

UNDER ROMAN LAW, THE ITALIANS WERE NOT CITIZENS, BUT *"ALLIES."* UNABLE TO SUE, THEY DECLARED WAR IN 90 B.C.

I TELL YOU, NO LAWYER IN ROME WOULD *TOUCH* THIS CASE—HEY!!

AS ITALY BURNED, CONSERVATIVES KNEW WHOM TO BLAME.

LIBERALS.

FORCED TO END THE WAR BY GRANTING CITIZENSHIP TO THE ITALIANS, CONSERVATIVES CHEERED AS GENERAL *CORNELIUS SULLA* TURNED HIS FURY ON THE POPULAR PARTY.

TO ROME!

SULLA MARCHED AN ARMY TO ROME AND SUPERVISED THE ASSASSINATION OF *HUNDREDS* OF "ENEMIES OF THE STATE."

BUT WHEN SULLA LEFT FOR A FOREIGN WAR IN 86 B.C., *MARIUS* CAME BACK, RAVING LIKE A LUNATIC, AND SLAUGHTERED SULLA'S FRIENDS.

MARIUS DIED OF OLD AGE... SULLA RETURNED IN 82, AND THIS TIME, HE SYSTEMATICALLY KILLED *THOUSANDS*...

WAIT! THIS IS A REPUBLIC! LET'S TALK...

:AHEM: PAY IT NO MIND, SENATORS... JUST COMMON CRIMINALS...

AFTER REVERSING EVERY POPULAR REFORM OF THE PAST *200 YEARS*, SULLA RESIGNED AS DICTATOR AND RETURNED TO HIS COUNTRY HOUSE, WHERE HE EXPIRED FROM *OVEREATING* IN 78 B.C.

MORE BLOOD SAUSAGE, SIRE?

SULLA CALLED HIMSELF "LUCKY" (FELIX), AND IN A WAY HE WAS: HE DIDN'T LIVE TO SEE ALL HIS WORK COME TO NOTHING... IT STARTED WITH A SLAVE REVOLT...

IN 74, A GLADIATOR NAMED SPARTACUS LED A BREAKOUT FROM THE SLAVE PENS.

MAYBE WE SHOULDN'T HAVE TRAINED THEM TO FIGHT *QUITE* SO WELL...

SLAVES ROSE ACROSS ITALY, AND FOR TWO YEARS THEY OUTDUELLED THE ROMAN LEGIONS.

MAYBE WE SHOULD RETHINK THE GLADIATOR THING...

WHAT—AND ADMIT DEFEAT?

CRASSUS, THE GENERAL WHO FINALLY DEFEATED SPARTACUS, AND *POMPEY*, WHO SHARED THE CREDIT, SLAUGHTERED AND CRUCIFIED THOUSANDS OF SLAVES, MARCHED THEIR LEGIONS TO ROME, AND "REQUESTED" THE CONSULSHIP.

YESSIR! YESSIR! YESSIR! YESSIR!

CRASSUS (PLAYED BY LAURENCE OLIVIER IN THE MOVIE *SPARTACUS*) WAS ROME'S *RICHEST CITIZEN* AND *SHARPEST BUSINESSMAN*, WHOSE ENTERPRISES INCLUDED *AGRICULTURE*, *INSURANCE*, AND A *PRIVATE FIRE DEPARTMENT*.

HELP! FIRE!

WHENEVER A FIRE BROKE OUT IN ROME, CRASSUS'S BRIGADE WOULD RUSH TO THE SCENE...

BLESS YOU, CRASSUS!

BUT THEY WOULDN'T *DELIVER THE SERVICE* UNTIL THE *VICTIM* SIGNED UP WITH THE *INSURANCE COMPANY*!

UM... AH... WAIT... LET ME THINK... CAN'T THIS WAIT UNTIL TOMORROW? NO... BY *JUPITER*, THAT PRINT IS SMALL...

CAESARIAN SECTION

ALTHOUGH CRASSUS AND POMPEY HAD BOTH BEEN *SULLA'S* MEN, AS CONSULS THEY *UNDID* SULLA'S ENTIRE PROGRAM. GRAIN WAS *CHEAP*... VETERANS GOT *LAND*... THE SENATE COOPERATED... AND ROME WAS *STABLE*— FOR A WHILE.

THE LESSON WAS NOT LOST ON A 32-YEAR-OLD NEPHEW OF MARIUS NAMED *JULIUS CAESAR*.

FROM AN OLD PATRICIAN FAMILY, CAESAR SURPASSED EVERYONE IN *AMBITION, SHREWDNESS, ELOQUENCE, ENERGY,* AND *SEXUAL VORACITY*.

AND THE LESSON CAESAR LEARNED WAS... AHEM! PSST! CAESAR!

JUST A MINUTE!

YES... ER... THE *LESSON*: THE *SENATE* CAN'T GOVERN... A WARLORD CAN HAVE *HIS WAY*... THE PEOPLE *NEED ME*... RIGHT, MRS. POMPEY?

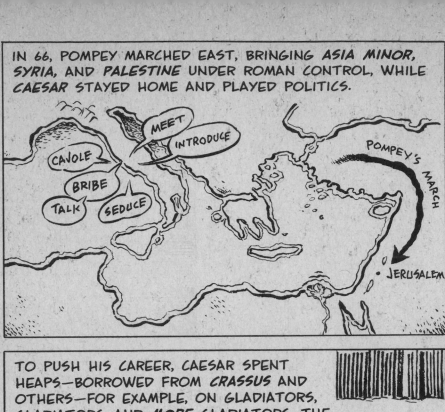

IN 66, POMPEY MARCHED EAST, BRINGING ASIA MINOR, SYRIA, AND PALESTINE UNDER ROMAN CONTROL, WHILE CAESAR STAYED HOME AND PLAYED POLITICS.

MEET
INTRODUCE
CAJOLE
BRIBE
TALK
SEDUCE
POMPEY'S MARCH
JERUSALEM

(WE'LL SEE SOME EFFECTS OF POMPEY'S TRIP TO JERUSALEM IN THE NEXT VOLUME.)

?

TO PUSH HIS CAREER, CAESAR SPENT HEAPS—BORROWED FROM CRASSUS AND OTHERS—FOR EXAMPLE, ON GLADIATORS, GLADIATORS, AND MORE GLADIATORS. THE CROWDS LOVED IT!

⸪ULP⸪ JULIE... THIS IS EXPENSIVE... YOU WOULDN'T FORGET TO PAY ME BACK— WOULD YOU?

DON'T BE CRASS, CRASSUS!

AND WHEN POMPEY CAME HOME, CAESAR PERSUADED CRASSUS AND POMPEY TO MAKE A THREE-WAY PARTNERSHIP ("TRIUMVIRATE") WITH HIMSELF.

IT'S SIMPLE... POMPEY HERE WILL DIVORCE HIS WIFE AND MARRY MY DAUGHTER, AND DON'T WORRY ABOUT YOUR EX... CAESAR WILL TAKE CARE OF EVERYTHING...

BUT

BUT

POMPEY, LIKE ALL ROMAN GENERALS, NEEDED LAND FOR HIS VETERANS.

THEY DESERVE NO LESS!

CAESAR NEEDED—WELL, IN HIS OWN WORDS, HE NEEDED ONLY ONE THING:

DIGNITY, ONLY MY DIGNITY!

CRASSUS NEEDED HIS MONEY BACK.

JULIE, PLEASE!

ELECTED CONSUL FOR THE YEAR 59, CAESAR INTRODUCED A LAND BILL FOR POMPEY'S MEN... HIS CO-CONSUL *BIBULUS* AND THREE TRIBUNES OPPOSED IT... IN A FACE-OFF IN THE FORUM, CAESAR'S PEOPLE DUMPED A BASKET OF *SOMETHING*, DESCRIBED AS "FILTH" BY POLITE HISTORIANS, ON BIBULUS'S HEAD.

DIGNITY, MY DEAR POMPEY, WE MUST MAINTAIN DIGNITY!

GAH!!

IT'S "REINVENTING GOVERNMENT!"

BIBULUS WENT HOME AND DIDN'T COME OUT AGAIN FOR THE REST OF THE YEAR.

NOW IT WAS CAESAR'S TURN TO WIN GLORY. HE RAISED AN ARMY AND INVADED *GAUL*.

I'LL GO DOWN IN HISTORY! BY JUPITER, I'LL **WRITE** THE HISTORY!!

PROVING HIMSELF A GREAT GENERAL, CAESAR CONQUERED THE GAULS' WITH A MIXTURE OF *DEFT MANEUVER*, ENGINEERING, DIPLOMACY, AND *AWESOME CARNAGE*. AT THE SAME TIME HE WROTE HIS *MEMOIRS*, WHICH HAVE *GALLED* 60 GENERATIONS OF LATIN STUDENTS.

GOD, I'M GOOD!

BUT NOW THE TRIUMVIRATE CRUMBLED: *CRASSUS* WAS KILLED WHILE IDIOTICALLY INVADING IRAQ...

JULEEE!

IN ROME POMPEY MADE UP WITH THE SENATE'S ANTI-CAESAR PARTY...

THE MAN *IS* A MENACE TO THE REPUBLIC!

AND CAESAR DREW THE OBVIOUS CONCLUSION...

MY *DIGNITY* IS IN DANGER...

I CAN TELL...IT'S LIKE A SIXTH SENSE...

IN THE WINTER OF 50-49, CAESAR MARCHED HIS ARMY ON ROME.

POMPEY FLED TO GREECE... CAESAR FOLLOWED...

AND FOR THE NEXT TWO YEARS, ROMAN BATTLED ROMAN.

CAESAR WON... WENT TO *EGYPT*... WHERE SOMEBODY BROUGHT HIM POMPEY'S PICKLED *HEAD*...

CAESAR CONSOLED HIMSELF BY CONQUERING EGYPT— AND ITS PRINCESS *CLEOPATRA*.

WHAT WOULD YOU SAY IF I TOLD YOU THAT SOMEDAY AFROCENTRIC HISTORIANS WOULD CLAIM YOU AS *AFRICAN*, EVEN THOUGH YOU'RE THE PRODUCT OF *EIGHT GENERATIONS* OF *MACEDONIAN INBREEDING*?

I'D SAY YOU SURE TALK A LOT FOR A GUY WITH YOUR REPUTATION...

IN *46*, CAESAR CAME HOME IN TRIUMPH.

CAESAR NOW RULED AS *DICTATOR*... BUT, UNLIKE SULLA, HE DIDN'T BELIEVE IN ANNIHILATING HIS ENEMIES.

I'M A GOOD GUY... YOU'LL SEE... BESIDES, I *NEED* YOU ALL, THERE'S SO MUCH TO BE DONE...

FIGHTING CORRUPTION... BUILDING INFRASTRUCTURE...

THIS LENIENCY MAY HAVE COST CAESAR HIS *LIFE*...

AND THE *CALENDAR* IS BADLY IN NEED OF A MONTH NAMED *JULY*...

ON MARCH 15, 44 B.C., CAESAR WAS APPROACHED BY A CROWD OF SENATORS, INCLUDING *JUNIUS BRUTUS*, DESCENDANT OF THE BRUTUS WHO TOPPLED THE TARQUINS, AND—

BUT NO SENATORIAL MOB TURNED OUT TO CELEBRATE... SO CAESAR'S LIEUTENANT, *MARC ANTONY* DARED TO MAKE A SPEECH.

FRIENDS, ROMANS, COUNTRYMEN! I COME NOT TO BURY CAESAR, BUT TO LEAVE HIM LYIN' AROUND IN THE OPEN A WHILE, UNTIL YOU COULDN'T FORGET ABOUT HIM IF YOU *TRIED...**

*EXACT WORDS NOT PRESERVED

NOW CAESAR'S MOB ROAMED THE STREETS, MURDERING SENATORS (AND ONE POET WITH A SENATOR'S NAME)...

I AM CINNA THE POET! CINNA THE POET!!

BRUTUS & FRIENDS FLED AND WERE HUNTED DOWN BY ANTONY AND HIS PARTNER, CAESAR'S SHORT AND SICKLY NEPHEW *OCTAVIAN*.

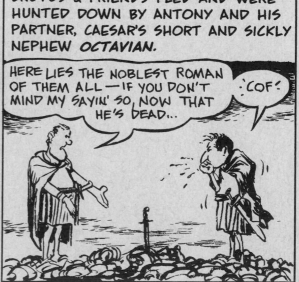

HERE LIES THE NOBLEST ROMAN OF THEM ALL — IF YOU DON'T MIND MY SAYIN' SO, NOW THAT HE'S DEAD...

COF!

ANTONY AND OCTAVIAN SWORE FRIEND-
SHIP, AS ANTONY MARRIED OCTAVIAN'S
SISTER *OCTAVIA.*

COF
COF!

UNLIKE UNCLE JULIUS, THEY ASSASSINATED
THOUSANDS OF SUSPECTED ENEMIES.

SORRY, SENATOR, BUT WE
REALLY DO WANT TO AVOID
"UNCLE JULIUS'S" MISTAKE—
YOU UNDERSTAND?

AT THE
GUT
LEVEL.

THEN OCTAVIAN AND
ANTONY EACH TOOK HALF
OF ROME'S VAST REALM.

I'LL STAY HERE IN ROME,
BROTHER-IN-LAW, *YOU*
CAN HAVE *EGYPT!*

WOW!
EGYPT!

IN EGYPT, ANTONY MET
AND MARRIED *QUEEN
CLEOPATRA.*

WOW!
EGYPT!

OCTAVIAN USED THIS AS
AN EXCUSE TO *ATTACK*
ANTONY.

THE ✰@# INSULTED
MY *FAMILY!*

AGAIN CIVIL WAR BROKE OUT... IT ENDED, IN 28 B.C.
WITH ANTONY'S DEFEAT AT *ACTIUM* AND CLEOPATRA'S
SNAKE-BITE SUICIDE.

HAIL, CAESAR OCTAVIANUS!
ANTONY—*DEAD!* CLEOPATRA—
DEAD! EGYPT—*YOURS!*

THANK YOU...
YOU MAY GO...

NOW ROME REALLY WAS
RULED BY *ONE MAN,*
COUGHING AND WEARING
PLATFORM SHOES.

HEE HEE HEE

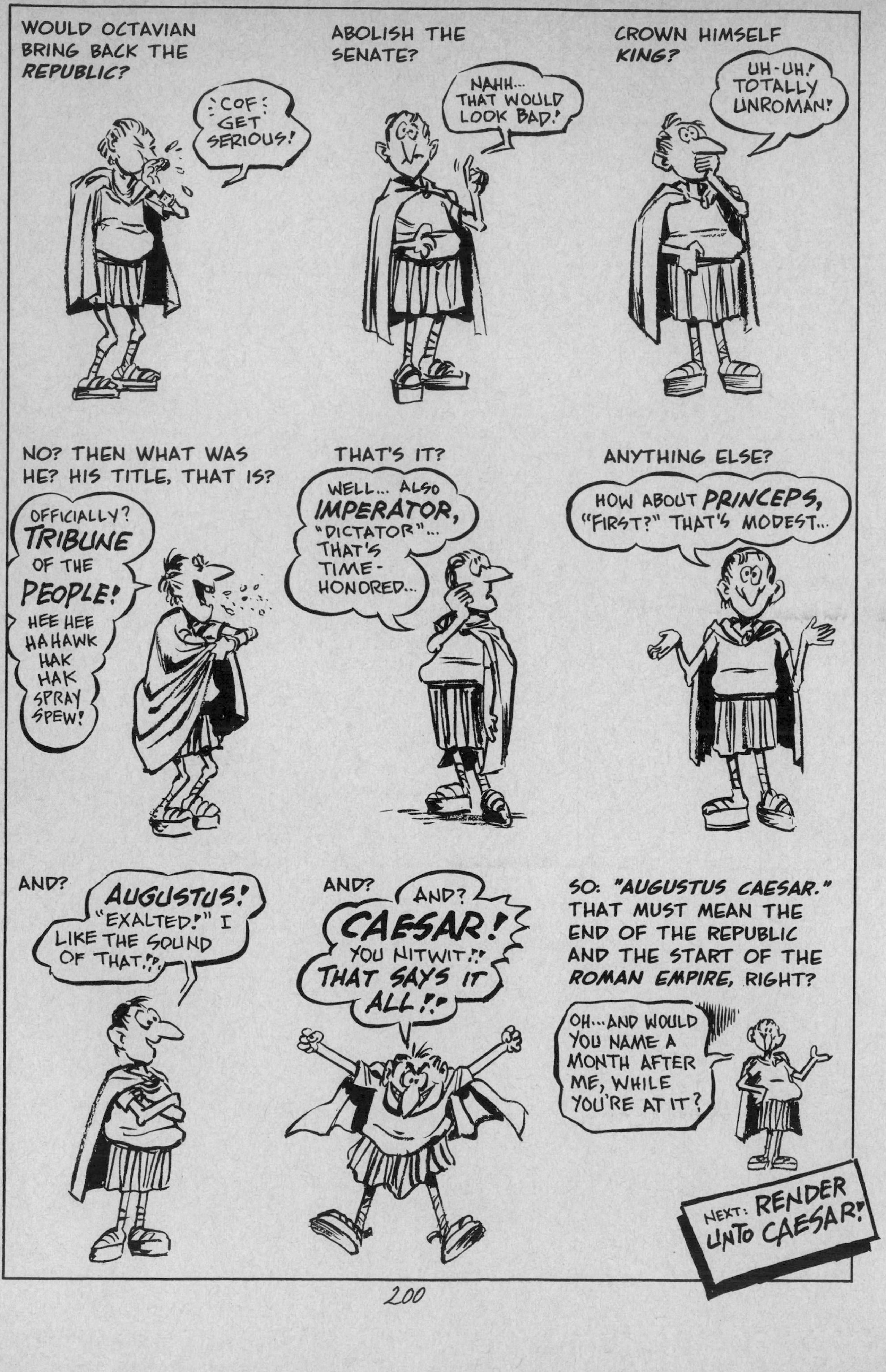
WOULD OCTAVIAN BRING BACK THE *REPUBLIC?*
COF GET SERIOUS!
ABOLISH THE SENATE?
NAHH... THAT WOULD LOOK BAD!
CROWN HIMSELF *KING?*
UH-UH! TOTALLY UNROMAN!
NO? THEN WHAT WAS HE? HIS TITLE, THAT IS?
OFFICIALLY? TRIBUNE OF THE PEOPLE! HEE HEE HAHAWK HAK HAK SPRAY SPEW!
THAT'S IT?
WELL... ALSO IMPERATOR, "DICTATOR"... THAT'S TIME-HONORED...
ANYTHING ELSE?
HOW ABOUT PRINCEPS, "FIRST?" THAT'S MODEST...
AND?
AUGUSTUS! "EXALTED!" I LIKE THE SOUND OF THAT!?!
AND?
AND? CAESAR! YOU NITWIT!?! THAT SAYS IT ALL!?!
SO: *"AUGUSTUS CAESAR."* THAT MUST MEAN THE END OF THE REPUBLIC AND THE START OF THE *ROMAN EMPIRE,* RIGHT?
OH...AND WOULD YOU NAME A MONTH AFTER ME, WHILE YOU'RE AT IT?
NEXT: RENDER UNTO CAESAR!

INTRODUCTION

THE TIME MACHINE'S ON THE BLINK... I'M NOT SURE WHY... COULD BE THE STRAIN OF THE *LAST* TRIP THROUGH ROME—OR THE *NEXT* ONE THROUGH ROMAN *PALESTINE* AND *JUDAEA!*

THINGS *CAN* HAVE CAUSES IN THE FUTURE, YOU KNOW!

ANY TIME YOU TRY TO *TIME TRAVEL* THROUGH AN ERA OF *HOLY STORIES,* YOU JUST *KNOW* YOU'RE ASKING FOR *ENGINE TROUBLE!*

HM... NOTHING SEEMS WRONG HERE...

TAKE *MIRACLES,* FOR EXAMPLE... WHAT'S A *HISTORIAN* TO MAKE OF *MIRACLES??!!*

START, YOU ☆@#$ *MACHINE!!*

BUNT

WHOA!

BURP CHUF CHUF HUMMM

IT'S *RUNNING!* THIS IS.... *AWESOME!*

WELL, EVEN HISTORIANS ADMIT THAT *SOME* THINGS ARE *HARD* TO EXPLAIN!

WAIT'LL I TELL 'EM ABOUT THIS AT *TECH SUPPORT...*

THE CARTOON HISTORY OF THE UNIVERSE

Volume 12

"RENDER UNTO CAESAR"

T WAS A NEW DAY FOR ROME! THE REALM SPREAD FURTHER THAN EVER BEFORE... ROMAN WEALTH HAD NEVER BEEN GREATER... AND THE ROMAN TRADITION OF FREEDOM WAS NOW ALL BUT EXTINGUISHED...

ALTHOUGH THE GOVERNMENT *APPEARED* TO FOLLOW THE OLD REPUBLICAN ROUTINES, IN REALITY EVERYONE—SENATORS, CONSULS, CENSORS, PRAETORS, QUAESTORS, AND ALL—OBEYED *ONE MAN: CAESAR AUGUSTUS,* DICTATOR, EMPEROR, PERPETUAL TRIBUNE OF THE PEOPLE—OR, IF YOU PREFER, JUST PLAIN *PRINCEPS: THE FIRST.*

HAVING WIPED OUT ALL HIS ENEMIES, AUGUSTUS COULD NOW "CONSULT" WITH THE SENATE IN COMFORT.

WHAT DO YOU THINK?

WELL... WHAT DO YOU THINK?

BUT—WHAT DO YOU THINK?

AFTER YOU...

I ASKED FIRST...

EXCEPT FOR A LOYAL 5000-MAN PRAETORIAN GUARD, ALL ROME'S ARMIES WERE STATIONED ON THE IMPERIAL FRONTIERS: GERMANY, GAUL, EGYPT, ASIA, ETC....

FAR FROM THE IMPERIAL THROAT!

WITH THE GROSS NATIONAL PRODUCT OF EGYPT AT HIS PERSONAL DISPOSAL, AUGUSTUS COULD LAVISH THE CAPITAL WITH SPLENDID BUILDINGS, GAMES, AND CHEAP BREAD.

DO YOU THINK THAT WATCHING MEN FIGHT TO THE DEATH DESENSITIZES US TO VIOLENCE?

STAB SHRIEK... BURBLE...

OH... I DUNNO...

A PATRON OF THE ARTS, THE EMPEROR ENCOURAGED PATRIOTIC WRITERS LIKE LIVY AND VERGIL.

ROME IS GREAT, ROME IS REALLY GREAT, AND SO ON AND SO ON FOR 5000 MORE LINES...

BUT HE BANISHED THE POET OVID TO A DESERT ISLAND FOR HIS "IMMORAL" VERSE...

(BY AND LARGE, AUGUSTUS'S EFFORTS TO IMPROVE PUBLIC MORALS FLOPPED UTTERLY.)

NOT EVEN AN EMPEROR CAN LEGISLATE FAMILY VALUES!

AS ROME'S FIRST CITIZEN, AUGUSTUS HAD THE PLEASURE OF *CHOOSING THE RULERS* OF THE LITTLE KINGDOMS ON THE FRINGES OF THE EMPIRE. FOR INSTANCE, WHEN KING *HEROD OF JUDAEA* DIED IN *4 B.C.,* AUGUSTUS WAS EXECUTOR OF HIS ESTATE!

THE HERODIAN HEIRS APPEARED IN PERSON: PRINCE *ARCHELAUS,* WHO CLAIMED THE KINGDOM...

HEROD'S SURVIVING SISTER *SALOME* HAD ANOTHER IDEA...

A DELEGATION OF *JUDAEAN CITIZENS* HAD A THIRD OPINION.

HONEY, I KILLED THE KIDS!

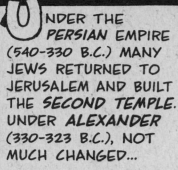

UNDER THE **PERSIAN** EMPIRE (540-330 B.C.) MANY JEWS RETURNED TO JERUSALEM AND BUILT THE **SECOND TEMPLE.** UNDER **ALEXANDER** (330-323 B.C.), NOT MUCH CHANGED...

AFTER HE DIED, THE **SELEUCID** DYNASTY OF SYRIA RULED, UNTIL, AROUND 170 B.C., THE SELEUCID KING TRIED TO FORCE ALL HIS SUBJECTS TO WORSHIP **ZEUS.**

HEY, GUYS! GOOD NEWS! I SACRIFICED TO ZEUS, AND IT REALLY WASN'T THAT BIG A DEAL!

SOMETIME IN THE 400S B.C., THE PERSIAN SHAH ISSUED ORDERS PUTTING JERUSALEM UNDER JEWISH RULE. AS THE WALLS ROSE, SO DID A QUESTION: WHO EXACTLY WAS A JEW, ANYWAY?

WHO'S IN?

AND WHO'S OUT?

NEHEMIAH THE GOVERNOR AND **EZRA THE SCRIBE** COMPILED A COMPLETE **FAMILY TREE** OF THE JEWS... CERTIFIED JEWS WHO HAD MARRIED PEOPLE **OFF THE LIST** WERE ORDERED TO **SEND THEM AWAY,** INCLUDING ANY KIDS.

OW! BETTER GO, HON'! THEY MEAN BUSINESS!

"I BEAT THEM... I PULLED THEIR HAIR..." — NEHEMIAH 13:25

THIS EARLY EXAMPLE OF ETHNIC CLEANSING DID LITTLE TO WIN THE GOOD WILL OF THE NEIGHBORS...

GROWL...

SNARL...

UM... DID WE BUILD THE WALL HIGH ENOUGH?

IN 170 B.C. (OR 169?), A PRIEST AND HIS FIVE SONS **BUTCHERED** THE FIRST JEW WHO DARED TO SACRIFICE TO ZEUS.

HAVE YOU FORGOTTEN THE *FIRST COMMANDMENT?*

HAVE *YOU* FORGOTTEN THE *SIXTH?*

CALLING THEMSELVES THE *MACCABEES*, OR HAMMERS, THE SONS LED A REVOLT THAT WON BACK ISRAELI CONTROL OF JERUSALEM...

IN 165, JUDAH MACCABEE, CHIEF OF THE FIVE, SMASHED THE STATUE OF ZEUS, HAD THE TEMPLE CLEANED UP, AND INVENTED THE FESTIVAL OF *HANNUKAH* TO COMMEMORATE THE EVENT.

THIS FAMILY, THE HASMONEANS* RULED FOR GENERATIONS, FIRST AS *HIGH PRIESTS*, LATER AS *KINGS* AND *QUEENS*...

NOTE: THIS WAS DURING THE TIME THAT ROME WAS RISING IN THE WEST!

*AFTER THE FIVE'S GRANDFATHER ASAMON

... BUT IN 69 B.C., A YOUNGER BROTHER, *ARISTOBULUS*, GRABBED THE THRONE FROM THE RIGHTFUL KING, *JOHN HYRCANUS*. TO KEEP FAMILY PEACE, HYRCANUS WAS LEFT ALIVE AND NAMED HIGH PRIEST.

IT SUITS YOU, BRO'! LITTLE TUCK HERE, LET OUT THE WAIST...

ENTER *ANTIPATER*, A WARRIOR FROM THE IDUMAEAN SOUTH, WHO BEFRIENDED JOHN HYRCANUS.

NEED ANY HELP?

AHH...

MAYBE?

TROMP TROMP TROMP

MAKING WAR ON ARISTOBULUS, ANTIPATER INVITED THE *ROMANS* IN TO HELP.

WELL...NO...NOT REALLY...NAH... TOO LATE, PAL!

IN 63 B.C., *POMPEY THE GREAT*, WITH ANTIPATER IN TOW, FORCED HIS WAY INTO JERUSALEM, KILLING THOUSANDS, AND HORRIFIED THE PRIESTS BY ENTERING THE TEMPLE'S FORBIDDEN *HOLY OF HOLIES*—THE INNER SANCTUM WHERE *MOST* RELIGIONS KEPT A STATUE OF THE GOD... SURPRISE!

THERE'S NOTHING HERE!

OY.

POMPEY MARCHED OFF, LEAVING JUDAEA UNDER JOHN HYRCANUS—AND ANTIPATER.

WAVE GOOD-BYE TO YOUR NEW FRIENDS!?

SPOOKIEST THING I EVER SAW, BY THE BEARD OF ZEUS...

(A FEW YEARS LATER, POMPEY'S PAL *CRASSUS* VISITED THE TEMPLE, TOO... HE MAY HAVE BEEN AWED BY THE IMAGELESS GOD, TOO, BUT NOT VERY... HE LOOTED THE TEMPLE TREASURY BEFORE MARCHING OFF TO DIE IN PARTHIA...)

WHAT? AN ARMY NEEDS CASH!

IN THE ROMAN CIVIL WARS, WHEN POMPEY FELL TO CAESAR, ANTIPATER DEFTLY *SWITCHED SIDES.*

NEED HELP, CAESAR?

HIS ENEMY ARISTOBULUS ALSO HOPED TO BEFRIEND CAESAR, BUT WAS *POISONED* BY ANTIPATER'S AGENTS AND EMBALMED IN A *TUB OF HONEY...*

VICTORY *IS* SWEET!

AFTER CAESAR'S ASSASSINATION, ANTIPATER'S SON *HEROD* BECAME MARK ANTONY'S LIEUTENANT...

WHEN ANTONY FELL TO *AUGUSTUS,* HEROD SHOWED HIMSELF JUST AS PLIANT AND ADAPTABLE AS HIS FATHER!

:AHEM: *AT YOUR* SERVICE, GUS!

HONEY, A COMMON INGREDIENT IN ANCIENT EGYPTIAN MEDICINE, DOES IN FACT KILL BACTERIA. (SAMPLES OVER 2500 YEARS OLD HAVE TURNED UP IN TOMBS.)

HAVE YOU EVER SEEN A PUTRID BEE?

BUT AS *EMBALMING FLUID?* THE MEDICAL HISTORIAN *GUIDO MAJNO* EXPERIMENTED BY IMMERSING PIECES OF RODENT MEAT IN HONEY FOR PERIODS OF TIME.

HE WRITES: "VERY SMALL PIECES MIGHT BE PRESERVED INDEFINITELY. BUT WITH LARGER PIECES, DEEP DOWN WHERE THE HONEY CANNOT REACH, PUTREFACTION IS RAMPANT, GAS DEVELOPS, AND THE RESULT IS A TERRIBLE WASTE OF WORK... THEY MUST HAVE BURIED HASMONAEAN (I.E., ARISTOBULOS) IN A HURRY."

AND HE WAS :CHOKE: ALL *GOOEY!!*

THE ROMANS APPOINTED HEROD *KING* OF *JUDAEA, IDUMEA* & ENVIRONS—*IF* HE COULD CONQUER IT!

PIECE OF MATZO!

SYRIA

JUDAEA

DEAD SEA

IDUMAEA

IN *37 B.C.*, HE ATTACKED JERUSALEM, AND FOR THE SECOND TIME IN 25 YEARS, HUMAN BLOOD SPLASHED THE TEMPLE COURTS...

HYRCANUS, BUDDY OF MY DAD! SORRY ABOUT ALL THIS! SORRY ABOUT YOUR DEAD BROTHER! SORRY YOU CAN'T BE KING! BUT WHAT SAY I *MARRY YOUR DAUGHTER?!*

DOUBLE-OY...

AFTER HIS VICTORY, HEROD RAISED A *GOLDEN EAGLE* ABOVE THE TEMPLE GATE—A SYMBOL OF ROME.

FOR THE NEXT *33 YEARS* HEROD RULED WITH A HARD HAND: *TAXING* HEAVILY, *OPPRESSING* MERCILESSLY, *BUILDING* SPLENDIDLY, AND DEDICATING WHOLE CITIES TO HIS ROMAN PATRON. AUGUSTUS REWARDED HIM WITH MORE TERRITORY!

YOU'RE A GOOD ROMAN, HEROD!

MANY PIOUS PATRIOTS LONGED FOR THE PRIEST-KING HASMONEANS AND *HATED* HEROD, HIS TOWNS FULL OF IDOLS, AND HIS GOLDEN EAGLE.

BESIDES, HE'S NOT *REALLY* JEWISH!

TRUE... HIS MOTHER WAS AN ARAB...

BUT THEN, WHAT WAS KING SOLOMON'S MOTHER...?

TO MAKE NICE, HEROD MARRIED *TWO* HASMONEANS: *MIRIAM*, DAUGHTER OF JOHN HYRCANUS, AND *MIRIAM*, GRANDDAUGHTER OF ARISTOBULUS. THIS DIDN'T WORK FOR A MINUTE...

HI... UM... HONEY!

SOB! *DON'T CALL ME THAT!!*

HE LOVED MIRIAM (ARISTOBULUS' GRANDDAUGHTER) MADLY, BUT THE FEELING WAS NOT MUTUAL!

WHY CAN'T YOU LOVE ME, HONEY?

I DON'T KNOW... IS IT BECAUSE YOU KILLED MY BROTHER? OR BECAUSE YOU KILLED MY UNCLE? OR BECAUSE YOUR FATHER KILLED MY GRAND-FATHER? OR BECAUSE YOU KEEP CALLING ME "HONEY?"

STILL, THEY HAD FIVE CHILDREN: TWO GIRLS AND THREE BOYS.

WHY DO I PUT UP WITH THIS??

BUT THE KIDS HATED HIM, TOO... SO, INCITED BY HIS SISTER SALOME, HE HAD MIRIAM AND THE TWO OLDER BOYS EXECUTED!

SHE TRIED TO POISON YOU, BROTHER... THIS IS SIMPLE SELF-DEFENSE!!

BUT, HEY, HE HAD EIGHT MORE WIVES AND PLENTY OF SONS! HE NAMED A NEW CROWN PRINCE, BUT THIS KID HATED HIM, TOO.

IT'S HARD TO BE THE KING!!

IN 4 B.C., ON HIS DEATHBED, HEROD HEARD THE NEWS THAT REBEL RABBIS HAD BEEN CAUGHT IN THE ACT OF CUTTING DOWN THE EAGLE OVER THE TEMPLE GATE.

HE ORDERED THEM TO BE BURNED ALIVE... ORDERED THE CURRENT CROWN PRINCE EXECUTED... ORDERED ALL THE LEADING CITIZENS OF JUDAEA TO BE ROUNDED UP AND SLAUGHTERED IMMEDIATELY AFTER HIS OWN DEATH.

NO ONE WILL MOURN ME, BUT I'LL MAKE 'EM WEEP!!

(ONLY THE FIRST TWO ORDERS WERE CARRIED OUT.)

AND SO DIED HEROD THE GREAT. HIS *WILL*, REVISED AT THE LAST MINUTE, PASSED THE CROWN TO HIS OLD-EST SURVIVING SON, *ARCHELAUS*, IF AUGUSTUS AGREED.

ARCHELAUS WENT STRAIGHT TO THE TEMPLE TO BUTTER UP THE MULTITUDE.

YES YES YES YES...

THAT NIGHT, ARCHELAUS' DINNER WAS DISTURBED BY *GROANS* AND *SHOUTS*.

JUSTICE OR DEATH!

JUSTICE OR DEATH!

JUSTICE OR DEATH!

REVOLUTIONARIES HAD SEIZED THE TEMPLE, DEMANDING PUNISHMENT FOR THE EXECUTIONERS OF THEIR FRIENDS, THE EAGLE STEALERS.

JUSTICE OR DEATH! JUSTICE OR DEATH!

WHEN NEGOTIATIONS FAILED, ARCHELAUS SENT IN THE TROOPS, AND ONCE AGAIN—

THE NEXT DAY, *ARCHELAUS* SAILED FOR ROME!

'BYE!

NOW ALL ISRAEL, IT SEEMS, LONGED FOR A *MESSIAH*: A *SAVIOR* WHO WOULD *DELIVER THE NATION* FROM HEROD'S HATED HOUSE AND THE ROMAN YOKE... ACROSS THE LAND, *WOMEN HEARD VOICES!!!*

THIS WAS THE POINT AT WHICH ARCHELAUS, SALOME, AND ALL ARGUED THEIR CASE BEFORE CAESAR AUGUSTUS!

AUGUSTUS'S JUDGMENT WAS **SOLOMONIC**: HE CHOPPED UP HEROD'S KINGDOM AND GAVE PIECES TO EVERYONE: JUDAEA FOR ARCHELAUS, ANOTHER CHUNK FOR HIS HALF-BROTHER, A CITY FOR SALOME, ETC....

THERE WERE SO DARN MANY OF THEM TO KEEP HAPPY...

BUT SALOME WAS *RIGHT*: ARCHELAUS *WAS* A SHNOOK. REBELLIONS CONTINUED... WOULD BE MESSIAHS WERE *EVERYWHERE!*

WOE! REPENT!!

IN THE YEAR 6, AUGUSTUS *DEPOSED* ARCHELAUS AND BANISHED HIM FOREVER TO GAUL.

I TRIED I TRIED I TRIED

EAT SNAILS!

JUDAEA CAME UNDER **DIRECT ROMAN CONTROL** FOR THE FIRST TIME...

UM... WE DID ASK FOR THIS, RIGHT?

NOW AUGUSTUS COULD TURN TO SOME OTHER PRESSING ISSUES, LIKE A WAR IN *GERMANY* THAT DESTROYED *THREE ROMAN LEGIONS* IN THE DEPTHS OF THE FOREST...

HERMANNSDENKMAL, 19TH CENTURY GERMAN MONUMENT TO THE ANCIENT VICTORY.

NOT TO MENTION THE SITUATION IN HIS *OWN HOUSEHOLD*...

MY LEGIONS... BRING BACK MY LEGIONS...

DARLING!! AHEM!!

CRASH

BUMP

JIGGLE

STARTING WITH JULIUS, THE FIRST FEW CAESARS ALL HAD *TROUBLE GETTING SONS*...

THE FAMILY HAS LAZY SPERM, OR SOMETHING...

(AUGUSTUS WAS JULIUS'S NEPHEW, REMEMBER.)

AUGUSTUS HAD JUST ONE CHILD, *JULIA*, FROM HIS FIRST MARRIAGE. ON HER SHOULDERS* RESTED THE EMPIRE'S FUTURE.

UM... DARLING... COULD YOU DO ME A TEENTSY FAVOR?

*OR SOMEWHERE

FIRST, AUGUSTUS MARRIED HER TO HER COUSIN *MARCELLUS*, BUT MARCELLUS DIED YOUNG...

UM... ANOTHER FAVOR?

HUSBAND #2 WAS AUGUSTUS'S RIGHT-HAND MAN *MARCUS AGRIPPA*. THEY HAD FIVE CHILDREN, BUT THE TWO OLDER BOYS, CAESAR'S HEIRS, ALSO DIED YOUNG.

NOW WHAT, DAD??

WHO WAS LEFT? WELL, AUGUSTUS'S SECOND WIFE *LIVIA* HAD A SON FROM *HER* FIRST MARRIAGE...

EXCUSE ME, ARE YOU FOLLOWING THIS?

YEH... HOW COME YOU AND I DON'T HAVE ANY KIDS?

THIS WAS *TIBERIUS*, A SOUR SORT OF FELLOW, WHO HAD SPENT THE LAST TEN YEARS SULKING FAR FROM ROME.

I HAD A HARD CHILDHOOD! LEAVE ME ALONE!!

ONE LAST FAVOR, JULIA....

AUGUSTUS COMMANDED TIBERIUS TO *DIVORCE* HIS *WIFE*, MARRY *JULIA*, AND *INHERIT THE EMPIRE*.

I MISS MY FIRST WIFE...

GO CONQUER ENGLAND AND BRING ME WHISKEY!!

JULIA HAD HAD ENOUGH! DRINKING HEAVILY, SHE STARTED HAVING *ADULTEROUS ALL-NIGHTERS*—IN VARIOUS *PUBLIC BUILDINGS*...

WOW!

WILL THIS ANNOY DAD!

AUGUSTUS BANISHED HER TO A SMALL, ROCKY ISLAND WITHOUT ALCOHOLIC BEVERAGES.

IN *14*, AUGUSTUS DIED, AND TIBERIUS DULY BECAME EMPEROR. HIS FIRST SPEECH TO THE SENATE WAS FAMOUS FOR ITS *DIRECTNESS*.

COMPARED TO THE EMPEROR, YOU'RE ALL *SCUM*... DON'T FORGET TO KEEP CRINGING...

TIBERIUS HATED POLITICS... ENTERTAINMENT... THE SOCIAL ROUND... HE PREFERRED TO BE ALONE ON THE ISLE OF *CAPRI*, WHERE HE COULD INDULGE HIS PEDOPHILIC PREDILECTIONS— AND ROME HATED HIM BACK!

GO AWAY!!

BUT FROM A *DISTANCE* HE DIDN'T LOOK SO BAD... HIS ADMINISTRATION WAS EFFICIENT, AND THANKS TO HIS THRIFT HE HAD NO NEED TO BLEED THE PROVINCES DRY. *JUDAEA*, FOR EXAMPLE, WAS FAIRLY QUIET UNDER TIBERIUS (14-37).

AHHHH...

IN THE YEAR *21*, TIBERIUS APPOINTED A NEW PROCURATOR FOR PALESTINE: *PONTIUS PILATE.*

GO... TRY TO KEEP THEM REASONABLY QUIET, BUT DON'T BREAK THE BANK DOIN' IT...

YO!

IN THE HISTORIES, ONLY TWO OF PILATE'S ACTS ARE MENTIONED, BOTH RATHER TO HIS CREDIT...

FIRST, ALTHOUGH HE ORDERED ROMAN EMBLEMS HUNG IN THE JERUSALEM TEMPLE...

SHRIEK!! GRAVEN IMAGES! FORBIDDEN!!!

TUT TUT... MERELY A FORMALITY... WE DO IT EVERYWHERE... REALLY...

HE REMOVED THEM TO SPARE LOCAL FEELINGS.

YOU'LL HAVE TO KILL ALL OF US!

WOA!

TAKE 'EM DOWN!

SECOND, HE BUILT A *50-MILE AQUEDUCT* TO BRING WATER TO JERUSALEM—PAID FOR FROM *TEMPLE FUNDS.*

DRINK?

AGH! UNCLEAN! SACRILEGE!

OTHERWISE, SAY THE HISTORIES, *NOTHING HAPPENED* IN JUDAEA DURING HIS TENURE... WHICH JUST GOES TO SHOW, HISTORIANS DON'T ALWAYS CATCH EVERYTHING...

218

"IT IS WRITTEN"

IN THOSE DAYS, THE BIBLICAL TRADITION OF *PROPHECY* STILL LIVED...
THE JEWS LONGED FOR *ELIJAH'S* RETURN... THEY REMEMBERED
THAT *ISAIAH* HAD PROMISED A SAVIOR FOR ISRAEL... AND NOW,
DESPITE THE DANGER, A NUMBER OF *FREE-LANCE PREACHERS* ADDED
THEIR VOICES TO THE MAINSTREAM OF JEWISH THOUGHT...
HERE'S ONE: *JOHN*, WHO TAUGHT THAT *SINS* COULD BE *WASHED*
AWAY BY A *BATH* IN THE *JORDAN RIVER*.

219

FOR AT LEAST ONE PERSON, *JESHUA BEN JOSEPH*, BAPTISM DELIVERED THE **ENLIGHTENMENT EXPERIENCE.**

LIKE OTHERS WHO HAVE SEEN "IT," JESHUA NEEDED TO HEAD FOR THE WILDERNESS TO THINK THINGS OVER...

HOW ABOUT "THANK YOU?"

TOO MUCH!

YOU *COULD* BE KING OF THE WORLD!

GET BACK!!

AFTER A WHILE, HE RETURNED TO RECRUIT FOLLOWERS—FROM JOHN THE BAPTIST'S FLOCK!

ANDREW... FOLLOW *ME...*

UM... WHAT DO YOU OFFER?

STRANGELY ENOUGH, THE BAPTIST DIDN'T SEEM TO MIND.

HOW ABOUT— *ETERNAL LIFE?*

WOA! DEAL!!

IF IT'S OF *GOD*, IT'S *GOOD*... OTHERWISE, IT WON'T WORK! THAT'S HOW I SEE IT...

GLUB

YUP. JUST GIVE ME A HAIR SHIRT, AND I'M HAPPY!!

221

IT BECAME CLEAR THAT JESHUA HAD THE *TOUCH:* HE COULD CURE THE AFFLICTED, OR AT LEAST *EXORCISE* THEIR *DEMONS...* ✱

PHEW! I FEEL BETTER...

COME OUT!!

PEOPLE BEGAN TO SEEK HIM OUT...

JESHUA BEN JOSEPH?

JUST PAST THE POSSESSED PIGS, AND LEFT AT THE LEPERS...

SOON THERE WAS SO MUCH WORK THAT JESHUA HAD TO DEPUTIZE *TWELVE ASSISTANT EXORCISTS.*

SIMON, WE'LL CALL YOU *"ROCK..."*

JAMES AND JOHN, YOU'LL BE *THUNDERSONS...*

MM! SOUNDS *SWEDISH!*

HOW 'BOUT *ME,* RABBI? DO *I* GET A NICKNAME, TOO? I WANT A NICKNAME!

AH! *JUDAS!* YOU CAN BE *ISCARIOT!*

WHICH MEANS?

THAT YOU CARRY A *CONCEALED DAGGER...*

ALSO, YOU CAN BE *TREASURER...*

THANK YOU THANK YOU...

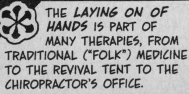

THE *LAYING ON OF HANDS* IS PART OF MANY THERAPIES, FROM TRADITIONAL ("FOLK") MEDICINE TO THE REVIVAL TENT TO THE CHIROPRACTOR'S OFFICE.

EVEN LAYING ON OF FEET!?

POP

ONCE I TOOK MY LOWER BACK PROBLEM TO A MODERN, BOARD-CERTIFIED ORTHOPEDIC M.D. TYPE. DURING OUR CONVERSATION, I SAID—

WHATEVER YOU THINK OF *CHIROPRACTORS,* THEY *DO* PRACTICE LAYING ON OF HANDS, WHICH HAS SOME HEALING POWER...

THE M.D. BACKED AWAY FROM ME TO THE FARTHEST CORNER OF THE ROOM!

¿ AHEM ⸮ WE LIKE TO THINK THAT ⸮ COUGH ⸮ *MODERN MEDICINE* PROVIDES A... AH... *CARING ENVIRONMENT...*

BUT THE HEALER WAS ALSO A *RABBI*, OR TEACHER. HIS TEACHING COVERED A LOT OF GROUND, AND IN FACT IT SOMETIMES SEEMED AS IF THERE WERE *SEVERAL JESHUAS:*

THE PREACHER OF PEACE, LOVE, AND *FORGIVENESS:*

BLESSED ARE THE *MEEK*...

TURN THE OTHER *CHEEK*...

YOU'LL FIND IF YOU WILL *SEEK*...

THE JUDGMENTAL, FURIOUS *THUNDERER:*

WOE UNTO YE, HYPOCRITES!

THE RABBI AMONG RABBIS:

BUT ACCORDING TO I SAMUEL CH. 8, PARA. 14, SUBPARA. 9, IT'S *OKAY* FOR MY PEOPLE TO *STEAL GRAIN* ON THE *SABBATH*, IF THEY'RE HUNGRY.

BUT BUT BUT—

THE VISIONARY:

THE *KINGDOM OF GOD* IS LIKE A *MUSTARD SEED*...

?

THE ICONOCLAST:

NO, WE DON'T WASH OUR HANDS BEFORE MEALS!

EW. WHY NOT?

IT'S NOT WHAT GOES *INTO* YOUR MOUTH THAT DEFILES YOU, IT'S WHAT *COMES OUT!!*

PUKE AND DROOL — I KNOW WHAT YOU MEAN...

NO, YOU DON'T!

THE MEDICAL MAN:

AFTER *ONE* DEMON GOES OUT, IT USUALLY COMES BACK WITH *SEVEN FRIENDS*...

THE COMMIE:

IT IS EASIER FOR A CAMEL TO PASS THROUGH THE EYE OF A NEEDLE THAN FOR A RICH MAN TO ENTER THE KINGDOM OF HEAVEN!!

AND — YOU MAKE THE CALL!!

ONLY BY *DRINKING MY BLOOD* AND *EATING MY FLESH* SHALL YE BE SAVED!

MM!

? ?

IS THIS A *RELIGION*, A *POLITICAL PARTY*, OR SOME *WEIRD KIND* OF *MEDICAL SCHOOL*?

EVEN THE TWELVE WERE CONFUSED!

FOR EXAMPLE, THIS "KINGDOM OF GOD." WAS THE RABBI PROMISING TO RESTORE A RIGHTEOUS THRONE TO ISRAEL? WAS HE CLAIMING TO BE THE *MESSIAH* HIMSELF?

JUST IN CASE, I'M ARMED!

YOU *ARE* A ROCK!

TO SOUND OUT HIS POLITICS, SOMEONE ASKED HIM A QUESTION ABOUT *TAX POLICY*.

RABBI, SHOULD WE PAY TAXES BOTH TO THE *ROMANS* AND THE *TEMPLE*?

THE DOUBLE WHAMMY IS A KILLER!

THE FAMOUS REPLY:

RENDER UNTO CAESAR WHAT IS CAESAR'S; RENDER UNTO GOD WHAT IS GOD'S...

THAT WOULD CERTAINLY *SEEM* TO SETTLE THE QUESTION IN FAVOR OF *CAESAR*...

UNTIL YOU STARTED THINKING ABOUT IT, THAT IS!

WAIT A MINUTE — WHAT *ISN'T* GOD'S?

WAIT... I'LL THINK OF SOMETHING...

THAT WOULDN'T SEEM TO LEAVE MUCH FOR CAESAR...

WHAT *DID* HE MEAN?

WHAT DID HE MEAN?

JESHUA ALSO HAD A SORT OF *13TH DISCIPLE*, A WELL-TO-DO WOMAN NAMED *MARY MAGDALENE*.

WHAT'S THE ATTRACTION, HONEY?

EVER SINCE HE RAISED MY BROTHER LAZARUS FROM THE DEAD, IT'S BEEN *MAGIC* BETWEEN US...

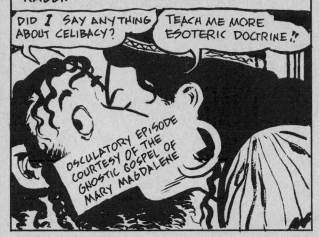

ACCORDING TO SOME TRADITIONS, MARY MAGDALENE HAD A *VERY SPECIAL* RELATIONSHIP TO THE RABBI.

DID *I* SAY ANYTHING ABOUT CELIBACY?

TEACH ME MORE ESOTERIC DOCTRINE!!

OSCULATORY EPISODE COURTESY OF THE GNOSTIC GOSPEL OF MARY MAGDALENE

ONE NIGHT, SHE WAS MASSAGING HIM WITH THE MOST *EXPENSIVE* OINTMENT MONEY COULD BUY...

JUDAS, WHO HANDLED THE RABBINICAL *FINANCES*, WAS OUTRAGED.

RABBI! WE COULD *SELL* THAT GUNK AND GIVE THE MONEY TO THE *POOR!*

PLEASE TRY TO BE *FISCALLY RESPONSIBLE!!*

OH, YOU'LL *ALWAYS* HAVE THE *POOR*... BUT YOU *WON'T* ALWAYS HAVE *ME*... AAAH... DO THAT THING WITH YOUR HAIR AGAIN...

"YOU'LL ALWAYS HAVE THE POOR?" WHAT KIND OF KINGDOM OF GOD IS *THAT??* CAN IT POSSIBLY BE THAT OUR RABBI IS JUST ANOTHER LUXURY-LOVING *POWER-TRIPPER??*

WELL, *WAS* HE THE MESSIAH, OR *WASN'T* HE? IT WASN'T EASY TO GET A DIRECT ANSWER!

WHEN THE SON OF MAN COMES, IT'LL BE A *BIG* SURPRISE!

WHY DOESN'T HE JUST SAY STRAIGHT OUT?

WHERE HAVE YOU *BEEN* THE LAST 30-40 YEARS?

BUT AS THE BAND PREPARED TO VISIT JERUSALEM FOR PASSOVER, THE DISCIPLES WERE LEANING TOWARD *"YES!"*

:SIGH: I CAN SEE CLEARLY WHERE THIS IS GOING...

AN IDIOT COULD SEE WHERE THIS IS GOING...

I CAN'T SEE WHERE THIS IS GOING...

THIS MESSIAH BUSINESS WAS *DANGEROUS*, AND JESHUA WAS SHOWING DEFINITE SIGNS OF *STRAIN*...

NO FRUIT? ☆※@ FIG TREE! I'M *HUNGRY!* TAKE THAT!

BUT MASTER... IT'S ONLY *APRIL*...

HRRFF! THAT'S BETTER! NOW GO "APPROPRIATE" ME A YOUNG DONKEY! IT IS WRITTEN *!!*

YESSIR YESSIR YESSIR!

NOW THEY WERE FILLED WITH HOPE! HADN'T THE PROPHET ISAIAH HIMSELF PROMISED THAT THE MESSIAH WOULD ARRIVE ON A *JUVENILE BURRO?*

226

AT LAST, THEY BEHELD THE MOTHER TEMPLE, WITH ITS GOLDEN GATES, TEEMING COURTYARDS, COLONNADES FULL OF MERCHANTS, INCENSE, AND OFFERINGS, AND BUREAUS OF FOREIGN EXCHANGE...

FOR SOME REASON, IT WAS THE MONEY-CHANGERS THAT REALLY SET HIM OFF—

IT WASN'T LONG BEFORE THE AUTHORITIES DECIDED TO GET RID OF THE TROUBLEMAKER.

THIS MESSIAH STUFF IS POLITICAL DYNAMITE!!

BUT WE CAN'T BUST HIM BY DAY, OR WE'LL HAVE ANOTHER SLAUGHTER IN THE MARKET!!

BUT HOW CAN WE *FIND* HIM IN THE MIDDLE OF THE NIGHT?

I'LL HELP!

THE MAN IS A MENACE TO SOCIETY!

JUDAS IDENTIFIED JESHUA TO THE ARRESTING OFFICERS WITH A KISS...

HERE HE IS — STILL SMELLS LIKE THAT ☆©#$ OINTMENT!!

SMIRT

IN THE STRUGGLE, SIMON CUT OFF THE EAR OF THE HIGH PRIEST'S SERVANT...

THE NEXT THING THEY KNEW, JESHUA HAD BEEN *TRIED, CONVICTED, TORTURED,* AND, BY ORDER OF PONTIUS PILATE HIMSELF, *CRUCIFIED* BETWEEN TWO COMMON THIEVES...

GUYS — THIS IS *NOT* GOING ACCORDING TO PLAN!!

HOW CAN YOU BE SURE?

HE COULDN'T BE THAT IMPORTANT, IF THEY LET ALL HIS FOLLOWERS GO...

THE BODY WAS CUT DOWN EARLY BECAUSE *FRIDAY NIGHT* WAS COMING—NO EXECUTIONS ON THE SABBATH—AND INTERRED IN A CAVE WITH A ROCK OVER ITS MOUTH.

SUNDAY MORNING—

THE BODY'S GONE!!

MARY MAGDALENE WAS THE FIRST TO SAY IT—

HE'S *ALIVE!* I SAW HIM!! HE *ROSE* FROM THE *DEAD!!* HE LOOKED JUST LIKE THE GARDENER, BUT...

NO! WHAT? WHAT DID HE SAY?

ACCORDING TO ONE TRADITION, AN *ARGUMENT* NOW BROKE OUT—

HE SAID—

WAIT! ARE *WE MEN* GOING TO TAKE THE *WORD* OF *GOD* FROM A :SHUDDER: PATRONIZE :SNEER: *WOMAN??*

AT THIS POINT, MARY M'S NAME VANISHES FROM THE BIBLE!

IF ANYONE'S GOING TO SEE HIM, IT'LL BE *US!!*

SOON...

AFTERNOON, GENTLEMEN!

HEY!‼ DID YOU SEE WHO *THAT* WAS?!!

WHO?

ELVIS... IT WAS ELVIS...

WE PASS OVER THE NEXT COUPLE OF MONTHS... *WHATEVER* HAPPENED DURING THAT TIME, JESHUA'S REMAINING ELEVEN DISCIPLES STUCK TOGETHER...

THEY RETURNED TO THE TEMPLE TO PREACH THE GOSPEL: JESHUA HAD *DIED* ON THE CROSS, *RISEN* FROM THE DEAD, AND *ASCENDED* TO HEAVEN—BUT HE MIGHT COME BACK AT ANY TIME!!!!

REPENT! AND BE BAPTIZED IN HIS NAME!

GAH! THEM AGAIN!

SOAP

AND GRADUALLY, THE FOLLOWERS OF *THE WAY,* AS THEY CALLED THEMSELVES, ATTRACTED CONVERTS...

ROME, A FEW YEARS LATER

IN THE YEAR 37, THE EMPEROR TIBERIUS PASSED AWAY... THE STINGY, SOUR OLD TYRANT WAS REPLACED BY HIS CHARMING YOUNG NEPHEW GAIUS, NICK-NAMED **CALIGULA**, WHO SHOWERED THE DELIRIOUS ROMANS WITH THE RICHES HIS UNCLE HAD HOARDED!

LET THE PARTY BEGIN!!

WHATEVER YOU SAY!!

ALAS, CALIGULA WAS *DEMENTED*. HE CON-SORTED WITH HIS OWN SISTERS... MADE LOVE TO HIS DINNER GUESTS' WIVES... AND OFTEN BURST INTO *INAPPROPRIATE LAUGHTER*.

AHAHAHAHAHAHAHA HAHAHAHAHAHA HEOOHOOHOOHEEHEEHEEE...

WHAT IS IT, SIRE?

I WAS JUST LOOKING AT YOUR *NECK* AND THINKING I COULD HAVE IT *SLIT* WITH A SINGLE WORD... UH-HUH- *HAHA*... YOU LAUGH TOO... *HA HA HA*...

HEH HEH

AMONG CALIGULA'S MANY INSANE AND EXPENSIVE PROJECTS WAS A FULL-SCALE "INVASION OF BRITAIN" THAT MARCHED TO THE ENGLISH CHANNEL—AND *BACK*.

RIGHT, THEN! SCOOP UP AS MANY SEASHELLS AS YOU CAN!! THEY'LL LOOK GREAT IN A PARADE!

AFTER WASTING UNTOLD WEALTH AND KILLING MORE CLOSE FRIENDS THAN NECESSARY, CALIGULA WAS MURDERED BY ONE OF HIS GUARDS IN THE YEAR 41.

CURED! MY HEADACHES ARE CURED!!

THE PRAETORIAN GUARDS PROWLED THROUGH THE PALACE LOOKING FOR A NEW EMPEROR...

BEHIND A CURTAIN QUIVERED *CLAUDIUS*, A ROYAL COUSIN WHO HAD SURVIVED CALIGULA BY FEIGNING *FEEBLE-MINDEDNESS*...

CONGRATULATIONS! YOU'RE IT!

SHADDUP!

WH-WH-WHO, ME? OH, N-NO... I MEAN, NO THANK Y-YOU!

DRAGGED TO THE PRAETORIAN CAMP, CLAUDIUS RECEIVED THEIR SALUTE!

HAIL, CAESAR!

J-J-JUST DON'T KILL ME, P-PLEASE...

232

SUDDENLY, THE **SENATE**, SO LONG DORMANT, DECIDED THAT NOW WAS A GOOD TIME TO BRING BACK THE **REPUBLIC!**

SENATORS‼ SHALL WE NOT TAKE OUR STAND AS **MEN**?

CLAUDIUS'S FRIEND **HEROD AGRIPPA**— GRANDSON OF HEROD THE GREAT—RAN BACK AND FORTH, MEDIATING THE SQUABBLE BETWEEN CLAUDIUS AND THE SENATE.

GENTLEMEN... GENTLEMEN... STOP THIS FOOLISH- NESS... AND CLAUDIUS WILL LET YOU LIVE... PROBABLY...

IN THE END, THE SENATE AVERTED CIVIL WAR BY ACCEPTING CLAUDIUS.

AS I SAID—WE TAKE OUR STAND AS RICH, OLD, SUBMISSIVE MEN‼

HAIL CAESAR!

ROME'S GREATEST ACHIEVEMENT DURING CLAUDIUS'S 13-YEAR REIGN WAS THE **CONQUEST OF BRITAIN.** IN 43, THE ROMANS FOUNDED **LONDON.**

NOW SAY "PIP PIP" AND LOOK SUPER- CILIOUS...

ROME'S MOST EFFECTIVE COMMANDER IN BRITAIN, **VESPASIAN,** WILL TURN UP AGAIN IN THIS STORY.

PIP PIP

AND **HEROD AGRIPPA** WAS REWARDED FOR HIS NEGOTIATING SKILL BY THE RETURN OF MOST OF HIS GRANDPA'S KINGDOM...

HEY! *I'M* THE MESSIAH‼

JESUS CHRIST

THESE WERE CRUCIAL YEARS FOR THE FOLLOWERS OF *THE WAY.* AT FIRST, THE GROUP WAS JUST ANOTHER JEWISH SECT WITH SOME UNORTHODOX PRACTICES, SUCH AS NOT WASHING BEFORE MEALS, AND *SPEAKING IN TONGUES,* WHICH THEY CALLED "POSSESSION BY THE HOLY SPIRIT..."

SOME ROMANS, CURIOUS ABOUT LOCAL BELIEFS, INVITED SIMON THE ROCK TO PREACH AT AN OFFICER'S HOME...

SIMON AGONIZED ALL NIGHT...

AFTER A VISION OF PORK CHOPS, SIMON ACCEPTED THE INVITATION.

THE RESULTS CAME AS A COMPLETE SURPRISE!

SHANANANA, SHANANANANA... GET A JOB...

SHEDOOP 'N' SHOOBEE DOOP!

HEYBOP A REE BOP!!

CONCLUDING THAT THE HOLY SPIRIT COULD POSSESS **ANYONE**, SIMON BAPTIZED THE LOT OF THEM...

THIS IS AMAZING!

AND HUSTLED BACK TO JERUSALEM WITH THE NEWS!

GUYS! THE GENTILES ARE EATIN' IT UP!!!

BUT SUCCESS DIDN'T COME SO EASILY... FOR ONE THING, THE SECT KEPT CHALLENGING **TRADITIONAL AUTHORITY**... AS WHEN A CONVERT NAMED **STEPHEN** INSULTED THE HIGH PRIESTS TO THEIR FACES.

YOU WOULDN'T KNOW THE TRUTH IF IT **BIT** YOU!

FOR THIS, STEPHEN WAS IMMEDIATELY STONED TO DEATH.

HERE...HOLD MY COAT...

BONK BONK THUD

HOUSE-TO-HOUSE SEARCHES BEGAN... BELIEVERS WERE JAILED... JAMES THE APOSTLE WAS EXECUTED ON ORDERS OF HEROD AGRIPPA...

BUT PLEASE... ONE CLEAN WHACK... NONE OF THIS LINGERING ROMAN CRUCIFIXION STUFF... ECH!

O.K...

BUT *SAUL*, ONE OF THE PERSECUTORS, HAD A VISION ON THE WAY TO DAMASCUS...

WHY DO YOU PERSECUTE ME — *HAH?!*

HEH... MADE YOU LOOK!

:GASP: *I CAN'T SEE!*

DON'T EVER LOOK STRAIGHT AT THE SUN LIKE THAT, CHILD...

WITHOUT AUTHORIZATION FROM JERUSALEM, SAUL ANNOUNCED IN DAMASCUS THAT JESHUA WAS THE *SON OF GOD*...

I *SAW* HIM!? WELL... NOT EXACTLY, BUT...

BOO!

SSSS!

GET OUTA HEAH!

HE ANNOYED THE SYRIAN JEWS SO MUCH THAT HE HAD TO FLEE BY NIGHT.

IN A BASKET OVER THE WALL... HOW HUMILIATIN'!

BUT BACK IN JERUSALEM, THE APOSTLES WOULDN'T LET HIM INTO THE CONGREGATION!

I LIKE YOU NOW... REALLY!

WE DOUBT IT.!!

NOTHING DAUNTED, SAUL LEFT TOWN TO PREACH THE GOSPEL ELSEWHERE—AND HE GOT *RESULTS*, AMONG THE *GREEKS* AS WELL AS THE JEWS.

THIS RAISED A TICKLISH PROBLEM: DID THE *GREEK CONVERTS* HAVE TO OBEY THE *JEWISH LAWS?*

A SIMPLE MATTER OF AVOIDING *PORK*, CELEBRATING SOME NEW HOLIDAYS, KEEPING TWO SETS OF DISHES...

OH... AND THE *MEN* ALL HAVE TO BE *CIRCUMCISED*...

WHAT?

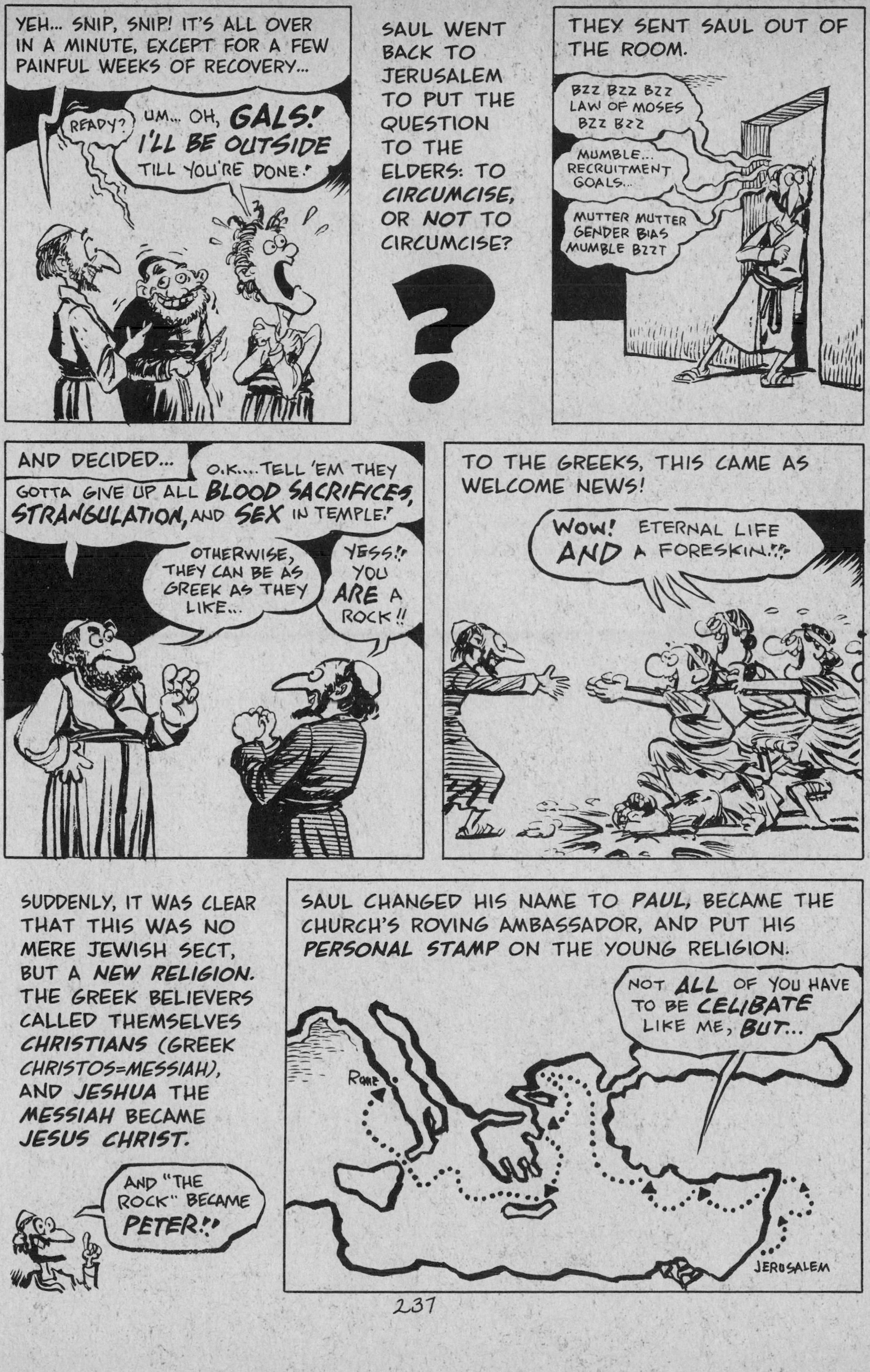
YEH... SNIP, SNIP! IT'S ALL OVER IN A MINUTE, EXCEPT FOR A FEW PAINFUL WEEKS OF RECOVERY...
READY?
UM... OH, GALS! I'LL BE OUTSIDE TILL YOU'RE DONE!
SAUL WENT BACK TO JERUSALEM TO PUT THE QUESTION TO THE ELDERS: TO CIRCUMCISE, OR NOT TO CIRCUMCISE?
?
THEY SENT SAUL OUT OF THE ROOM.
BZZ BZZ BZZ LAW OF MOSES BZZ BZZ
MUMBLE... RECRUITMENT GOALS...
MUTTER MUTTER GENDER BIAS MUMBLE BZZT
AND DECIDED...
O.K.... TELL 'EM THEY GOTTA GIVE UP ALL BLOOD SACRIFICES, STRANGULATION, AND SEX IN TEMPLE!
OTHERWISE, THEY CAN BE AS GREEK AS THEY LIKE...
YESS!! YOU ARE A ROCK!!
TO THE GREEKS, THIS CAME AS WELCOME NEWS!
WOW! ETERNAL LIFE AND A FORESKIN!!!
SUDDENLY, IT WAS CLEAR THAT THIS WAS NO MERE JEWISH SECT, BUT A NEW RELIGION. THE GREEK BELIEVERS CALLED THEMSELVES CHRISTIANS (GREEK CHRISTOS=MESSIAH), AND JESHUA THE MESSIAH BECAME JESUS CHRIST.
AND "THE ROCK" BECAME PETER!!
SAUL CHANGED HIS NAME TO PAUL, BECAME THE CHURCH'S ROVING AMBASSADOR, AND PUT HIS PERSONAL STAMP ON THE YOUNG RELIGION.
NOT ALL OF YOU HAVE TO BE CELIBATE LIKE ME, BUT...
ROME
JERUSALEM

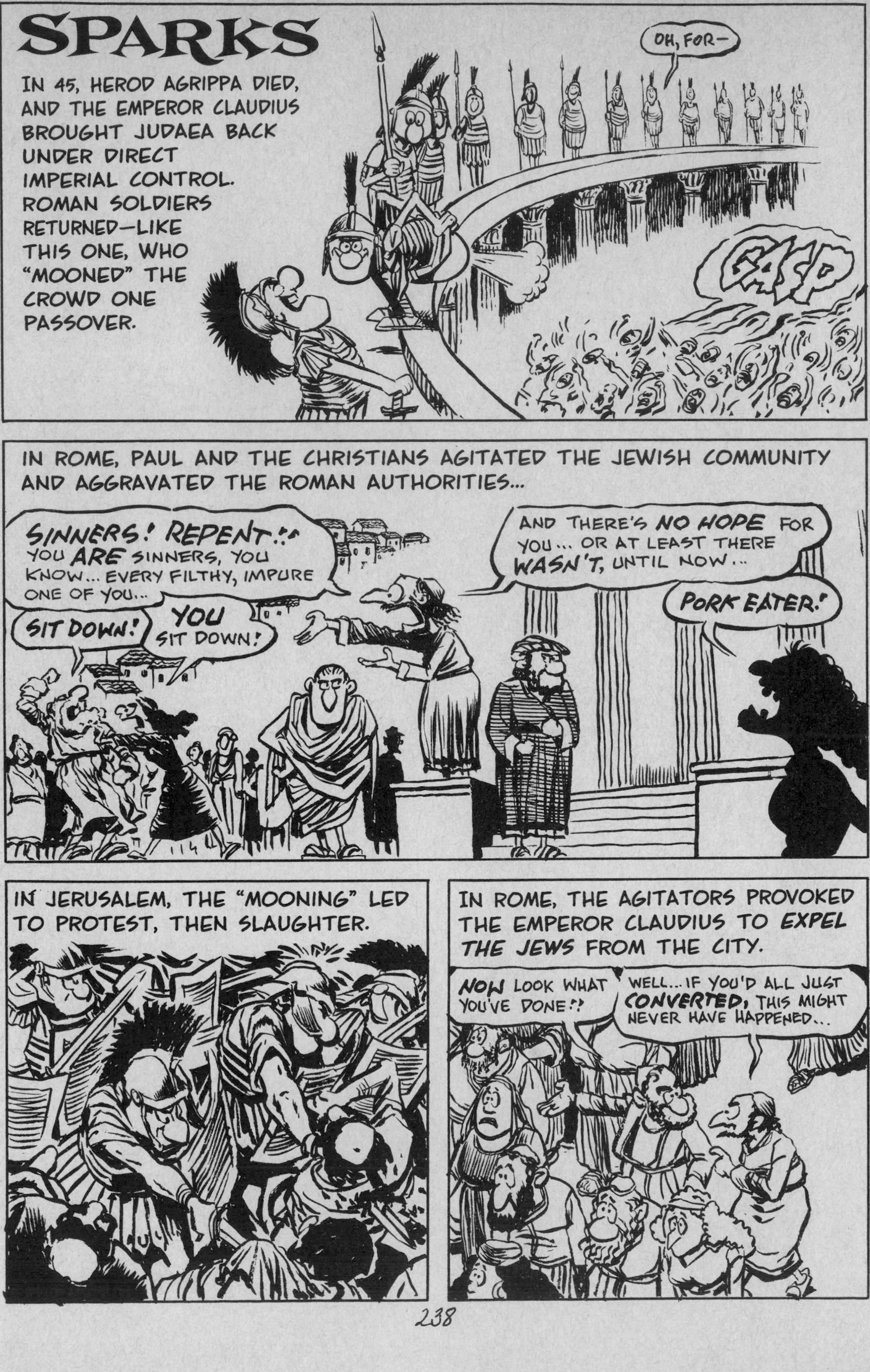
SPARKS
IN 45, HEROD AGRIPPA DIED, AND THE EMPEROR CLAUDIUS BROUGHT JUDAEA BACK UNDER DIRECT IMPERIAL CONTROL. ROMAN SOLDIERS RETURNED—LIKE THIS ONE, WHO "MOONED" THE CROWD ONE PASSOVER.
OH, FOR—
GASP
IN ROME, PAUL AND THE CHRISTIANS AGITATED THE JEWISH COMMUNITY AND AGGRAVATED THE ROMAN AUTHORITIES...
SINNERS! REPENT!!! YOU ARE SINNERS, YOU KNOW... EVERY FILTHY, IMPURE ONE OF YOU...
SIT DOWN!
YOU SIT DOWN!
AND THERE'S NO HOPE FOR YOU... OR AT LEAST THERE WASN'T, UNTIL NOW...
PORK EATER!
IN JERUSALEM, THE "MOONING" LED TO PROTEST, THEN SLAUGHTER.
IN ROME, THE AGITATORS PROVOKED THE EMPEROR CLAUDIUS TO EXPEL THE JEWS FROM THE CITY.
NOW LOOK WHAT YOU'VE DONE!?
WELL... IF YOU'D ALL JUST CONVERTED, THIS MIGHT NEVER HAVE HAPPENED...

IN 54, A BAD MUSHROOM FELLED CLAUDIUS, AND ROME HAD A NEW EMPEROR: THE YOUNG, DISSOLUTE *NERO*—AND HIS MOTHER *AGRIPPINA*.

STRAIGHTEN YOUR WREATH!

SIT UP!

AS USUAL ROMAN LUXURY MEANT PROVINCIAL POVERTY! IN JUDAEA, HIGH TAXES CREATED UNREST, ARRESTS, AND EXECUTIONS.

CATCH 'EM AND KILL 'EM SLOWLY— THAT'S THE ROMAN WAY...

IN ROME, NERO PUT ON A GOOD SHOW. HE GAVE PUBLIC PERFORMANCES, AND NOT JUST ON GUITAR. A HUGE AUDIENCE WITNESSED HIS MARRIAGE TO HIS SLAVE *DORYPHORUS*, WITH NERO IN THE ROLE OF THE *BRIDE*...

IF YOU CAN'T DO IT IN PUBLIC, YOU SHOULDN'T DO IT AT ALL!

BY THE WAY, WHERE'S YOUR MOM?

OH, WE HAVEN'T SEEN HER FOR A WHILE, POOR WOMAN.

HE ALSO *MURDERED* HIS OWN *MOTHER*...

IN JUDAEA, ROME STRIPPED WHOLE CITIES OF WEALTH... PEOPLE TOOK TO THE HILLS... THE GOVERNOR ARRESTED REBEL RINGLEADERS—AND THEN LET THEM *BUY* THEIR WAY OUT OF JAIL...

THESE ROMANS ARE *CRAZY!*

..12, ...13... Y'ALL BE GOOD NOW!

JUST LIKE JESUS SAID — IT'S THE END OF THE WORLD!

NERO OPENED HIS ESTATE TO THE HOMELESS AND WONDERED *WHICH SUBVERSIVES* HAD STARTED THE FIRE.

SIRE, THE SECT OF THE *CHRISTIANS* SEEMED AWFULLY PLEASED!"

OOO...THAT IS *TOO* NASTY!

FOR THE NEXT FEW NIGHTS, NERO MADE *HUMAN TORCHES* OF THE CHRISTIANS, AND CHRISTIANITY WAS *OUTLAWED.*

A PROPHECY FULFILLED

IN 66, A PARTY OF RADICALS, OR *ZEALOTS*, SEIZED THE JERUSALEM TEMPLE, SURROUNDED THE ROMAN GARRISON, AND, AFTER PROMISING SAFE PASSAGE TO THE ROMANS IF THEY DISARMED, SLAUGHTERED THEM TO A MAN...

ANOTHER ROMAN ARMY SOON APPEARED... THEY PUSHED *HALFWAY* INTO THE CITY AND THEN GOT SPOOKED...

THE ROMANS FLED, AND THE JEWS PURSUED.

IN THIS WAY, THE REBELS GOT THEIR HANDS ON THE ROMAN HEAVY ARTILLERY.

ACROSS THE COUNTRY, ARMED BANDS SEIZED HEROD'S FORTS, LIKE THE MASSIVE *MASADA*... IN JERUSALEM, THE REBELS ORGANIZED A MILITARY GOVERNMENT FOR THE NATION.

MASADA

TO LEAD *GALILEE* THEY CHOSE A 29-YEAR-OLD PRIEST NAMED *JOSEPHUS*, WHO, BY HIS OWN ACCOUNT, NEVER BELIEVED THEY COULD WIN IN THE FIRST PLACE.

ULP!

COMBINING *FORCE* AND *TRICKERY*, JOSEPHUS BROUGHT GALILEE UNDER HIS CONTROL.

GIVE UP! YOU'RE *OUTNUMBERED!*

HERE HE THREATENS THE TOWN OF TIBERIAS WITH HIS "NAVY" OF 230 BOATS—EACH WITH NO MORE THAN FIVE MEN ON BOARD.

NERO (THEN ON A CONCERT TOUR OF GREECE) APPOINTED *VESPASIAN*, HERO OF BRITAIN, TO PUT DOWN THE REVOLT. VESPASIAN, WITH HIS SON *TITUS*, MARCHED AN ARMY FROM SYRIA STRAIGHT TOWARD *GALILEE*.

CHINK CHINK CHINK CHINK

JOSEPHUS' BATTLE LINES BROKE AT THE MERE *SIGHT* OF THE ROMAN FORMATIONS.

CHINK CHINK CHINK CHINK

THEY FLED TO THE CLIFF-HANGING VILLAGE OF *JOTAPATA*, WHERE VESPASIAN SURROUNDED THEM.

THAT SOUND IS DRIVING ME NUTS!

CHINK CHINK CHINK CHINK CHINK CHINK CHINK

JOSEPHUS RESISTED THE ROMAN ASSAULT IN EVERY WAY POSSIBLE...

EVENTUALLY, THE ROMANS BROKE DOWN THE WALL AND LOWERED A GANGWAY.

CREAK
RATTLE

JOSEPHUS' ORDERS: "STOP YOUR EARS WHEN THEY MAKE THEIR BATTLE CRY, AND GET UNDER YOUR SHIELDS WHEN THEIR ARROWS FLY...

ROAR

THWIP
THWIP
THWIP
THWIP
THWIP
THWIP

... AND THEN ATTACK THEM *FIRST!*"

YAHU!

BUT FINALLY, AFTER *47 DAYS,* THE ROMANS ENTERED THE TOWN, AND JOSEPHUS DISAPPEARED DOWN A HOLE!

AAGH!

EEK

BYE!

THIS WAS A SECRET HIDING PLACE FOR JOTAPATA'S LEADERS.

HEY! IT'S ME!

SHHH!

SOMEONE TIPPED OFF THE ROMANS, WHO MADE JOSEPHUS AN OFFER, WHICH STARTED AN ARGUMENT.

JOSEPHUS! COME OUT! VESPASIAN WANTS YOU ALIVE!!

THAT MAKES TWO OF US! BE RIGHT UP!

FERGEDDABOUDIT, JO!

JOSEPHUS MADE A SUGGESTION.

OH... RIGHT... COUGH... DEATH BEFORE DISHONOR... I FORGOT... BUT LET'S BE SYSTEMATIC... WE'LL DRAW LOTS IN TURN... IN EVERY ROUND, THE LOSER DIES... AND THE LAST ONE ALIVE COMMITS SUICIDE... HOW ABOUT IT?

MUMBLE... WELL... O.K...

ONE BY ONE, THEY KILLED EACH OTHER.

STAB THUD

NEXT!

HISTORIANS ARE FAIRLY SURE THAT JOSEPHUS "COOKED" THE LOTTERY SOMEHOW—BECAUSE WHEN IT WAS OVER HE WAS ONE OF TWO LEFT ALIVE...

WHAT SAY WE STOP THIS FOOLISHNESS?

THEY BOTH SURRENDERED, AND JOSEPHUS, AT LEAST, WAS MARCHED OFF.

JOSEPH, YOU TRAITOR! AAAAAGH!

IN VESPASIAN'S TENT, JOSEPHUS ASKED TO BE ALONE WITH THE GENERAL, AND THEN PUT ON HIS *MOST AMAZING PERFORMANCE* YET...

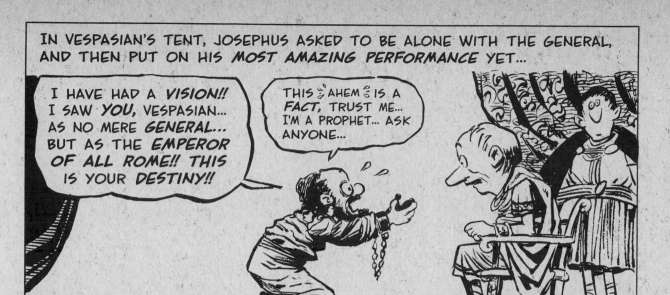

I HAVE HAD A *VISION!!* I SAW *YOU*, VESPASIAN... AS NO MERE *GENERAL*... BUT AS THE *EMPEROR OF ALL ROME!!* THIS IS YOUR *DESTINY!!*

THIS ≷AHEM≷ IS A *FACT*, TRUST ME... I'M A PROPHET... ASK ANYONE...

VESPASIAN HAD GOOD REASON TO PONDER THIS PROPHECY...

BY THE WAY, I *ALSO* SEE MY CHAINS COMING OFF SOON!

IN GAUL, THE LEGIONS OF *VINDEX* HAD DECLARED WAR ON NERO... THEY DECLARED *GALBA*, A SPANISH GOVERNOR, AS *THEIR* EMPEROR.

HAIL!!

IN ROME, NERO'S DEFENSE PREPARATIONS WENT SLOWLY.

STAGE EQUIPMENT? CURTAINS? LUTES? MASKS?

AT LAST, ALL ROME TURNED AGAINST NERO, AND HE FLED WITH A FEW FRIENDS.

YOU DON'T THINK THEY'D LET ME STAY ON AS, SAY, GOVERNOR OF EGYPT?

NO, SIRE...

THEY TUNNELED THEIR WAY INTO A COUNTRY VILLA.

WHAT A *TACKY* WAY TO GO...

AND THERE, IN THE SLAVE QUARTERS, NERO CLUMSILY STABBED HIMSELF IN THE THROAT.

MISSED! UGH! MISSED AGAIN! SOMEBODY GIVE ME A HAND...

GALBA, IT'S SAID, WAS *TERRIBLY EXCITED* BY THE NEWS OF THE SUICIDE.

BUT BY JANUARY, 69, HE WAS MURDERED AND REPLACED AS EMPEROR BY *OTHO*.

IN APRIL, OTHO FELL TO *VITELLIUS* AND HIS LEGIONS.

69 WAS THE YEAR OF *THREE EMPERORS*—SO WHY NOT *FOUR*? VESPASIAN'S OFFICERS NOW SALUTED *HIM* WITH ALL THE HIGH TITLES!

VESPASIAN LEFT JUDAEA TO WOO THE EASTERN LEGIONS AND CUT OFF ROME'S *GRAIN SUPPLY* FROM *EGYPT*, WHILE HIS ALLY *ANTONIUS PRIMUS* HEADED FOR ITALY.

VESPASIAN'S FRIENDS OVERWHELMED VITELLIUS'S DEFENSES.

246

BACK IN ROME, VITELLIUS'S TROOPS MINDLESSLY TORCHED THE CITY, DESTROYING ANCIENT TEMPLES AND A FEW OF VESPASIAN'S RELATIVES.

AT LAST, VITELLIUS WAS KILLED, AND *ALL ROME* HAILED VESPASIAN EMPEROR IN ABSENTIA. (HIS SON DOMITIAN STOOD IN FOR HIM.)

HAIL WHAT'S-HIS-NAME!

IN THE EAST, VESPASIAN CELEBRATED BY HAVING *JOSEPHUS'S* CHAINS STRUCK OFF!!!

SPANGK!

IN THE SPRING, VESPASIAN SAILED FOR ROME, SENDING TITUS, WITH JOSEPHUS, BACK TO *JERUSALEM* TO FINISH IT OFF.

THEY ARRIVED DURING THE *PASSOVER FESTIVAL*, AS GARDENS BLOOMED AND VISITORS THRONGED TO THE CITY...

THE ROMANS ARE COMING!!

(THE CHRISTIANS HAD FLED THOUGH: THEY HAD A PROPHECY OF THE OUTCOME!)

IN HIS HISTORY, JOSEPHUS DEVOTES NEARLY *100 PAGES* TO THE FIVE-MONTH SEIGE OF JERUSALEM... HE DESCRIBES THE CROWDS TRAPPED IN THE CITY... THE SURROUNDING HILLS STRIPPED OF TREES FOR THE ROMAN CAMP... ROMAN MOVEMENTS OUTSIDE... CIVIL WAR INSIDE... SORTIES AND AMBUSHES... HIS OWN PLEAS FOR A JEWISH SURRENDER... JERUSALEM'S SHORTAGE OF FOOD... THEN STARVATION... A MOTHER EATING HER OWN CHILD... ESCAPING JEWS SLIT OPEN BY SOLDIERS LOOKING FOR SWALLOWED GOLD... *115,800* CORPSES COUNTED BY THE CORONER'S OFFICE... THE ROMAN ASSAULT... THE ATTACK ON THE TEMPLE... A ROMAN SOLDIER'S HOBNAIL BOOTS SLIPPING ON THE POLISHED STONES... THE TEMPLE IN FLAMES... THE CITIZENS MASSACRED... BUT I'M GOING TO SKIP IT—*HOW MANY GORY DRAWINGS DO YOU WANT IN ONE BOOK?*

248

IN AUGUST 70, THE TEMPLE FELL... IN SEPTEMBER, TITUS ORDERED THE CITY'S *COMPLETE DEMOLITION*, EXCEPT FOR HEROD'S TOWERS AND PART OF THE WALL, TOKENS OF JERUSALEM'S FORMER GLORY...

TENS OF THOUSANDS OF PRISONERS WENT OFF IN CAGES...

TO BE SOLD AS SLAVES, OR TO FIGHT TO THE DEATH IN THE "GAMES" HELD FOR TITUS' AMUSEMENT.

ENJOYING THE SHOW, JO?

YEH...

A FEW HUNDRED ZEALOTS STILL HELD OUT AT MASADA. THE ROMANS BUILT A HUGE EARTHEN RAMP UP THE FORT...

...ONLY TO FIND THAT THE ZEALOTS HAD COMMITTED *MASS SUICIDE* RATHER THAN SURRENDER.

NO FAIR!

FANATICS DON'T LIKE "GAMES," I GUESS...

TITUS REJOINED HIS FATHER VESPASIAN IN ROME FOR A *TRIUMPHAL PARADE*, IN WHICH REBEL LEADERS, CHAINED TO MODELS OF THEIR TOWNS, ROLLED OFF TO EXECUTION... JOSEPHUS JOINED VESPASIAN'S HOUSEHOLD AND WROTE A HISTORY OF THE REVOLT... ROME HAD ENDURED... THE JEWS HAD LOST THEIR NATION... AND THE CHRISTIANS CARRIED ON—IN *SECRET*...

INTRODUCTION

SO HERE'S THE STORY: IN A GREAT CAPITAL, A CROSSROADS OF CIVILIZATION, AN *ALIEN CULT* ARRIVES FROM THE EDGE OF THE EMPIRE...

AS THE EMPIRE BEGINS TO *DECAY*, ITS OLD GODS NO LONGER SEEM QUITE AS *POTENT* OR *RELEVANT* AS THEY USED TO... SOME PEOPLE TURN TO THE NEW RELIGION, WHICH EMPHASIZES *SPIRITUALITY*, *PURITY*, AND *SALVATION*...

PLAGUES AND *INVASIONS* RAVAGE THE IMPERIAL FRONTIER! CHAOS SPREADS TO THE VERY *CENTER!!!*

THE PEOPLE UNDERGO A *SPIRITUAL TRANSFORMATION*... THE LITTLE CULT GROWS WITHOUT BOUNDS... JUST BEFORE— OR JUST AFTER?—THE EMPIRE COLLAPSES COMPLETELY, THE *WHOLE COUNTRY* EMBRACES THE NEW FAITH!

WHAT A STORY! IT'S GOT *EVERYTHING:* PATHOS, CONFLICT, HOPE, NEW IDEAS, VAST MOVEMENTS OF PEOPLES, SOME GREAT ART...

IN FACT, IT'S *SO GOOD,* I'M GONNA TELL IT *TWICE* IN ONE VOLUME!

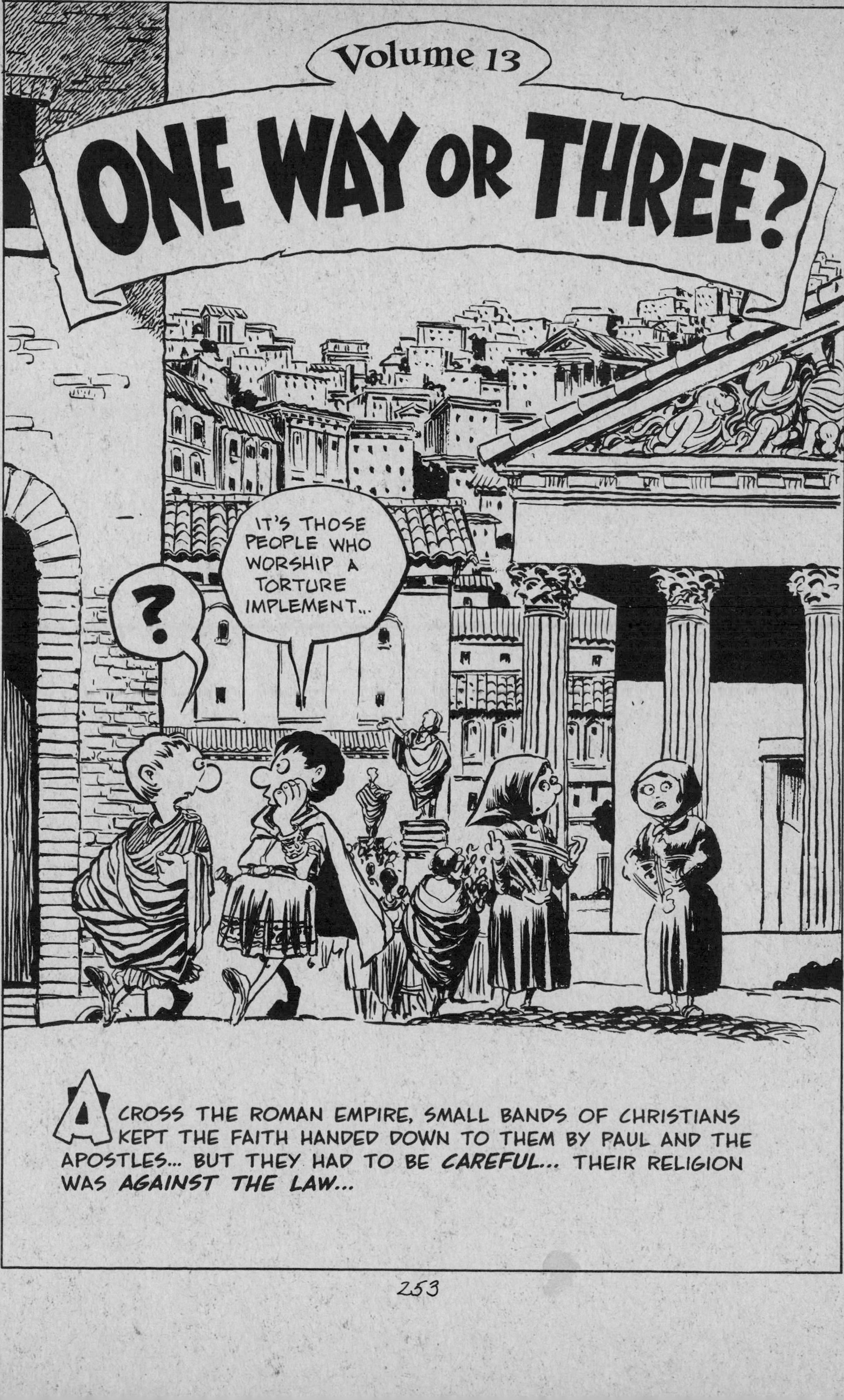
Volume 13
ONE WAY OR THREE?
?
IT'S THOSE PEOPLE WHO WORSHIP A TORTURE IMPLEMENT...

ACROSS THE ROMAN EMPIRE, SMALL BANDS OF CHRISTIANS KEPT THE FAITH HANDED DOWN TO THEM BY PAUL AND THE APOSTLES... BUT THEY HAD TO BE ***CAREFUL...*** THEIR RELIGION WAS ***AGAINST THE LAW...***

THIS WAS *UNUSUAL!* IN THOSE DAYS, PEOPLE RESPECTED EACH OTHER'S GODS, AND THE ROMANS RARELY BANNED RELIGIONS. ASIDE FROM THE CHRISTIANS, ONLY ONE OTHER CULT WAS OFF-LIMITS: THE *DRUIDS*, PRIESTS TO THE GAULS...

IT AIN'T FAIR!!

BUT THE DRUIDS PERFORMED *HUMAN SACRIFICE*—*ROMAN* HUMAN SACRIFICE, WHENEVER POSSIBLE.

DETAILS, DETAILS!!

THE CHRISTIANS DIDN'T DO ANYTHING LIKE THAT! THEIRS WAS MORE OF AN *ATTITUDE PROBLEM*...

IT'S NOT THAT WE DON'T BELIEVE IN YOUR GODS... WE *DO*... WE BELIEVE THEY'RE *DEMONS* FROM *HELL*...

WHICH IS WHERE ALL OF *YOU* ARE GOING TO *BURN* FOR *ETERNITY!*

BUT WE LOVE YOU...

CHRISTIANS ABSOLUTELY REFUSED TO SACRIFICE TO THE *GODS OF THE ROMAN STATE.* THIS WAS A KIND OF *TREASON.*

IMAGINE IF PEOPLE LIKE THIS WERE IN THE *ARMY*... IT WOULD JUST *DESTROY* UNIT COHESION...

BEGINNING WITH NERO IN 64, EVERY EMPEROR OUTLAWED THE CHRISTIAN CULT.

THEY POSITIVELY *ENJOYED* THE BIG FIRE!

THE GOVERNMENT'S USUAL PROCEDURE WAS TO "INVITE" THE SUSPECT TO OFFER SOME INCENSE TO THE SPIRIT OF ROME OR THE EMPEROR.

MUMBLE MUMBLE GET THEE BEHIND ME, SATAN...MUMBLE MUMBLE MUMBLE...

COMPLIANCE MEANT FREEDOM.

OH, COME ON... JUST A LITTLE PINCH OF INCENSE ON THE FIRE... A LITTLE OATH... AND THERE'S THE DOOR...

REFUSAL MEANT *BROWBEATING, PERSUASION, WHEEDLING, YELLING,* AND *THREATS,* FOLLOWED BY *TORTURE.*

WHY WON'T YOU BE REASONABLE?

LISTEN!

YEEEOUCH OUCH OUCH OUCH OUCH!

MUMBLE MUMBLE

...AND FINALLY *EXECUTION* IN ONE OF THE ROMAN WAYS: BURNING, BOILING, BEASTS, ETC.

MAN, IF THEY AREN'T HOLIER THAN THOU ALREADY, THEY'RE ABOUT TO BE...

THE AUDIENCE COULDN'T HELP NOTICING THAT THE CONDEMNED CHRISTIANS ACTUALLY SEEMED TO *WELCOME* DEATH.

C'MON! WHAT ARE YOU WAITING FOR??

INSTEAD OF *STIFLING* THE CHURCH, EACH FRESH BATCH OF MARTYRS ACTUALLY *ENLARGED* IT.

MAN! HOW DO THEY *DO* THAT?

MUST...FIND... OUT...

CHOMP

AS CHRISTIAN RANKS SWELLED OVER THE YEARS, THE OTHER ROMANS EVENTUALLY GOT *USED* TO THEM—AND EVEN CAME TO RESPECT THEIR *RADICAL ALTERNATIVE* TO ROMAN VALUES.

CHARITY, NOT CHARIOT RACES!

COMPASSION, NOT COMPULSION!

GLORY, NOT GLADIATORS!

SPIRITUALITY, NOT SENSUALITY!

FASTING, NOT FEASTING!

WHAT'S WRONG WITH THAT??

BIBLES, NOT BULIMIA!

WAIT... :BURP: I'M THINKING...

BUT WHAT TO DO? THEY *STILL* REFUSED TO SACRIFICE TO THE GODS, SO THEY COULDN'T BE *LEGALIZED*.

IT'S OUT OF THE QUESTION!!

THERE'S A RELIEF!

IN THE 110s, THE EMPEROR TRAJAN COMPROMISED WITH A *"DON'T ASK, DON'T TELL"* POLICY. THE POLICE JUST STOPPED LOOKING FOR CHRISTIANS.

HEY! WAIT UP! I ONLY JOINED TO BE *PERSECUTED!* REALLY!!

TRAJAN COULD AFFORD TO BE MAGNANIMOUS. IN HIS REIGN (98–117) THE EMPIRE REACHED ITS GREATEST EXTENT, CROSSING THE DANUBE RIVER INTO DACIA (MODERN RUMANIA). TRAJAN'S FORUM IN ROME DWARFED THE REST, AND, UNUSUAL FOR A ROMAN EMPEROR, TRAJAN FOUNDED A *DYNASTY*, CALLED THE *ANTONINES*.

NOW, FOR THE *FIRST TIME IN HISTORY*, THERE WERE *LARGE, CIVILIZED EMPIRES* ALL THE WAY FROM WESTERN EUROPE TO THE CHINA SEA, EXCHANGING THEIR GOODS, IDEAS—AND *GERMS*.

COFF COFF

TRAJAN'S SUCCESSOR *HADRIAN* PUT DOWN THE LAST OF THE *JEWISH REVOLTS*. WHEN HADRIAN TRIED TO IMPOSE THE ROMAN RELIGION IN JUDEA, RESISTANCE WAS LED BY *SIMON BAR-KOCHBA*, WITH MORAL SUPPORT FROM THE RABBI *AKIBA*.

THIS TIME, IT'S THE *MESSIAH*, FOR SURE!

THIS REVOLT WENT MUCH LIKE THE LAST ONE: THREE YEARS' COMBAT, HALF A MILLION DEAD, BAR-KOCHBA KILLED, THE RABBI TORTURED TO DEATH...

BAR-KOCHBA COIN

HADRIAN BUILT A NEW CITY, AELIA CAPITOLINA, ON JERUSALEM'S RUINS AND *BARRED ALL JEWS* FROM COMING ANYWHERE NEAR IT. AND SO, ALL OVER THE WORLD, JEWS HAVE MOURNFULLY PRAYED, "NEXT YEAR IN JERUSALEM..."

UM...WELL... MAYBE THE YEAR *AFTER* NEXT...

BOOM

CRACK

THE BIG PICTURE

HERE IS SOME OF WHAT WAS HAPPENING IN THE TERRITORY THAT CONNECTED—AND SOMETIMES SEPARATED—ROME AND CHINA.

IN THE FORESTS BEYOND THE RHINE LIVED THE *GERMANS*. DESPITE ROMAN INFLUENCE, SOME OF THESE TRIBES STILL PRACTICED HUMAN SACRIFICE, SUBMERGING THEIR VICTIMS ALIVE IN BOGS.

IN *PERSIA*, THE PARTHIAN DYNASTY INTRODUCED *PLATE ARMOR* TO THE WORLD OF WAR.

THE OVERLAND, INTERCONTINENTAL TRADE ROUTE—THE "SILK ROAD"—HAD ONE END HERE.

ALEXANDRIA WAS THE EMPIRE'S MELTING POT. GREEKS, JEWS, SYRIANS, NATIVE EGYPTIANS, AND A FEW HINDUS LIVED PEACEFULLY SIDE BY SIDE, EXCEPT FOR THEIR REGULAR RIOTS.

THE KINGDOM OF *GHANA* WAS FOUNDED AROUND THIS TIME, POSSIBLY BY NORTH AFRICANS FLEEING ROMAN RULE.

Britain

Germany

Rhine R.

Gaul

Danube R.

Byzantium

Spain

Rome

Antioch

Babylon

Alexandria

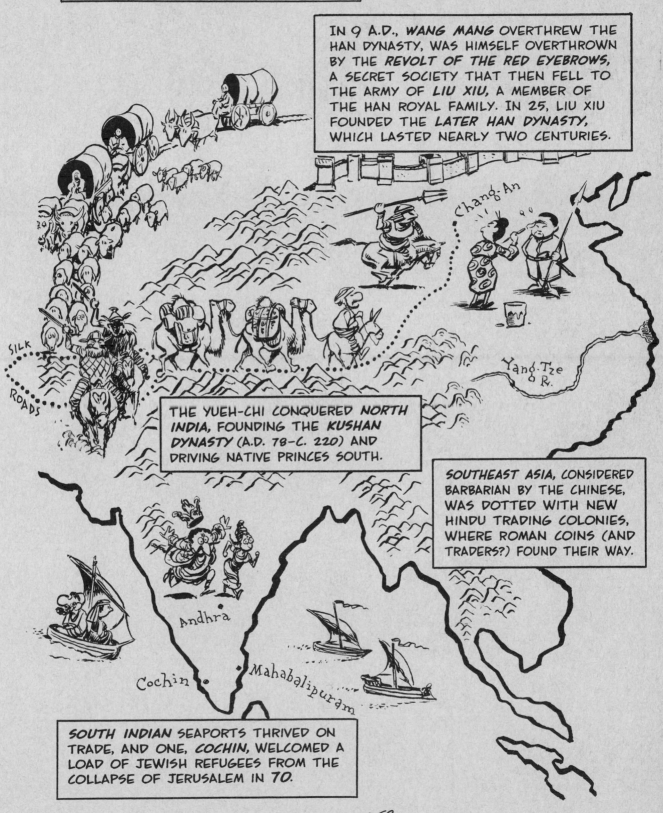

WHEN *CHINA* BATTERED THE *HUNS* AROUND 150 B.C., SOME HUN SUBJECTS, THE YUEH-CHI, WENT ON A LONG TREK THAT BROUGHT THEM ALL THE WAY TO THE HINDU KUSH MOUNTAINS.

IN 9 A.D., *WANG MANG* OVERTHREW THE HAN DYNASTY, WAS HIMSELF OVERTHROWN BY THE *REVOLT OF THE RED EYEBROWS*, A SECRET SOCIETY THAT THEN FELL TO THE ARMY OF *LIU XIU*, A MEMBER OF THE HAN ROYAL FAMILY. IN 25, LIU XIU FOUNDED THE *LATER HAN DYNASTY*, WHICH LASTED NEARLY TWO CENTURIES.

THE YUEH-CHI CONQUERED *NORTH INDIA*, FOUNDING THE *KUSHAN DYNASTY* (A.D. 78–C. 220) AND DRIVING NATIVE PRINCES SOUTH.

SOUTHEAST ASIA, CONSIDERED BARBARIAN BY THE CHINESE, WAS DOTTED WITH NEW HINDU TRADING COLONIES, WHERE ROMAN COINS (AND TRADERS?) FOUND THEIR WAY.

SOUTH INDIAN SEAPORTS THRIVED ON TRADE, AND ONE, *COCHIN*, WELCOMED A LOAD OF JEWISH REFUGEES FROM THE COLLAPSE OF JERUSALEM IN *70*.

SILK ROADS

Chang-An

Yang-Tze R.

Andhra

Cochin

Mahabalipuram

259

THE WAY OF PEACE

IN CHINA, THE HAN COURT LOOKED MORE SPLENDID THAN EVER... BUT THOSE INTERNATIONAL TRAVELERS, THE *MICROBES*, WERE ABOUT TO BRING IT DOWN...

IN 161, AN *EPIDEMIC* RAVAGED NORTHERN CHINA. IT'S IMPOSSIBLE TO SAY NOW WHAT DISEASE IT WAS, BUT WHEREVER IT STRUCK, IT KILLED *THREE* OUT OF *TEN*. THIS CAN REALLY MESS UP A SOCIETY!

THE PLAGUE DIDN'T WRECK THE GOVERNMENT—IT JUST SAPPED ITS ABILITY TO COPE.

SQUEEZING PEOPLE IS HARD WHEN YOU'RE NOT FULLY STAFFED!

AT THIS POINT, A HEALER NAMED *CHANG CHIO* WON A FOLLOWING WITH HIS MAGIC AND MEDICINE. HIS BOOK WAS CALLED *"THE WAY OF PEACE."*

HEAL!

AS "THE MYSTIC OF THE WAY OF PEACE" HE SOON HAD AN IMMENSE FOLLOWING, ORGANIZED UNDER 36 DISCIPLES.

SHE DIED, BUT HAPPY!

HOORAY!

IN VEILED LANGUAGE, THEY PREACHED THE *OVERTHROW OF THE HAN DYNASTY.*

THE BLUE HEAVEN IS *DYING!* THE TIME HAS COME TO SET UP THE *YELLOW!!*

YES! RIGHT!

WHAT?

THE FOLLOWERS OF THE WAY OF PEACE PUT ON *YELLOW TURBANS* AND PREPARED FOR WAR.

IT'S A POLITICAL STATEMENT *AND* A FASHION STATEMENT!

THERE WERE SO MANY OF THEM THAT THE IMPERIAL ARMIES FLED WITHOUT A FIGHT.

FROM THE CAPITAL CHANG-AN CAME AN ALL-OUT CALL TO ARMS...

ACROSS THE EMPIRE, FREE-LANCE WARLORDS RAISED FORCES—FOR EXAMPLE, THE EMPEROR'S DISTANT, IMPOVERISHED COUSIN *LIU PEI*, FAMOUS FOR LONG EARLOBES.

WE'LL HELP! FOR PURELY SELF-LESS, PATRIOTIC, CONFUCIAN REASONS, OF COURSE!

THESE ARMIES TOOK ON THE YELLOW TURBANS IN A SERIES OF BATTLES.

THE MEDICAL REBELS WERE BEATEN, AND CHANG CHIO'S CORPSE BEHEADED.

AND NOW, INSTEAD OF *YELLOW TURBANS*, THE GOVERNMENT HAD TO WORRY ABOUT ALL THE *PRIVATE ARMIES* IT HAD JUST CONJURED UP!

GLEEP!

DISCLAIMER:

THE NEXT FEW PAGES, THROUGH THE BATTLE OF RED BLUFF, ARE NOT *STRICTLY HISTORI-CAL*... THEY'RE TAKEN FROM A BOOK, *THE ROMANCE OF THE THREE KINGDOMS*, WHICH IS USUALLY DESCRIBED AS A *HISTORICAL NOVEL!*

UNLIKE THE HISTORICAL NOVELS OF THE WEST, THE *ROMANCE* HAS NO *FICTIONAL CHARAC-TERS*... EVERYONE IN IT WAS *REAL*... THE BOOK WEAVES TOGETHER ALL THE HISTORI-CAL SNIPPETS HANDED DOWN FROM THE *COLLAPSE* OF THE HAN DYNASTY... SO IT'S MORE LIKE *KING ARTHUR* THAN *WAR AND PEACE*...

SO WHAT YOU ARE ABOUT TO READ IS REALLY AN EXCERPT FROM ONE OF CHINA'S *LITER-ARY* CLASSICS... I COULDN'T RESIST SHARING IT WITH YOU, AND BESIDES, I COULDN'T FIND ANY "REAL" HISTORIES OF THE TIME IN A *LANGUAGE* THE *TIME MACHINE* UNDERSTANDS...

I GOTTA UPGRADE THIS THING'S LANGUAGE MODULE!..

MEANWHILE, IN THE PALACE, THE EMPEROR WAS DYING, AND HIS TWO LIKELY HEIRS WERE BOTH *LITTLE BOYS.*

PRINCE *PIEN'S* MOTHER WAS THE LOW-BORN QUEEN, LADY *HO,* WHOSE BROTHER *HO CHIN* HAD RISEN STRAIGHT FROM *DOG BUTCHER* TO *GENERALISSIMO.*

PRINCE *HSIEH,* A CONCUBINE'S SON, HAD THE BACKING OF THE OLD EMPEROR'S *MOTHER* AND THE POWERFUL PALACE *EUNUCHS.*

WHEN THE EMPEROR DIED, *HO CHIN* BARGED INTO THE ROOM WHERE THE CORPSE WAS DISPLAYED, KILLING A EUNUCH ALONG THE WAY, AND PROCLAIMED *PIEN* THE *NEW EMPEROR.*

HE EASILY BANISHED AND MURDERED THE OLD EMPRESS, BUT HE JUST COULDN'T SEE A WAY TO DESTROY ALL THE *EUNUCHS.*

THERE ARE SO *MANY* OF 'EM!

AT LAST, HO CHIN CAME UP WITH A *BAD PLAN:* ISSUE ANOTHER *CALL TO ARMS,* INVITING ALL THOSE PRIVATE ARMIES TO THE CAPITAL!

HO CHIN, THIS IS LIKE *LIGHTING A FURNACE* TO *BURN A HAIR!!*

YEH... WELL... THAT WOULD WORK...

AN ARMY ARRIVED—HEADED BY *TUNG CHO*, THE LATE EMPRESS'S RELATIVE AND FRIEND OF THE EUNUCHS. TUNG CHO CAMPED OUTSIDE THE CITY WALLS...

OOPS!

INSIDE, THE EUNUCHS INVITED HO CHIN INTO THE WOMEN'S QUARTERS TO VISIT HIS SISTER THE QUEEN. HO CHIN'S MEN WAITED AND WAITED... FINALLY—

HEY! WHERE'S HO CHIN??

HERE'S PART OF HIM!!

AFTER HO CHIN'S *HEAD* SAILED OVER THE GATE, HIS MEN STORMED IN AND *SLAUGHTERED* THE *EUNUCHS.*

TUNG CHO NOW ATTACKED, CRUSHED HO'S PARTY, REPLACED *PIEN* WITH *HSIEH* AS EMPEROR, AND *EXTERMINATED* THE HO CLAN, BOY, MOM, AND ALL.

NOW BE A GOOD BOY, MY EMPEROR!

PLOTTING AGAINST TUNG BEGAN... THE OFFICIAL *TSAO TSAO* PLANNED TO KILL HIM... BUT THE GLEAM OF HIS SWORD GAVE HIM AWAY.

WHUZZAT?

SOMEHOW, TSAO TSAO TALKED HIMSELF OUT OF *INSTANT DEATH.*

I SAID— WHUZZAT?

THIS? UM... THIS? HEEHEEHAHO... WHY...IT'S A *SWORD*... A *SURPRISE PRESENT* FOR *YOU,* YOUR EMINENCE...

UNDER SUSPICION, TSAO TSAO FLED... HE AND A FRIEND TOOK SHELTER IN TSAO'S UNCLE'S FARMHOUSE... THE UNCLE WAS *SUSPICIOUSLY APOLOGETIC*...

PLEASE PARDON MY POOR HOSPITALITY!! I HAVE NOTHING WITH WHICH TO WELCOME YOU... PLEASE WAIT HERE WHILE I GO TO TOWN FOR SOME *WINE!*

HE WENT OUT FOR WHAT SEEMED LIKE A *LONG TIME.*

I DON'T LIKE THE SMELL OF THIS... LET'S LOOK AROUND...

OUT BACK THEY HEARD—

TRUSS BEFORE KILLING! TRUSS BEFORE KILLING!

TAKING NO CHANCES, THEY LEAPED IN AND KILLED HALF A DOZEN SERVANTS OR SO.

ONLY THEN DID THEY NOTICE:

OOPS... THEY WERE TALKING ABOUT THIS *PIG!!*

WHAT A COUPLE OF DUMMIES!

AGAIN THEY FLED—AND MET THE UNCLE COMING HOME WITH THE WINE.

GENTLEMEN! WHAT'S YOUR HURRY? HERE'S THE WINE... LET'S *EAT!*

WITHOUT HESITATION, TSAO TSAO KILLED HIS OWN UNCLE AND SPED OFF.

BEST NOT TO TAKE CHANCES!

THIS GUY HAS A FUTURE IN POLITICS...

TSAO TSAO SENT OUT AN INVITATION TO *REBEL AGAINST TUNG CHO.* THOUSANDS RESPONDED...

THIS ARMY MARCHED ON THE CAPITAL...

TUNG CHO FLED, TAKING THE BOY EMPEROR AND MOST OF THE POPULATION WITH HIM.

BUT TUNG CHO WAS MURDERED BY ONE OF HIS AIDES IN AN ARGUMENT OVER A WOMAN.

THE EMPEROR ESCAPED INTO THE COUNTRYSIDE, WHERE CROPS HAD FAILED AND THE *YELLOW TURBANS* HAD REVIVED.

AT LAST, THE ROYAL HOUSEHOLD WAS "RESCUED" BY *TSAO TSAO.*

IN A STARVING VILLAGE, *TSAO TSAO* BECAME *CHIEF MINISTER OF HAN.*

MEANWHILE, IN OTHER PARTS OF THE COUNTRY, A COUPLE OF STORIES SHOW HOW PEOPLE DREADED AND RESPECTED *MAGICIANS* IN THOSE TROUBLED TIMES...

WHLE TSAO TSAO BOSSED THE NORTH, THE *SUN* FAMILY GAINED POWER DOWN SOUTH WITH A NAVY ON THE *YANG-TZE RIVER.*

ONE DAY, THE FAMILY HEAD, *SUN-TSE,* HEARD A COMMOTION IN THE STREET.

ON INQUIRING, HE FOUND PEOPLE THRONGING AROUND A TAOIST SAGE, *YU ZHI,* FAMED FOR HIS MEDICAL MAGIC.

HE'S WORKED THESE PARTS FOR DECADES... PERFECTLY HARMLESS... A *SAINT,* REALLY...

DON'T BE NAIVE... THESE "SAINT-HEALERS" ARE A *MENACE!*

YU ZHI'S MEDICAL TEXTBOOK WAS *THE WAY OF PEACE,* BIBLE OF THE *YELLOW TURBANS.* TOO BAD FOR HIM!

PEOPLE THEY CURE BECOME *REBELS...* PEOPLE THEY DON'T CURE *DROP DEAD!*

BURN HIM AT THE STAKE!

AS THE TORCH WAS APPLIED, GOES THE LEGEND, YU ZHI CONJURED UP *THREE FEET* OF *RAIN,* AND HE WAS BEHEADED INSTEAD.

THIS IS *NOT* A CONTROLLED EXPERIMENT!

AND PEOPLE SAID THAT YU ZHI'S *GHOST* HAUNTED SUN TSE TO DEATH WITHIN WEEKS.

I'M NOT REAL! YOUR *WAR WOUNDS* ARE INFECTED!!

267

A *DIFFERENT* ATTITUDE TOWARD THE TAO WAS SHOWN BY THE SWASHBUCKLING *LIU PEI*, THE IMPERIAL COUSIN WITH THE PENDULOUS EARLOBES...

IN THE REIGNING CHAOS, LIU PEI AND HIS BAND WERE NOT DOING WELL. THE PROBLEM, IT SEEMED, WAS THAT HE WAS TOO *POLITE*, TOO *HONORABLE*, TOO *NOBLE*.

YOU'RE TOO *CONFUCIAN*, BROTHER!

YOU WON'T STAB *ANYBODY* IN THE BACK!

THIS SITUATION CALLS FOR *LESS BENEVOLENCE!*

YOU NEED A *TAOIST...*

HE SOUGHT OUT *CHUKO LIANG*, A YOUNG HERMIT/SCHOLAR/WIZARD WITH NO EXPERIENCE IN POLITICS.

GO AWAY! COME BACK TOMORROW!

WOW! WHAT A GREAT NEGOTIATOR!

BUT CHUKO LIANG HAD A *LONG-TERM PLAN...*

TSAO TSAO IS SUPREME IN THE NORTH... THE SUNS RULE THE SOUTH... WHILE THE TIGER FIGHTS THE PHOENIX, A LONG EARLOBE MIGHT SWING TO THE *WEST...* GET IT??

COOL!

CHUKO EMPLOYED THE MAGICIAN'S ARTS OF *DECEPTION* AND *MISDIRECTION* IN THE ART OF WAR, AND HE ADDED *WIND* AND *FIRE* TO LIU PEI'S OTHER WEAPONS...

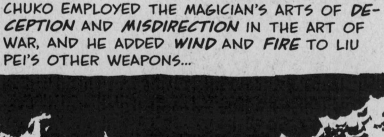

AND SOON LIU PEI WAS A FORCE TO BE RECKONED WITH...

MY MAN!

AFTER A SERIES OF STRATAGEMS, AMBUSHES, AND NARROW ESCAPES, LIU PEI HEADED SOUTH TO JOIN FORCES WITH THE SUNS AND THEIR NAVY.

UP NORTH, TSAO TSAO MARSHALED ALL HIS ARMIES AND WENT AFTER HIM.

THE CAMPS STRETCHED FOR MILES ALONG BOTH SIDES OF THE YANG-TZE RIVER.* TSAO TSAO'S NAVY FAR OUTNUMBERED THE SOUTHERNERS, BUT HAD LITTLE EXPERIENCE WITH LIFE ON THE WATER.

☆@## KNOTS!!

THE SOUTHERN ADMIRAL, ZHOU YU, CHALLENGED CHUKO LIANG TO CONTRIBUTE SOME WEAPONS TO THE CAUSE. CHUKO PROMISED TO BRING HIM *100,000 ARROWS* IN *THREE DAYS.*

GREAT! I CAN'T WAIT TO SEE THIS GUY FALL FLAT ON HIS FACE!

HE LASHED BUNDLES OF STRAW TO THE SIDES OF 20 BOATS, THEN WAITED... ON THE THIRD NIGHT, THEY SAILED OUT INTO A DENSE FOG.

NEARING TSAO TSAO'S CAMP, THE SAILORS BEAT THEIR DRUMS AND SHOUTED. THE PANICKING NORTHERNERS OPENED FIRE.

BOM BOM

CHUKO LIANG'S BOATS RETURNED WITH 100,000 ARROWS, GIVE OR TAKE A FEW!

EVEN BETTER, IT'S 100,000 OF *THEIR* ARROWS!

CHUKO LIANG SENT A **SECRET AGENT** ACROSS THE RIVER, HOPING TO TRAP TSAO TSAO INTO A BLUNDER.

THOUGH NUMEROUS, YOUR MEN ARE **CLUMSY** ON **WATER**. WHY NOT **CHAIN YOUR SHIPS TOGETHER** FOR **STABILITY?** THAT WOULD BE LIKE FIGHTING ON **LAND!!**

I SEE THROUGH THIS!! CHAINED TOGETHER, WE CAN BE **BURNED** BY THE &*%# **CHUKO LIANG!!** IS THIS A TRICK?

NONONONO... IT'S **WINTER**... AND AROUND HERE THE WINTER WIND **ALWAYS** BLOWS FROM OUR **BACKS!**

ANY ATTEMPT TO FIRE **YOUR** SHIPS WOULD **BACKFIRE** ON YOUR **ENEMIES...**

TSAO TSAO TOOK THE BAIT.

JUST LIKE SOLID GROUND!

CHUKO LIANG RETIRED TO A SHRINE TO WORK HIS STUFF.

ON THE THIRD DAY, THE WIND SHIFTED.

WITH THE BREEZE SUDDENLY BLOWING TOWARD TSAO TSAO, THE SOUTHERNERS SAILED OUT, PUSHING THEIR *FIRE SHIPS* STRAIGHT AT THE IMMOBILIZED NORTHERN NAVY. THE *TOTAL INCINERATION* THAT FOLLOWED IS KNOWN AS THE *BATTLE OF RED BLUFF.* THE YEAR WAS 208.

THIS BATTLE SEALED CHINA'S FATE: FOR THE NEXT FORTY YEARS, THE EMPIRE BROKE INTO *THREE KINGDOMS.* TSAO TSAO'S FAMILY RULED THE NORTH... LIU PEI RULED THE WEST (WITH CHUKO LIANG AS HIS BRAIN TRUST)... AND THE SUN FAMILY HELD POWER IN THE SOUTH.

AFTER **265,** AN ASSORTMENT OF OUTLANDERS GALLOPED OVER THE WEAKENED REGION: *TIBETANS, HUNS,* THE MYSTERIOUS *HSIEN-BI* IN 316, AND THE CENTRAL ASIAN *TOBA* IN 386. MASSES OF CHINESE FLED SOUTH, WHERE THEY STRUGGLED TO ADJUST TO THE HOT, SWAMPY ENVIRONMENT.

THE *TOBA*, WHO RULED NORTH CHINA FOR OVER A CENTURY (400—530), HAD A *LASTING IMPACT:* THEY WERE *BUDDHISTS.*

WHAT?

UNTIL THEN, BUDDHISM IN CHINA HAD BEEN AN *ALIEN RELIGION,* BUT THE TOBA PUSHED IT HARD.

HERE...TALK TO THIS CONFUCIAN... SEE IF YOU CAN TRANSLATE *RUPA, VEDANA, SAMJÑA, SAMSKARA, VIJÑANA, DHARMA, SAMBHOGA, NIRVANA,* ETC., ETC..., INTO A LANGUAGE HE CAN UNDERSTAND...

I'LL TRY.

BUDDHISM BECAME THE *STATE RELIGION* OF NORTH CHINA, AS THE TOBA SPONSORED MONASTERIES AND HUGE *ART PROJECTS,* LIKE THESE INDIAN-INSPIRED CAVE SCULPTURES.

THE WEIRDEST PART IS...I'M GETTING USED TO IT...

ALTHOUGH THE TOBA ADOPTED CHINESE MANNERS, THEY COULD NEVER ADOPT *CONFU-CIANISM,* WHICH WOULD ALWAYS REGARD THEM AS *BARBARIANS.* *BUDDHISM* EMBRACED *ALL* CLASSES AND PEOPLES EQUALLY.

273

HERE, IT WOULD SEEM, WERE THE INGREDIENTS OF *RELIGIOUS WAR*: A NEW FAITH, *BUDDHISM*, TRYING TO CONVERT A NATION RAISED ON *CONFUCIAN BEHAVIOR* AND THE *TAO*.

THE THREE WAYS CERTAINLY HAD DIFFERENT IDEAS.

EXCUSE ME. DO I BOW TO YOU, OR DO YOU BOW TO ME??

WHO CARES?

THE TAO OF THE BOW— WOW!

CONFUCIANS BASED EVERYTHING ON *FAMILY VALUES*: EVERYONE NEEDS CHILDREN—IN ORDER TO KEEP UP THE SACRIFICES TO THE ANCESTRAL SPIRITS.

BUDDHISTS DIDN'T BELIEVE IN ANCESTRAL SPIRITS, AND EVEN ENCOURAGED *CELIBACY*.

LUST IS A KIND OF *ATTACHMENT*, AND ATTACHMENT CAUSES *SUFFERING!*

OH, HONESTLY!

TAOISTS SOUGHT ENLIGHTMENT BY CONTEMPLATING *NATURE*. THEY DABBLED IN MAGIC, MEDICINE, AND CHEMISTRY.

TO MAKE *SCIENTIFIC PROGRESS*, YOU HAVE TO MUCK ABOUT WITH THE TAO!

BUDDHISTS WERE *ANTI-SCIENTIFIC*, VIEWING REALITY, AS PERCEIVED BY THE SENSES, AS AN *ILLUSION*.

SPIRITUAL PROGRESS— THAT'S WHAT COUNTS!

274

BUDDHISTS ALSO DISAGREED WITH OTHER *BUDDHISTS.*
SECTS SPLINTERED OFF, EACH WITH ITS ANCIENT,
"AUTHENTIC" SCRIPTURES...

BUT *SOMEHOW* THE INEVITABLE FRICTION NEVER FLARED INTO ALL-OUT PERSECUTION.*

*EXCEPT FOR ONE ANTI-BUDDHIST CAMPAIGN MUCH LATER

INSTEAD, CHINESE INTELLECTUALS OF ALL STRIPES PREFERRED TO *DISCUSS* THINGS OVER A GLASS OF WINE OR TWO OR THREE...

TELL ME: *HOW* DO YOU BUDDHISTS BELIEVE IN *REINCARNATION* IF YOU DON'T BELIEVE IN AN *INDIVIDUAL SOUL?*

YEAH.

IT ISN'T EASY...

AND DESPITE THEIR DIFFERENCES, THEY FOUND A FEW THINGS IN *COMMON...*

YOU BELIEVE IN COMPASSION AND SALVATION... *WE* BELIEVE IN –HIC– BENEVOLENCE...

THERE'S NO QUESTION THE ULTIMATE REALITY IS BEYOND KNOWING...

ESPECIALLY AT THE MOMENT!

SO... BY THE TIME CHINA WAS REUNIFIED IN 589, THE CHINESE HAD MANAGED TO EMBRACE ALL THESE DOCTRINES AT THE SAME TIME, WITH THE SLOGAN: *ONE TRUTH, THREE WAYS.*

ANYWAY, IN IMMORAL TIMES LIKE THESE, WE CONFUCIANS ARE PRETTY *USELESS!!*

WHA'S WRONG WITH BEING USELESS?

IN *ROME,* THINGS WENT A LITTLE DIFFERENTLY...

PARALLEL CHAOS

JUST AS IN CHINA, A *KILLER DISEASE* SWEPT THE ROMAN WORLD IN THE 160s... LIKE THE YELLOW TURBANS, THE CHRISTIANS NURSED THE SICK, WON CONVERTS, AND SUFFERED PERSECUTION.

THEY DON'T RUN AWAY FROM SUFFERING AND DEATH!

SUBSERSIVE!

THE ANTONINE DYNASTY, LIKE THE HAN, HUNG ON FOR 25 MORE YEARS, UNTIL THE EMPEROR *COMMODUS* WAS STABBED BY A WRESTLER IN 192.

GOSH! MAYBE THESE REALLY *ARE* THE LAST DAYS!

GOODY!

IN THE UNSTABLE CENTURY THAT FOLLOWED, THE *ARMY* AGAIN AND AGAIN CHOSE A NEW EMPEROR.

HAIL, MAXIMUS, ILLITERATE THRACIAN GIANT, IMPERATOR!!

ONLY TO DISPOSE OF HIM WHEN HE FAILED TO DELIVER THEIR PAY.

NEXT!

BETWEEN THE YEARS 192 AND 285, ONLY *ONE EMPEROR* (SEPTIMIUS SEVERUS) DIED OF NATURAL CAUSES...

IN THIS CENTURY, ASSASSINATION SEEMS PRETTY "NATURAL..."

IN CHAOTIC TIMES LIKE THESE, THE *NEIGHBORS* WILL TAKE ADVANTAGE!! IN THE 250s, THE *PERSIANS* ATTACKED FROM THE EAST AND SUCCEEDED IN DRAGGING THE EMPEROR *VALERIAN* OFF TO THEIR DUNGEONS... AND WORSE WAS TO COME...

WORSE?

THE FOREST FOLK

NEITHER *PLAGUE* NOR *PERSIAN* RUINED ROME. THAT HONOR WAS RESERVED FOR THE TRIBES FROM THE DENSE FORESTS BEYOND THE RIVER *RHINE*: THE *MARCOMANNI, FRANKS, JUTHUNGI, GREUTHUNGI, VANDALS, SUEBI, GOTHS,* AND THE CONFEDERATION CALLED THE ALLAMANI— IN SHORT, *GERMANS.*

CONQUER THE ROMANS! CONQUER THE ROMAAAANS! ♪

WHILE THE EMPIRE SUFFERED, THE GERMANS WERE THRIVING. IN THE *250s,* WAVES OF GERMAN TRIBES INVADED *GAUL,* WHILE OTHERS SAILED DOWN THE *DANUBE* TO THE *BLACK SEA.*

AT THE MOUTH OF THE DANUBE, THEY BUILT A NAVY OF 500 OR 2,000 SHIPS, DEPENDING ON WHO DID THE COUNTING.

1... 2... 3...

IN 268, SOME 320,000 MEN SAILED OUT THROUGH THE BOSPHORUS AND OVERRAN GREECE, THREATENING ROME ITSELF.

319,998... 319,999... 320,000!

IT LOOKED LIKE THE *FALL OF THE ROMAN EMPIRE*—BUT IT WASN'T. THE EMPEROR *GALLIENUS* HAD INTRODUCED SOME *NEW CONCEPTS* INTO THE ROMAN CALVARY. BARE-BACKED MOORISH *JAVELIN PITCHERS*, SYRIAN *ARCHERS*, AND MOST IMPORTANT, PERSIAN-STYLE *TOTALLY ARMORED KNIGHTS.*

IN *268*, THE ROMANS MET THE GERMANS AT NAISSUS (NOW NISH, SERBIA), AND WON A *COMPLETE VICTORY* IN ROME'S MOST IMPORTANT BATTLE OF THE THIRD CENTURY.

BONG BONG BONG

SOMEHOW THE HEAVY KNIGHT HAD TO STAY ON HIS STEED WITHOUT BENEFIT OF *STIRRUPS*, WHICH HADN'T BEEN INVENTED YET.

TAKE THA·A·AA

TO *MOUNT* A HORSE, A SKILLFUL LIFTER WAS ESSENTIAL. THE EMPEROR *VALENTINIAN* ONCE ORDERED HIS GROOM *EXECUTED* FOR BOTCHING THIS JOB.

MAKE *ME* LOOK BAD, WILL YOU?

THE STIRRUP, A *CHINESE* INVENTION, WAS FIRST USED STRICTLY AS A WAY TO STEP ONTO THE ANIMAL WITHOUT HELP.

HOW'D YOU THINK OF *THAT*?

THE BOSS HAS BEEN KIND OF CRANKY LATELY...

GALLIENUS HAD ENDED THE INVASION OF GREECE, AND—AFTER HIS INEVITABLE *ASSAS-SINATION*—HIS SUCCESSORS WON BACK GAUL. BY *280*, THE EMPIRE WAS QUIET AGAIN...

SOME GERMANS FLED FOR HOME, SOME SETTLED IN ROMAN TERRITORY, AND SOME ENLISTED IN THE ROMAN ARMY.

IN *284*, AFTER A SPASM OF *MUTINY* AND *CONSPIRACY* THAT CHEWED UP *FIVE EMPERORS* IN *TEN YEARS*, THE ARMY CROWNED *DIOCLETIAN*. DIOCLETIAN PERSONALLY KILLED THE CHIEF PLOTTER OF THE PREVIOUS CONSPIRACY.

WITH DIOCLETIAN, THE EMPIRE BEGAN A NEW ERA OF *SPLENDOR* AND *WRETCHEDNESS.*

AN ENERGETIC AND FORCEFUL EMPEROR, DIOCLETIAN IS FAMOUS FOR SEVERAL REASONS:

HE **SPLIT** THE EMPIRE IN **HALF.** DIOCLETIAN TOOK THE **EAST** FOR HIMSELF AND MADE HIS FRIEND **MAXIMIAN** THE **AUGUSTUS OF THE WEST.** THERE WERE ALSO TWO UNDER-EMPERORS, OR **CAESARS.**

HE INVENTED **SERFDOM.** TO ENSURE **TAX PAYMENTS** FROM THE DEPOPULATED COUNTRYSIDE, DIOCLETIAN DECREED THAT **NO TENANT FARMER COULD MOVE FROM HIS LANDLORD'S FARM.** THIS RESTRICTION ON RENTERS PASSED FROM GENERATION TO GENERATION FOR OVER **1000 YEARS!!**

HELP! I'VE FALLEN IN STATUS, AND I CAN'T GET UP!!

HE RETIRED FROM OFFICE **ALIVE.** IN **305,** AFTER **20** YEARS' RULE, HE **ABDICATED,** TO SPEND HIS LAST YEARS GARDENING IN AN UNIMAGINABLY HUGE PALACE IN **SPLIT, CROATIA.**

AND HE STARTED THE **LAST PERSECUTION OF CHRISTIANS.*** IN NICOMEDIA, DIOCLETIAN'S CAPITAL, A CHRISTIAN CHURCH SAT DIRECTLY ACROSS FROM THE PALACE. THERE WERE CHRISTIANS IN THE IMPERIAL BUREAUCRACY AND EVEN IN DIOCLETIAN'S OWN FAMILY.

ONE DAY IN 298, THE IMPERIAL FORTUNETELLERS WERE UNABLE TO READ THE OMENS OF THE GODS...

THEY BLAMED THE **CHRISTIANS** IN THE ROOM, WHO HAD BEEN FRANTICALLY CROSSING THEMSELVES TO DRIVE OUT THE "DEMONS".

AT FIRST, DIOCLETIAN REACTED MILDLY. BUT, EGGED ON BY HIS UNDER-EMPEROR **CAESAR GALERIUS**, HE ORDERED CHURCHES DEMOLISHED, BIBLES BURNT, BISHOPS ARRESTED.

REPENT!

WHO CAN INTERPRET INTESTINES WITH PEOPLE LIKE THAT AROUND?

AFTER THE ABDICATION OF 305, GALERIUS TURNED EVEN MORE VICIOUS, SENDING CHRISTIANS TO THE **MINES**— AFTER **CUTTING ONE HAMSTRING**—OR PITCHING THEM INTO **DUNGEONS**.

YOOOU'LL BE SORRRY!

CHRISTIAN SOLDIERS!?

WHEN OUT OF THE WEST CAME **CONSTANTINE**, THE FIRST **CHRISTIAN EMPEROR**.

HURRY!

HURRY!

CONSTANTINE'S FATHER HAD BEEN **AUGUSTUS OF THE WEST**. WHEN HE WAS DYING, CONSTANTINE RUSHED TO HIS SIDE JUST IN TIME.

DAD! I'M HERE! YOU CAN DIE NOW!!

JUST IN TIME, THAT IS, TO BE HAILED **CAESAR** BY THE TROOPS—WITHOUT DIOCLETIAN'S PERMISSION!!

HAIL, CONSTANTINE!

OO, IT'S BRIGHT OUT HERE—YOW! THERE'S A CROSS IN THE SUN!!

BUT NEVER MIND! CONSTANTINE WAS READY TO FIGHT! AS SOON AS GALERIUS DIED (311), CONSTANTINE'S ARMIES TOOK ON ALL RIVALS.

MEN! LET ME EXPLAIN A **NEW CONCEPT**: DRAWING THE SWORD FOR THE PRINCE OF PEACE!

Xρ = "CHI RHO" = GREEK ABBREVIATION OF "CHRIST"

BY **312**, HE HAD ENTERED **ROME**, UNDISPUTED MASTER OF THE WEST.

THROUGHOUT THE EMPIRE, THE PERSECUTION OF CHRISTIANS ABRUPTLY STOPPED... AND NOT ONLY THAT... BUT WHEN THE CHRISTIAN PRISONERS EMERGED FROM THE DUNGEONS, CONSTANTINE SHOWERED THEM WITH FAVORS!

EMOLUMENTS? SUBSIDIES? CHANGE OF CLOTHES? WHAT WOULD YOU LIKE?

TEAR... DOWN... TEMPLE...

AND WHEN, IN THEIR ZEAL, THEY DE-STROYED A PAGAN TEMPLE OR TWO, HE *FORGAVE* THEM.

FORGIVENESS IS A VIRTUE, AFTER ALL...

THE ONLY CHRISTIAN THING CONSTANTINE *WOULDN'T* DO WAS BE *BAPTISED.*

I'M A *KING*... SIN IS PART OF MY *JOB*... YOU UNDERSTAND...

PERFECTLY... JUST KEEP THOSE EMOLU-MENTS AND SUBSIDIES COMING...

CHRISTIAN OR NO, CONSTANTINE WASN'T SATISFIED WITH HALF AN EMPIRE. HE PICKED A FIGHT WITH THE EASTERN EMPEROR *LICINIUS,* AND BY 325, CONSTANTINE RULED *ALL.* CHRISTIANS CHEERED AND PAGANS TREMBLED!

STRANGE CROWD AT THE PARADE TODAY...

CONSTANTINE NOW ORDERED HIMSELF A *BRAND NEW CAPITAL CITY,* AN EASTERN ROME, DECORATED WITH SPLENDOR LOOTED FROM THE *PAGAN TEMPLES* ACROSS THE EMPIRE.

AND THE CITY SHALL BE NAMED... HM... *CHRISTOPOLIS?* NO... *JESUSVILLE?* UH-UH... *NEW JERUSALEM?* TOO ETHNIC... WAIT! I HAVE IT... *CONSTANTINOPOLIS!*

AS THE CITY ROSE FAST AND SLOPPY, CONSTANTINE TURNED TO THE NEXT AGENDA ITEM:

MAKING EVERYBODY *THINK ALIKE?!*

UNLIKE ROME, CONSTANTINOPLE *WAS* BUILT IN A DAY!

CRASH

THE NEW RELIGION REQUIRED *EVERYONE TO HAVE THE SAME OPINIONS.* DISAGREEMENT, OR *HERESY,* WAS *NOT O.K.*

MAKES SENSE— HOW CAN THERE BE MORE THAN *ONE TRUTH??*

YOU HAVE QUITE A POINT THERE...

THUD

WHERE DID HERESIES COME FROM? A TYPICAL ONE ORIGINATED WITH THE EGYPTIAN BISHOP *MELITUS,* WHO HAD SPENT *NINE YEARS* IN A *DUNGEON* FOR HIS FAITH.

YOU GET SOME FUNNY IDEAS DOWN HERE!

NOW HE WAS OUT, HE SAW A LOT OF *WEAKER SOULS* COMING BACK TO THE CHURCH— PEOPLE WHO HAD DODGED PERSECUTION BY SACRIFICING TO THE ROMAN GODS!

WE CAN'T ALL BE AS CRAZY— UH, STRONG AS YOU...

MELITUS DIDN'T APPROVE!

YOU I'M IGNORING... BUT I HAVE A *BIG PROBLEM* WITH THE GUY WHO *LET YOU BACK IN!!*

OH, LIGHTEN UP, MEL...

AN ARGUMENT OVER POLICY TURNED INTO A DISAGREEMENT ABOUT DOCTRINE.

I AGREE WITH MY BELOVED BISHOP IN ALL THINGS *BUT ONE*...

GAH!

MELITUS' FOLLOWER *ARIUS* OPINED THUSLY ABOUT THE TRINITY OF *FATHER, SON,* AND *HOLY SPIRIT.*

THE SON WAS CREATED BY THE *FATHER*... SO, COMING AFTER THE FATHER, HE IS NOT OF THE *SAME SUBSTANCE* AS THE FATHER. *SIMILAR,* MAYBE, BUT *NOT THE SAME*...

SUCH A LOVELY VOICE...

FURIOUS ARGUMENTS FOLLOWED... LETTERS FLEW... TEMPERS FLARED. IN ALEXANDRIA, ARIUS WAS *EXPELLED* FROM THE CHURCH.

TO SETTLE THIS (AND OTHER) QUESTIONS, CONSTANTINE CALLED A MEETING OF **ALL THE BISHOPS** IN THE EMPIRE. ABOUT **300** OUT OF **500** SHOWED UP AT **NICAEA**, ASIA MINOR.

THEIR FINDINGS FORM THE *NICENE CREED,* A STATEMENT OF ORTHODOXY STILL HELD BY THE CATHOLIC CHURCH.

AND HERE'S THE *COMPLETE LIST* OF HERETICAL IDEAS...

TO DATE...

ON THE ARIAN QUESTION, THEY ANNOUNCED THAT FATHER AND SON WERE THE **SAME SUBSTANCE** (IN GREEK, *HOMO-OUSION*). TO BELIEVE, WITH ARIUS, THAT THEY WERE MERELY OF *SIMILAR SUBSTANCE* (*HOMOI-OUSION*) WAS **HERESY.**

AS I SAID, I AGREE WITH YOU, EXCEPT FOR ONE LETTER!

BUT, FOR SOME REASON, ARIANISM REMAINED A POPULAR OPINION IN THE EAST, WHERE THE DISCUSSION CONTINUED IN THE STREETS.

SO-O-O... WHICH CAME FIRST — THE, UM, CHICKEN OR THE EGG?

AFTER A LAST MINUTE BAPTISM, CONSTANTINE DIED IN *337*.

QUICK!

SPLAT

HIS TWO SONS, *CONSTANS* AND *CONSTANTIUS*, DIVIDED THE EMPIRE, KILLED MANY RIVALS AND COUSINS, AND PROMOTED CHRISTIANITY.

I KNOW! NOW LET'S BAN *ANIMAL SACRIFICE!*

MISSIONARIES, LIKE THE SAINTED, THOUGH ARIAN, *ULFILAS*, WENT OFF TO CONVERT THE *GERMANS*, WITH SOME SUCCESS.

ACH! FEELS GOOD! WHERE'S MY *SWORD?*

UNFORTUNATELY, THIS DID NOTHING TO STOP THE GERMANS FROM INVADING *GAUL* AGAIN... IN FACT, *NOTHING* COULD STOP THEM.

I'M NOT EVEN *TRYING*, AND I'LL TELL YOU WHY *NOT!*

IF YOU *BEAT 'EM*, YOU JUST HAVE TO FACE THOSE TWO *PARANOID EMPERORS.*

AFTER SEVERAL DEFEATS, CONSTANTIUS PUT *JULIAN* IN CHARGE OF THE ARMY— THE SON OF ONE OF THOSE *MURDERED COUSINS*.

I HAVE COMPLETE FAITH IN YOU!

BUT YOU MURDERED MY DAD...

FORGIVENESS IS A VIRTUE, SO I FORGIVE YOU!

JULIAN, RAISED AS A PHILOSOPHER WITH NO MILITARY EXPERIENCE, SURPRISED *EVERYONE*, ESPECIALLY THE *GERMANS*.

LET'S GO!!

MOVING "FASTER THAN RUMOR," HE POUNCED, BLOODILY CHASING THEM FAR INTO THEIR OWN LAND.

HAD ENOUGH?

ONKEL!

NEXT SURPRISE: HE NOW MOVED ON THE CAPITAL, AND SUDDENLY (361) JULIAN WAS THE *NEW EMPEROR!* ANY MORE SURPRISES?

JUST ONE: I WORSHIP *ZEUS!!*

JULIAN ORDERED THE CHRISTIAN CHURCHES TO *GIVE BACK* ALL THE PROPERTY THEY HAD LOOTED FROM THE PAGANS.

B-BUH-B-BUH-BUH...

JUST THE *LAND, BUILDINGS,* AND *GOLD!*

OTHER THAN THAT, HE DIDN'T REALLY PERSECUTE THE CHRISTIANS.

YOU'RE *QUITE* EFFECTIVE ENOUGH AT PERSECUTING *EACH OTHER!*

THAT EVIL, EVIL MAN!!

A BELIEVER IN THE *SIMPLE LIFE,* JULIAN DROVE A HORDE OF *HAIR-DRESSERS, CHEFS,* AND *EUNUCHS* OUT OF THE IMPERIAL PALACE, WITH NO JOB RETRAINING.

THAT *EVIL, EVIL* MAN!!

THERE'S NO SAYING WHAT MIGHT HAVE HAPPENED IF JULIAN HADN'T LAUNCHED AN IMMENSE INVASION OF *PERSIA* IN 362... PLUNGING RASHLY INTO THE UN-KNOWN, THE EMPEROR WAS KILLED, ALONG WITH MOST OF HIS ARMY—A CATASTROPHE THAT MAY HAVE CHANGED EUROPEAN HISTORY FOREVER...

OOPS.

AFTER JULIAN'S DEATH, THE CHRISTIANS REVIVED WITH THE EMPEROR **VALENTINIAN**, A FURIOUS, PARANOID CHARACTER OBSESSED WITH CONSPIRACIES AND EVIL MAGICIANS—BUT A CHRISTIAN!

FUME SNARL

PET BEAR ↓

IT'S HARD TO KNOW IF JULIAN, VALENTINIAN, OR **ANYONE** COULD HAVE COPED WITH WHAT CAME NEXT... YOU'LL RECALL THAT THE FOURTH CENTURY WAS WHEN **CHINA** WAS OVER-RUN AGAIN AND AGAIN!

CENTRAL ASIA WAS IN TURMOIL... THERE'S EVIDENCE THAT **COOLING CLIMATE** WAS PUSHING PEOPLE OUT OF THEIR USUAL HOMES...

IT'S HARD TO TRACE ALL THE MIGRATIONS, BUT THERE'S NO QUESTION THAT **PRESSURE** WAS **BUILDING UP...**

'SCUSE!

OW!

MOVE IT!

VALENTINIAN WAS DIMLY AWARE OF ALL THIS, BUT NO MATTER—DURING A TEMPER TANTRUM, HE BURST A BLOOD VESSEL AND DIED.

SPLUT
SPLUT
SPLUT
SPLAT

HIS BROTHER, THE NEW EMPEROR **VALENS**, RECEIVED A DELEGATION OF **VISIGOTHS**, GERMANS FROM ACROSS THE DANUBE RIVER.

THEY DESCRIBED HORRIBLE RAIDS ON THEIR FARMS AND TOWNS BY TRIBES CALLED THE **ALANS** AND **HUNS**.

THEIR REQUEST WAS **AMAZING**: TO MOVE THE WHOLE **VISIGOTHIC NATION** ACROSS THE RIVER INTO ROMAN TERRITORY.

VALENS SAID YES...

BUT YOU'LL HAVE TO CHECK YOUR **WEAPONS** AT THE BORDER!!

RIGHT!

IN THE SPRING OF 376, THE VISI-GOTHS CROSSED—WHILE UPRIVER, A **SECOND TRIBE** OF GERMANS ALSO CROSSED, SECRETLY...

289

WHAT POSSESSED VALENS TO ADMIT AN ENTIRE—SOMETIMES *HOSTILE*—NATION INTO HIS MIDST? IN A WORD:

MANPOWER NEEDS!

THAT'S TWO WORDS!

MANY GERMANS ALREADY SERVED IN THE ROMAN ARMY, FROM FOOT-SOLDIERS TO GENERALS, AND VALENS WANTED *MORE!*

THAT ONE!

JA

BUT HE HAD FORGOTTEN TO THINK ABOUT ONE THING: *FOOD*... WITH ALMOST A MILLION PEOPLE IN CAMPS, SUPPLIES RAN SHORT... AND *HUNGER* TURNED TO *ANGER* WHEN SOME ROMANS TRADED ROMAN *DOGS* FOR GOTHIC *CHILDREN*...

DON'T WORRY... I'LL FEED HIM AND THRASH HIM JUST AS IF HE WERE MY OWN!

THE GOTHS DID WHAT ANY SELF-RESPECTING PEOPLE WOULD HAVE DONE.

HEY! I THOUGHT YOU GAVE UP YOUR WEAPONS!

YA, SOME OF THEM!

THEY PILLAGED *THRACE*... THE *HUNS* AND *ALANS* JOINED THEM... BATTLES RAGED... THE EMPEROR RUSHED TO THE SCENE WITH REINFORCEMENTS.

GLEEP!

VALENS MET THE GOTHS AT *HADRIANOPLE*, ON AUGUST 9, 378, A DECISIVE DAY FOR THE ROMAN EMPIRE.

WHEN IT WAS OVER, MOST OF THE ROMAN ARMY WAS DEAD, INCLUDING THE *EMPEROR*, WHOSE BODY WAS NEVER FOUND.

DOWN WITH CIVILIZATION AS WE KNOW IT!!

WHEN THE NEWS REACHED CONSTANTINOPLE, A QUICK-THINKING GENERAL SENT *SECRET ORDERS* TO ALL THE COMMANDERS OF THE *EAST*.

OUR ARMIES IN ASIA ARE FULL OF GOTHS... A CLEAR THREAT TO *NATIONAL SECURITY*...

GOOD THING WE ROMANS ARE RUTHLESS...

ON THE ASSIGNED DAY, ALL THEIR GOTHIC UNITS WERE MUSTERED AT DAWN...

TEN·*HUT!!*

AND *ANNIHILATED* BY THE ROMANS FROM AMBUSH...

THE NEXT EMPEROR, *THEODOSIUS*, INHERITED A MESS, BUT HE WAS NOT WITHOUT RESOURCES.

I STILL HAVE THE WEALTH OF THE EAST, MY NATIVE WIT, AND PRIESTS WHO SPEAK GOTHIC!

HE ALSO HAD *STILICHO*, A GERMAN OF THE VANDAL TRIBE, WHO BECAME THEODOSIUS'S RIGHT-HAND MAN.

MY MAN!

THE EMPEROR USED HIS ASSETS TO WIN OVER AS MANY GERMAN CHIEFS AS POSSIBLE...

LOOK TO YOUR SOUL, ALARIC! THIS WILL HELP...

THINK... YOU CAN *ENJOY* CIVILIZATION, NOT *WRECK* IT...

AND THEN SET THE FRIENDLY GERMANS ON THE UNFRIENDLY ONES!

SCHWEIN!

HUND!

BY 385, MILLIONS OF GERMANS HAD SETTLED INSIDE THE EMPIRE, NEAR THE GREAT CITIES, AND ALL WAS QUIET, OR AT LEAST QUIETER...*

ACH, DU LIEBER *AUGUSTINE*, AUGUSTINE... ♪ ETC ETC...

MOAN...

WE CAN GET A GLIMPSE OF DAILY LIFE IN THE LATE 300S FROM THE *CONFESSIONS* OF ST. AUGUSTINE, SON OF A CHRISTIAN MOTHER SO *STRICT* THAT SHE ALLOWED HER CHILDREN ONLY *THREE SMALL GLASSES OF WATER* PER DAY.

THE FLESH IS OUR ENEMY!

YOUNG AUGUSTINE *REBELLED*, FALLING IN LOVE WITH—BUT NOT MARRYING—AN "INAPPROPRIATE" WOMAN, WHO BORE HIS CHILD.

BUT WHEN HIS MOTHER DIED, AUGUSTINE FLIPPED WITH GRIEF.

MOM! I WAS BAD... BUT NOW I'LL BE *GOOD!*

SO HE DID THE "RIGHT" THING: *DITCHED HIS MISTRESS* AND LEFT FOR ROME TO *SEEK TRUTH!!*

WHERE'S MY ✶@# CHILD SUPPORT?

AT THIS POINT, THEODOSIUS TURNED TO ANOTHER PROJECT: BRINGING *PAGANISM* AND *HERESY* TO AN END *FOREVER.*

HE ENCOURAGED THE FOLLOWERS OF THE ROMAN CHURCH TO TAKE OVER THE EASTERN CHURCHES AND KICK OUT THE ARIANS.

IF YOU LOVE GOD, GIVE ME EVERYTHING AND GET OUT!

HE APPLAUDED THE BANDS OF *DESTROYER MONKS* WHO ROAMED THE COUNTRYSIDE PILLAGING PAGAN SHRINES.

HE SUPPORTED THE RIOTING EGYPTIAN ZEALOTS WHO ATTACKED TEMPLES— AND LIBRARIES!—FULL OF THINGS PAGAN, SECULAR, OR JUST OLD.

...BUT THIS STUFF WAS *MILD* COMPARED TO WHAT HAPPENED WHEN BISHOP *AMBROSE* OF MILAN GOT THE EMPEROR'S EAR. IT HAPPENED LIKE THIS...

IN *390*, THEODOSIUS'S GENERAL *BUTHERIC* WAS LYNCHED IN *THESSALONICA*, GREECE.

IN REPLY, THE EMPEROR LET THE ARMY *MASSACRE* THE GOOD CITIZENS OF THESSALONICA.

BISHOP AMBROSE ORDERED THEODOSIUS TO DO A YEAR'S PENANCE. CHURCH NOW RULED STATE!

SAY 10,000 NOVENAS... AND...

YES! YES!

293

PRODDED BY GUILT (AND BY AMBROSE, NO DOUBT), THEODOSIUS NOW DECREED—ON FEB. 24, 391—THAT *ALL REMAINING PAGAN TEMPLES* WERE CLOSED TO THE PUBLIC.

GUESS WE'LL JUST HAVE TO SACRIFICE *ELSEWHERE!*

WHEN PAGANS MOVED THEIR RITES TO *GROVES* AND *FIELDS*, THEODOSIUS BANNED THAT PRACTICE, TOO (11/8/392).

GUESS NOT...

IN 395, THEODOSIUS MARCHED INTO ROME, STRIPPED THE TEMPLES, AND DRAGGED THE STATUES OF THE GODS THROUGH THE STREETS...

WHAT? NO THUNDER-BOLT??

WHAT A DRAG...

HE PUT THE QUESTION TO THE SENATE: WAS THE EMPIRE TO BE RULED BY *JUPITER* OR *JESUS?*

BY *YOU,* OH GLORIOUS LEADER!

THE SENATE CONVERTED... SO DID MOST CITIZENS... BUT WHO KNOWS HOW MANY OF THEM LONGED FOR ROME'S ANCIENT GODDESS OF *VICTORY* OR DARED TO RISK READING THE FUTURE FROM THE DANCES OF *CHICKENS??*

"NO MORE ROMAN VICTORIES"

A FEW MONTHS LATER, THEO-DOSIUS DIED. HIS TWO SONS DIVIDED THE EMPIRE, *ARCADIUS* IN THE EAST AND *HONORIUS* IN ROME. BUT ROME WASN'T WHAT IT USED TO BE...

SINCE DAD STRIPPED THE TEMPLES, EVERYONE EXPECTS THE WORST...

THE RECORD IS MURKY, BUT APPARENTLY HONORIUS HAD SOME SQUABBLE WITH A GOTHIC KING NAMED *ALARIC*. SO HONORIUS MOVED HIS CAPITAL TO *RAVENNA*, SAFELY SURROUNDED BY SWAMPS.

THE ONLY GOTHS WHO CAN GET IN *HERE* ARE GOTHIC *MOSQUITOS*...

AT THIS POINT, ALARIC MARCHED HIS GOTHS INTO ITALY, IGNORING RAVENNA AND HEADING FOR *ROME*.

PIL-LAGE!

AT THE GATES OF ROME, HE DEMANDED 5,000 LBS. OF *GOLD* AND 3,000 LBS. OF *PEPPER*(!). THE DIALOG WAS THIS:

BEWARE ALARIC! THERE ARE LOTS OF US, AND WE'RE *DESPERATE!*

THE THICKER THE HAY, THE EASIER THE MOWING!!

WHEN THE PEPPER RAN OUT, THE GOTHS CAME BACK FOR A *SECOND* VISIT, AND THE CITIZENS OPENED THE GATES...

THEIR THIRD VISIT TO ROME WAS IN THE YEAR 410...

THIS IS TOO EASY!!

THIS TIME, THE GOTHS SPENT SIX DAYS THOROUGHLY **SACKING** THE PLACE—EXCEPT **CHURCH PROPERTY,** WHICH THEY SPARED!✳

I'M SORRY... THEODOSIUS TOOK MOST OF THE GOOD STUFF!

DURING THE FIRST SACK OF ROME, CHRISTIANS TOOK REFUGE IN THE **VATICAN** AND WERE SPARED BY ALARIC'S MARAUDERS. ALARIC, OF COURSE, WAS A CHRISTIAN!

IF YOUR MEN TOUCH CHURCH PROPERTY, ALARIC, THEIR SOULS ARE TOAST!

SO **AUGUSTINE,** BY THEN A CHRISTIAN BISHOP, WROTE **THE CITY OF GOD,** WHICH ARGUES THAT CHRISTIANITY UNITES PEOPLE IN A **SPIRITUAL, INVISIBLE CITY** GREATER THAN ANY PHYSICAL CITY.

WE LIVE ON A HIGHER PLANE, SAFE FROM PILLAGING!

IF AUGUSTINE HAD LIVED A FEW MORE YEARS TO SEE WHAT THE CHRISTIAN **VANDALS** DID TO HIS NATIVE AFRICA, HE **MIGHT** HAVE WANTED TO REVISE THIS BOOK...

OOPS!

THE SACK OF ROME DEMORALIZED THE EMPIRE AND ENCOURAGED THE *SUEBI, FRANKS, AND VANDALS,* WHO SWEPT ACROSS EUROPE WITHOUT RESISTANCE.

WHY BOTHER?

THE CITIZENS OF GAUL DIDN'T PEEP WHEN THE GERMANS DIVIDED UP THEIR PROPERTY...

ONE FOR ME, AND ONE FOR YOU... NO... MAKE THAT *TWO* FOR ME...

WHATEVER.

TO RETURN THE KINDNESS, MOST OF THE GERMANS RENOUNCED THE ARIAN HERESY AND BECAME CATHOLICS.

WHY NOT? AND I MEAN THAT SINCERELY.

AN EXCEPTION WERE THE *VANDALS,* WHO CONQUERED NORTH AFRICA. STUNG BY THE CATHOLICS' TONGUE-LASHINGS, THEY CUT OUT 2000 CATHOLIC TONGUES.

GOT ANYTHING TO SAY ABOUT IT?

MM·MM!

IN *453,* THE VANDALS SACKED ROME, COMMITTING MORE ACTS OF THE KIND NOW KNOWN AS VANDALISM...

THE PUMP DON'T WORK!

IN THE *440s,* THE *HUNS,* UNDER *ATTILA,* SCARED EUROPE SENSELESS...

BOOGIE BOOGIE!

BUT WHEN ATTILA DIED, THE HUN THREAT DID TOO...

...AND EUROPE BECAME A PATCHWORK OF "BARBARIAN" NATIONS, WITH GERMAN ROYAL HOUSES AND A POPE IN ROME. SO IT REMAINS TO THIS DAY...

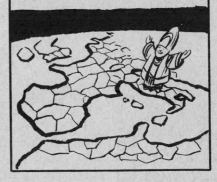

BUT THE *EASTERN* EMPIRE SURVIVED! HERE'S A GLIMPSE OF CONSTANTINOPLE IN THE *500*s, THANKS TO THE HISTORIAN *PROCOPIUS*... AT THE HIPPODROME, FANS ARE DIVIDED INTO RIVAL GANGS, THE *BLUES* AND THE *GREENS*. HAIR IS WORN *HUN-STYLE*.

AT A NIGHT CLUB, THE FAMED *THEODORA* AND A TRAINED GOOSE DO *"LEDA AND THE SWAN"*.

WITH THIS ONE SHE MANAGED TO MOCK *GREEK* MYTHOLOGY AND *CHRISTIAN* MORALITY ALL AT THE SAME TIME!

YOU'RE DIVINE!

IN THE AUDIENCE, PRINCE *JUSTINIAN** WAS IN LOVE!

*BORN "PETER SABBATH," JUSTINIAN WAS HIS ADOPTED NAME.

THE PRINCE MARRIED THE DANCER, AND JUSTINIAN AND THEODORA BECAME *EMPEROR* AND *EMPRESS*!

¡AHEM¡ HONEY... LOSE THE GOOSE...

298

THIS IDYLLIC SCENE WAS INTERRUPTED BY A RIOT OF THE BLUES AND GREENS THAT NEARLY OUSTED JUSTINIAN... (537 A.D.)

GAH! ANOTHER CROWD SCENE!

DON'T WORRY, DEAR... IT'S THE LAST ONE OF THE BOOK...

HIS GENERAL, *BELISARIUS*, PUT DOWN THE REBELLION, KILLING 30,000 RACING FANS.

CONGRATULATIONS, GENERAL! THE ODDS WERE 100 TO 1 AGAINST YOU!

FROM THERE, BELISARIUS SAILED WEST TO WIN BACK ITALY... HE FAILED, RUMOR HAS IT, BECAUSE THEODORA WANTED HIM TO FAIL...

YOU CAN READ THE *SCANDALOUS* DETAILS IN PROCOPIUS'S SECRET HISTORY...

BUT JUSTINIAN'S OTHER GENERALS DID SUCCEED AT PUTTING SOME OF THE OLD EMPIRE BACK TOGETHER...

IT'S THE DAWN OF A GLORIOUS, BUT VERY SHORT, NEW AGE...

YOU ARE HERE

IT DIDN'T LAST LONG. BEGINNING IN THE 540s, THE *BULGAR* INVASIONS BEGAN—

OH, FOR—

AT THE SAME TIME, EUROPE'S FIRST CASES OF *BUBONIC PLAGUE* ERUPTED.

:OOG: I FEEL THE *DARK AGES* COMING ON...

BY THE END OF JUSTINIAN'S REIGN (564), THE WESTERN END OF THE EMPIRE WAS IN TRULY WRETCHED SHAPE...

FARMS BURNT... WEALTH GONE... DEAD BULGARS ALL OVER THE PLACE...

EUROPE WAS MIRED IN POVERTY AND IGNORANCE... CHINA WAS RISING AGAIN UNDER THE *TANG* DYNASTY... AND MOST OF THE LAND IN BETWEEN WAS ABOUT TO SEE SOME *VISITORS* FROM A *SURPRISING DIRECTION*...

HM! EVER SINCE SWAMI TOOK MY *WATCH*, I DON'T *CARE* WHAT *TIME* IT IS!

THE FIRST CITIES BY D. HAMBLIN. EXCELLENT SOURCE FOR HARAPPAN MUD VOLCANOES.

THE RIG VEDA TRANSLATED BY W. O'FLAHERTY. EARLY ARYANS SING A SONG OF SOMA, ETC...

THE WONDER THAT WAS INDIA BY A.L. BASHAM. SUPERBLY DETAILED, JUDICIOUSLY ARGUED, WELL WRITTEN. ALSO SURVEYS TAMIL TRADITION

SOURCES OF INDIAN TRADITION ED. BY A.T. EMBREE. MANY SHORT EXCERPTS

INDIAN MYTHOLOGY BY V. IONS. GOOD PIX.

HINDU MYTHS TR BY W. O'FLAHERTY; VARIOUS VERSIONS OF EVERYTHING

THE PANCHATANTRA TRANSLATED BY A. RYDER. ANIMAL FABLES, RUMORED TO BE AESOP'S SOURCE

DAILY LIFE IN ANCIENT INDIA BY J. AUBOYER DESCRIBES SOCIETY IN ASHOKA'S TIME

INDIA: PAINTINGS FROM THE AJANTA CAVES N.Y. GRAPHIC SOCIETY + UNESCO; SUMPTUOUS BUDDHIST FRESCOES

GLIMPSES OF WORLD HISTORY BY J. NEHRU AN INCISIVE ALTERNATIVE TO H.G. WELLS

INDIAN ATHEISM BY D. CHATTOPADHYAYA REVEALS A SURPRISING GODLESS TRADITION IN INDIAN PHILOSOPHY

LOKAYATA, A STUDY OF ANCIENT INDIAN MATERIALISM BY D. CHATTOPADHYAYA A RECONSTRUCTION FROM SLENDER REMAINS

BHAGAVAD GITA TR. BY A. STAFFORD

KRSNA, THE SUPREME PERSONALITY OF GODHEAD BY A.C. BHAKTIVEDENTA SWAMI PRABHUPADA; AN ACCOUNT BY A TRUE BELIEVER

INDIA BY M. HÜRLIMANN BEST PHOTO BOOK I'VE SEEN

DEEDLE DEEDLE DEEDLE

NOW IF ONLY MY *PUBLISHER* FELT THE SAME WAY!!

THE MAYOR DIDN'T ANSWER MY LETTER! SO I'M MAKING *MY OWN* STREET SIGNS!!

CHANG, K.-C., *THE ARCHAEOLOGY OF ANCIENT CHINA* DARING SNIPPETS OF SPECULATION LIE BURIED AMONG THE POTS AND BONES. DIG THEM OUT!

CHUANG-TZU *COMPLETE WORKS* TR. BY B. WATSON. WHAT'S WRONG WITH BEING USELESS?

CONFUCIUS, *ANALECTS*, TR. BY A. WALEY BEST TRANSLATION OF THE OLD REPUBLICAN'S SAYINGS, COMPILED BY HIS STUDENTS

DEBARY, CHAN, + WATSON, EDS., *SOURCES OF CHINESE TRADITION.* MANY PITHY EXCERPTS.

EDITORS OF HORIZON MAGAZINE *THE HORIZON BOOK OF THE ARTS OF CHINA.* LAVISH PIX.

FITZGERALD, C.P., *THE HORIZON HISTORY OF CHINA.* MORE LAVISH PIX — PLUS THOUGHTFUL TEXT. AN EXCELLENT BOOK!

HSÜN-TZE, *WORKS.* NAKED DEFENSE OF HIERARCHY AND AUTHORITY

INSTITUTE OF THE HISTORY OF NATURAL SCIENCE, BEIJING, *ANCIENT CHINA'S TECHNOLOGY AND SCIENCE.* GOOD CHAPTER ON SILK

LAO-TSE, *TAO-TE CHING* GET AN EDITION WITH LOTS OF FOOTNOTES, IF YOU'RE SERIOUS.

LEGGE, J., TR., *THE CHINESE CLASSICS.* AN IMMENSE, 5-VOLUME TREASURE-TROVE: THE ANNALS OF YAO, SHUN, + YÜ, OLD POEMS, SPRING + AUTUMN ANNALS, SALTY FOOTNOTES, ALL SERVED UP WITH GREAT SCHOLARSHIP AND CRANKY, VICTORIAN OPINIONS BY THE REV. DR. LEGGE!

LI, D. *THE ESSENCE OF CHINESE CIVILIZATION*, MORE EXCERPTS

LOEWE, M, *EVERYDAY LIFE IN EARLY IMPERIAL CHINA.* SURPRISINGLY THIN.

SCHAFER, E., + TIME-LIFE EDS, *ANCIENT CHINA.* DISAPPOINTING

SMITH, B + WENG, W, *CHINA, A HISTORY IN ART.* GOOD, NON STANDARD PIX

SSU-MA CHIEN, *RECORDS OF THE HISTORIAN.* MY MAN! CHINA'S GREATEST HISTORIAN LAYS IT OUT FOR YOU! REPAYS REPEATED READINGS. IF POSSIBLE, GET THE EDITION FROM BEIJING FOR ITS BROADER SELECTION AND LIVELY TRANSLATION.

SUN-TZU *THE ART OF WAR.* A QUICK READ. POPULAR WITH CORPORATE "WARRIORS," TOO, I HEAR.

VER WILGHEN, A, *MENCIUS, THE MAN AND HIS IDEAS*

WATSON, W., *ANCIENT CHINA: DISCOVERIES OF POST-LIBERATION ARCHAEOLOGY*

ALSO: J. NEEDHAM'S *SCIENCE & CIVILIZATION IN CHINA* IS A MUST-READ, BUT I DIDN'T!

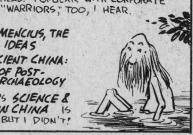

BUSH
CONFUCIUS
ME... TZU ST

GRANT

THE BEST THING ABOUT READING CHINESE HISTORY IS THAT HALF AN HOUR LATER YOU'RE HUNGRY FOR *MORE!!*

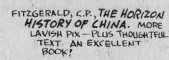

PLEASE ACCEPT MY HUMBLE APOLOGIES FOR NOT USING MORE BOOKS ON ASIAN HISTORY!

AUGUSTINE, *CONFESSIONS*, TR. BY J. G. PILKINGTON, N.Y., LIVERIGHT PUBLISHING CORP., 1943; JUICY, PIQUANT SELF-EXAMINATIONS.

AUERBACH, E., *MIMESIS*, TR. BY E. TRASK, GARDEN CITY, N.Y., DOUBLEDAY ANCHOR, 1953; A MASTERPIECE ON LITERATURE, FEELING, AND WESTERN CIVILIZATION.

BALSDON, J.P.V.D., *LIFE AND LEISURE IN ANCIENT ROME*, N.Y., MCGRAW-HILL, 1969.

BALSDON, J.P.V.D., *ROMAN WOMEN: THEIR HISTORY AND HABITS*, CONNECTICUT, GREENWOOD PRESS, 1975; WAY MORE THAN I COULD USE, SADLY, BUT A GOOD SOURCE.

DE BARY, W.T., *SOURCES OF CHINESE TRADITION*, N.Y., COLUMBIA UNIVERSITY PRESS, 1960, BRIEF EXCERPTS FROM A FEW OF THE CLASSICS.

DE CAMP, L. S., *THE ANCIENT ENGINEERS*, N.Y., DOUBLEDAY, 1963; BRICKS AND MORTAR.

CARCOPINO, J. *DAILY LIFE IN ANCIENT ROME*, TR. BY E.O. LORIMER, NEW HAVEN, YALE U. PRESS, 1963; DETAILED DESCRIPTIONS OF GARBAGE DISPOSAL, HORSE-RACING, ETC.

COOK, S.A., ADCOCK, F.E., CHARLESWORTH. M.P., EDS.,*THE CAMBRIDGE ANCIENT HISTORY. VOLUME VIII.,* CAMBRIDGE, THE UNIVERSITY PRESS, 1928; MASSIVE.

COOK, S.A., ADCOCK, F.E., CHARLESWORTH. M.P., EDS., *THE CAMBRIDGE ANCIENT HISTORY. VOLUME IX,* CAMBRIDGE, THE UNIVERSITY PRESS, 1966; MASSIVE.

CORNELL, T. & MATTHEWS, J., *ATLAS OF THE ROMAN WORLD*, N.Y., FACTS ON FILE, INC., 1982; SURPRISINGLY FINE HISTORICAL NARRATIVE PLUS GOOD PIX.

EBERHARD, W., *A HISTORY OF CHINA*, BERKELEY, U.C. PRESS, 1977; SOMEWHAT MORE DETAILED THAN SOME.

EUSEBIUS, *THE ECCLESIASTICAL HISTORY*, TR. BY J.E.L. OULTON, LOEB CLASSICAL LIBRARY, HARVARD U. PRESS, 1964; I DARE YOU TO READ THIS WITHOUT EXPLODING!

GIBBON, E., *THE DECLINE AND FALL OF THE ROMAN EMPIRE*, N.Y., MODERN LIBRARY, (3 VOLUMES); JUSTIFIABLY FAMOUS: SCHOLARLY, JUDICIOUS, & OPINIONATED, THOUGH HIS ROLLING STYLE EVENTUALLY WEARS.

HEICHELHEIM, F.M. AND YEO, C., *A HISTORY OF THE ROMAN PEOPLE*, ENGLEWOOD CLIFFS, N.J., PRENTICE-HALL, 1962; GOOD GENERAL HISTORY TO THE AGE OF CONSTANTINE.

HOLUM, K.G., *THEODOSIAN EMPRESSES*, BERKELEY, U.C. PRESS, 1982; SOME INTERESTING EASTERN CHURCH HISTORY.

JONES, A.H.M., *THE LATER ROMAN EMPIRE 284-602*, NORMAN, OKLA., U. OF OKLAHOMA PRESS, 1964; EVERYTHING YOU ALWAYS WANTED TO KNOW ABOUT LATE ROMAN TAX COLLECTION, PLUS SOME GOOD STUFF.

JOSEPHUS, *THE JEWISH WAR*, TR. BY G.A. WILLIAMSON, N.Y., PENGUIN, 1969; A MUST-READ!!!

LIVY, *A HISTORY OF ROME*. SELECTIONS TR. BY M. HADAS AND J.P. POE, N.Y., THE MODERN LIBRARY, 1962; A GOOD, IF UNTRUSTWORTHY READ.

LO KUAN-CHUNG, *ROMANCE OF THE THREE KINGDOMS, VOLUME ONE*, TR. BY C.H. BREWITT-TAYLOR, RUTLAND, VT., CHARLES E TUTTLE, 1976; SWASHBUCKLING EPIC.

MAENCHEN-HELFEN, OTTO J., *THE WORLD OF THE HUNS*, BERKELEY, U.C. PRESS, 1973; A SCHOLARLY *TOUR DE FORCE*.

MARCELLINUS, AMMIANUS, *HISTORY, VOLUMES I, II, III*, TR. BY J. ROLFE, LOEB CLASSICAL LIBRARY, HARVARD U. PRESS, 1939; A NEGLECTED, BLOOD-CURDLING, HAIR-RAISING CLASSIC BY A FOURTH-CENTURY EYEWITNESS.

McGOVERN, W.M., *THE EARLY EMPIRES OF CENTRAL ASIA*, CHAPEL HILL, UNIVERSITY OF N. CAROLINA PRESS, 1939; SOME SURPRISING INFO.

McNEILL, WILLIAM, *PLAGUES AND PEOPLES*, N.Y., ANCHOR BOOKS, 1976. BADLY WRITTEN BUT THOUGHT-PROVOKING SPECULATIONS.

METZGER, B.M. AND MURPHY, R.E., EDS., *THE NEW OXFORD ANNOTATED BIBLE*, N.Y., OXFORD U. PRESS, 1991; GOOD FOOTNOTES, BUT TRIES TO NEUTRALIZE THE ORIGINAL'S GENDER-BIASED LANGUAGE.

NEEDHAM, J., *SCIENCE AND CIVILIZATION IN CHINA*, CAMBRIDGE, CAMBRIDGE U. PRESS, 1988... AN ENCYCLOPEDIC, MAGNIFICENT LIFE'S WORK.

PAGELS, E., *THE GNOSTIC GOSPELS*, N.Y., VINTAGE, 1981; THE EARLY HERETICS AND WHAT THEY THOUGHT.

PAYNE, R., *THE HORIZON BOOK OF ANCIENT ROME*, N.Y., AMERICAN HERITAGE PUBLISHING CO., INC., 1966; GOOD PIX.

PLINY, *NATURAL HISTORY, VOLUME 8 & 9*, TR. BY H. RACKHAM, LOEB CLASSICAL LIBRARY, HARVARD U. PRESS, 1961; BAD SCIENCE, BUT VOL 9'S SECTION ON BIRDS IS NOT TO BE MISSED.

PROCOPIUS, *THE SECRET HISTORY*, TR. BY ???; I CAN'T FIND THE REFERENCE, BUT YOU SHOULD TRY, IF YOU WANT TO READ A FIRST-HAND ACCOUNT OF THEODORA'S SCANDALS.

RENAULT, M., *THE NATURE OF ALEXANDER*, N.Y., PANTHEON, 1975.

STRONG, D., *THE EARLY ETRUSCANS*, N.Y., G.P. PUTNAM'S SONS, 1968.

TACITUS, *THE ANNALS* AND *THE HISTORIES*, TR. BY A.J. CHURCH AND W.J. BRORIBB, ABRIDGED BY H. LLOYD-JONES, N.Y., WASHINGTON SQUARE PRESS, 1964; SEEMINGLY WRITTEN (AROUND THE YEAR 100) IN A SEETHING FURY.

TARN, W.W., *ALEXANDER THE GREAT*, CAMBRIDGE, CAMBRIDGE U. PRESS, 1979; GOOD, SHORT ACCOUNT

UH-OH! INFORMATION DENSITY'S GOIN' UP!

305

WAIT, THERE'S MORE!

"A delight."
—CARL SAGAN

"Obviously one of the great books of all time."
—TERRY JONES, *MONTY PYTHON'S FLYING CIRCUS*

"Not simply a comic, but a good story that I can recommend."
—RICHARD LEAKEY

"Hilariously informative...
Gonick manages to cover three billion years...
with casual erudition, silly humor and delightfully cartoony
black-and-white drawings."
—*PUBLISHERS WEEKLY*